Knowledge Management: Social, Cultural

CHANDOS
KNOWLEDGE MANAGEMENT SERIES

Series Editor: Melinda Taylor
(email: melindataylor@chandospublishing.com)

Chandos' new series of books are aimed at all those individuals interested in knowledge management. They have been specially commissioned to provide the reader with an authoritative view of current thinking. If you would like a full listing of current and forthcoming titles, please visit our web site **www.chandospublishing.com** or contact Hannah Grace-Williams on email info@chandospublishing.com or telephone number +44 (0) 1865 884447.

New authors: we are always pleased to receive ideas for new titles; if you would like to write a book for Chandos, please contact Dr Glyn Jones on email gjones@chandospublishing.com or telephone number +44 (0) 1865 884447.

Bulk orders: some organisations buy a number of copies of our books. If you are interested in doing this, we would be pleased to discuss a discount. Please contact Hannah Grace-Williams on email info@chandospublishing.com or telephone number +44 (0) 1865 884447.

Knowledge Management: Social, Cultural and Theoretical Perspectives

EDITED BY
RUTH RIKOWSKI

Chandos Publishing
Oxford · England

Chandos Publishing (Oxford) Limited
Chandos House
5 & 6 Steadys Lane
Stanton Harcourt
Oxford OX29 5RL
UK
Tel: +44 (0) 1865 884447 Fax: +44 (0) 1865 884448
Email: Rikowskigr@aol.com
www.chandospublishing.com

First published in Great Britain in 2007

ISBN:
978 1 84334 139 0 (paperback)
978 1 84334 189 5 (hardback)
1 84334 139 5 (paperback)
1 84334 189 1 (hardback)

Typeset by Domex e-Data Pvt. Ltd.
Printed and bound in the Great Britain by 4edge Ltd, Hockley. www.4edge.co.uk

Contents

List of figure and tables

Figure

Tables

Foreword

If the nineteenth century saw the beginning of data collection, and the twentieth century the beginning of data processing, it might be said that the twenty-first century will see the real beginning of data analysis. At present, we are engulfed with information with which we can barely cope. A keyword in a search engine produces millions of references, albeit rich with information but hardly manageable, while the Internet has generated vast amounts of connectivity but little real coherence – hence the plague of unwelcome e-mails that we all receive daily. The trick is to discover that intelligent navigation which, as far as possible, replicates human intellectual processes.

Meanwhile a new generation of social philosophers has begun to raise key questions about the way knowledge is used – from Alvin Tofler to Friedman. A common theme is the contraction of the world as a paradoxical consequence of the expansion of knowledge about it. Indeed, in his most recent work, Friedman asks whether history itself is diminishing and the world is, in a metaphorical sense, becoming 'flat'.

Another widely discussed theme in knowledge management is the notion of the democratic deficiency; that new forms of disadvantage have been created through an inability to gain access to knowledge or, indeed, from the exclusion of individuals and whole communities from the knowledge revolution. Indeed, this raises the question of the ownership of information as well as its dissemination.

In this new collection of essays which deal both with the theoretical and practical aspects of knowledge management, a number of these key themes are explored. Ruth Rikowski is, of course, known for her challenging and perceptive views as presented, for example, in her book *Globalisation, Information and Libraries*, and in her many published articles and presentations. Here she is joined by a number of academics and professionals to examine the extent to which knowledge management engages with social and political change. This book embraces a range of issues, global and local, political and intellectual, and in the process raises a number of questions about the function and utility of the way we manage and disseminate knowledge. In the process, it suggests an alternative agenda, one that commands real debate and discussion.

Professor Deian Hopkin
Vice-Chancellor, London South Bank University

About the contributors

Bob Bater trained initially as an industrial chemist, then later as an information scientist. He has worked in various capacities in the chemical, engineering and aerospace industries culminating in an eight-year period as IT manager and then information manager in the National Health Service. Bob left the NHS in 1994 to form his own company providing advisory and development services in knowledge management.

Isabelle Cabos has worked on the assessment of macro and micro sustainable development issues for the European Parliament, the European Commission and the United Nations Commission on Sustainable Development. She has a degree in environment and economics, and is now involved in the development of corporate responsibility issues at the European Investment Bank.

Paul Catherall works for a higher education institute in North Wales (NEWI) in the field of web systems and e-learning. Paul is the author of *Delivering E-learning for Information Services in Higher Education* (Chandos Publishing, 2004) and is currently engaged in a PhD on the same topic. Paul's other interests include web accessibility and career development issues in the LIS sector. He also has many poems published, most notably in his anthology *Foibles Frolics and Phantasms – Illustrated Poems 1995–2005* (PublishAmerica, 2006).

Bruce Lloyd spent over 20 years in industry and finance before joining the academic world a decade ago to help establish the Management Centre at what is now London South Bank University. Professor Lloyd has written extensively on a wide range of strategy/futures related issues, and undertaken over 30 interviews on leadership for *Leadership and Organization Development Journal*, as well as others for 'The Tomorrow Project Bulletin'.

Ruth Rikowski has been an information professional for some 25 years, working in a variety of organisations, in both the public and the private sector. For the last few years, she has been working in academia, at London South Bank University and the University of Greenwich. Her writing and research interests cover a wide range of subjects, including globalisation, knowledge management, and the knowledge revolution and information technology. She is the author of *Globalisation, Information and Libraries* (Chandos Publishing, 2005).

Leburn Rose is Head of the Department of Mathematics, Statistics and Foundation Studies at London South Bank University. He worked for several years in manufacturing and engineering before moving into academia. Dr Rose is deeply committed to teaching, with a portfolio that now includes management education in information technology and business. Furthermore, he also taught on the MSc in knowledge management systems at London South Bank University. His PhD is in the area of economic evaluation of human platelet dosing.

Mandy Webster gained her law degree at the University of Nottingham and an MA in librarianship at Loughborough University. For the last ten years she has been the library and information services manager at Browne Jacobson LLP, working as a legal information specialist. This work has included developing intranet resources, online services and information skills training. Her previous experience includes working in academic sector libraries and research and National Health Service information services.

The authors may be contacted care of the Editor:

E-mail: *rikowskigr@aol.com*

Preface

Knowledge management (KM) – so much has been written on this subject. Do we really need another book on it, you might be asking? My work and my writing courts controversy – there is absolutely no doubt about that. Take this headline from a review of my book, *Globalisation, Information and Libraries*, for example:

> Marxism mires debate: globalisation is unjust, unfair and threatens the existence of libraries... (Chillingworth, 2005: 61)

So, that is what Mark Chillingworth of *Information World Review* thinks about my first book – that it stops debate, when here I am, trying to encourage debate. So be it. Many others, though, have realised the depth and significance of my work. Toni Samek, Associate Professor, University of Alberta, for example, in her review of my book in *Feliciter*, the journal of the Canadian Library Association, says that:

> In a profession that is regrettably light on theory, the fresh Marxist analysis offered here is an exceptionally important contribution to our literature ... This is a remarkable book and I highly recommend it for all library sectors and constituencies, including LIS schools. (Samek, 2005: 246)

Thus, in one way or another, people are taking a real interest in my work!

But boring? A well-trodden path? Well, I have never been accused of that in my work. Will this book break the mould? Is this going to be another run-of-the-mill book on KM? Fear not – a radical element runs through it, and my alternative Marxist theoretical analysis forms an important part of it. A Marxist analysis of KM – now, that is something new and different. However, the book has contributions from a variety of KM experts, all from different backgrounds and perspectives, and on a variety of topics. Let's hope that buries the notion that Marxists are dogmatic and are unable to respect the work and ideas of others. Hopefully, then, this book will be an interesting, useful and enjoyable read for a wide variety of people.

Returning to Marxism, though, the point about Marxist theory and analysis, as far as I am concerned, is that it provides a *deeper* and more adequate explanation and analysis of capitalism than does any other social scientific theory. I would suggest, however, that social scientific theory itself also needs to be considered further today. The chapters in this book are all valuable and important contributions to KM, while at the same time they do not, in any way, undervalue the importance of Marxism. Instead, they provide a platform upon which my work, a Marxist analysis of KM can be built, which I hope I am able to demonstrate clearly in this book.

The knowledge revolution, as a concept, is still relatively new ground, particularly in certain circles, including academic circles. Furthermore, it needs to be accepted, in general, that it is, indeed, the latest phase of capitalism. Lancaster University has been one institution that has taken the initiative in this regard. The Institute for Advanced Studies (IAS) at Lancaster University has taken the 'knowledge-based economy' as its theme for its inaugural annual programme, 2005–06. It has been holding a series of workshops throughout the 2005–06 academic year, in which I have participated, followed by a conference in the summer of 2006. More information about the whole programme can be found at the IAS website (*http://www.lancs.ac.uk/ias/annualprogramme/kbe/2005-06.htm*).

This book is divided into four main parts, each of which examines KM from a particular perspective. Part 1 considers social, economic, political and philosophical perspectives; Part 2 examines practical perspectives; Part 3 focuses on cultural perspectives; and Part 4 examines wider theoretical perspectives. Obviously, these are all very big topics, so each part will only focus on a couple of themes, which, it is hoped, will give the reader food for thought and a desire to explore some of these and other related issues in more depth.

Thus, the first part of the book considers KM from a social, economic, political and philosophical perspective. The section begins from a philosophical perspective with a chapter on the topic of KM and wisdom, by Bruce Lloyd, Professor of Strategic Management at London South Bank University. Lloyd argues that more importance needs to be attached to the part that wisdom can, does and needs to play in KM, as well as the role that he thinks wisdom should play in KM in the future. Furthermore, he thinks that wisdom has been mistakenly excluded from much of the KM literature, and he is keen to reintroduce it. As such, he has published a variety of articles and given a number of talks on the topic of KM and wisdom (e.g. Lloyd 1999, 2003, 2006). Lloyd says that we 'need to be increasingly concerned with what is the core of knowledge, distilled through the experience of history into wisdom that is critically important for us to preserve and pass on to future generations'.

Furthermore, he adds that:

> ...we appear to be spending more and more time focusing on learning knowledge, or more strictly information/facts, that have a relatively short shelf-life, and less and less time on knowledge that overlaps with wisdom that has a long shelf-life.

Lloyd also considers this within the notion of 'values' (personal/subjective), as opposed to the objective definition of 'value' which has been the focus of my work on KM – building on Marx's concept of value, which I examine in some detail in Chapter 11. Lloyd argues that:

> All decisions involve the integration of the economics dimensions of value, with the ethical (i.e. 'right') dimension of 'values'. Of course, this is a dynamic process and there is continual feedback from the experience of our actions into whether we need more technical information (what and how much are also value-influenced decisions) and how values are assessed both as the ends and the means of the decisions/outcome itself.

Making wise decisions implies a 'values framework' and is important to Lloyd. He concludes by emphasising the point that we need to take the whole subject of wisdom much more seriously. Furthermore, we really need to focus on moving to 'the wise economy', rather than the traditional emphasis on 'the knowledge economy'.

Clearly then, wisdom is something that should be given further consideration within KM. Wisdom demands that we consider the KM topic at a deeper level. In addition, philosophical enquiry is very valuable when examining KM in general, and indeed, I consider the meaning of knowledge from a philosophical perspective elsewhere (R. Rikowski, 2000a, 2000b). To help us to answer the deeper questions, a philosophical enquiry into the meaning and value of wisdom can only be beneficial.

This is followed with a chapter by Bob Bater, KnowPlexity Ltd and Isabelle Cabos, European Investment Bank, Luxembourg, entitled 'Intangible value at work: personal, organisational and social dimensions'. Bater and Cabos argue that intangible value is very important today, and that companies need to take, and are taking, it more seriously. Furthermore, they also say that companies need to act, and are acting, more benevolently, giving more consideration to all their different stakeholders, and are appreciating the importance and utilisation of intangible value. Companies are now also measuring this value more in various ways.

In the first half of their chapter, Bater and Cabos examine how intangible value is likely to change how people relate to each other at work, while in the second half they consider how intangible value is 'demanding its rightful place in the corporate balance sheet...'

Bater and Cabos consider the fact that the spread of knowledge management practices has highlighted the role of intangible value, both within and outside of the organisation. They argue that intangible value questions the role of traditional business, with its emphasis on investment for shareholders. Furthermore, they suggest that shareholders are only one kind of stakeholder in the business, and that there are now many other stakeholders, such as employees themselves, the local economy and the environment. They say that focusing solely on profit oversimplifies the process, and that the psychological motivations of employees need to be taken into account instead, along with various other welfare and humane considerations.

Thus, they say that businesses are now becoming more people-centred, and more importance is being attached to ethical considerations and corporate responsibility. They also consider various ways in which intangible value is measured today, and emphasise that this now needs to be linked to positive impacts on society and the environment in general. Furthermore, they add that the role of management has changed, and that today it is less about managing and more about enabling and empowering employees to utilise their knowledge to best effect for the collective benefit.

Bater and Cabos begin their chapter by saying that:

> The growth of the knowledge economy has brought with it a whole new perspective. Increasingly, the notion of 'intangible value' as embodied and embedded in the diversity of corporate technologies, in corporate workflow cycles, and in governance and regulatory processes, is casting an informative light on the changes taking place.

They continue, arguing that:

> ...knowledge assets are all about creating future growth and environmental, sanitary and social risks require the application of responsibility and precaution management because the consequences might be worldwide and irreversible.

They emphasise the importance of 'managing' and 'measuring' intangible value, saying that:

> The need to manage intangible value induced by the advent of KM is requiring significant changes not only to the conventional ways of measuring value; it is requiring equally significant changes in organisational behaviour towards stakeholders and in perceptions of the organisational sphere of influence.

Bater and Cabos also consider organisations as social systems and the fact that organisations are dynamic, not just machines. Some useful comparisons could be drawn between their work and the related work of Dr Leburn Rose (in Chapter 10 of this book). They say that when considering an organisation as a social system, there is a need to recognise that employees are not just 'cog wheels in a machine'. This is in contrast to the traditional view of a business, which sees a business as simply an instrument for making profit.

They refer again to intangible value, emphasising the importance of:

> ...harnessing the full potential of the organisation's intangible value – the knowledge embodied in its people, and the capacity for value-generation arising from the creative relationships among them. In other words, it is not machines, not managers, not marketers, but people who are the key actors, and it is their knowledge that generates and sustains the flow of value among individual and groups of employees; among the business, its associate businesses and the local economy; and between the business and the environment.

Furthermore:

> The key source of value now is intangible and largely locked inside people's heads. You cannot command someone to think, be

effective or to innovate; cooperation cannot be coerced. Such behaviour has to be facilitated, encouraged and ultimately rewarded.

Bater and Cabos also emphasise the importance of corporate responsibility and the need to look beyond the simple profit motive, saying that:

> Corporate responsibility is the buzzword that has emerged to remind corporates that profit generation should not be their sole focus and that real costs and benefits, in environmental terms, in energy terms and in terms of global social justice need to be accounted for.

Bater and Cabos examine the work of Enid Mumford. Mumford's ethics model outlines five contracts: the knowledge contract, the psychological contract, the efficiency contract, the work structure contract and the value contract. With the knowledge contract, for example, the employee provides the skills, competences and knowledge required, while the employer ensures that they are utilised well and that the employee is adequately remunerated. According to Bater and Cabos, her model can be seen to be designing a system on the basis that people matter.

Bater and Cabos are also of the opinion that enlightened companies that are concerned with humane and moral issues can exist, flourish and thrive in capitalism. Furthermore, this is the direction in which companies are being forced to go, and as such, people working and living in capitalism today might well gain significant benefits; indeed, this can be a 'win-win' situation for everyone. They provide the example of Semco, a Brazilian company, which they say:

> ...has gone further than any other documented case towards building a fully democratic, humanitarian and sustainable business agglomerate ... Consider a business that has turned its back on the facile assumption that profits belong solely to those who invest the capital, and openly espouse profit sharing.

Bater and Cabos continue noting the fact that different companies have now adopted various ways in which to measure intangible value; these include Kaplan and Norton's Balanced Scorecard, Accenture's

Performance Prism, Skandia's Intellectual Capital Navigator and Triple Bottom Line Reporting. They say that:

> Traditional financial reporting methods disclose only a fraction of the information that is relevant to investors. Intangible assets have become key drivers of shareholder value in the knowledge economy, but accounting rules do not yet acknowledge this shift in the valuation of companies ... The problem they need to solve, though complex, can be stated quite simply: how to demonstrate a cause-and-effect link between improvement in non-financial areas and cash flow, profit, or stock price.

Kaplan and Norton began work in 1990 to 'explore new ways of measuring organisational performance', and they recognised the importance of knowledge-based assets in this regard. The Balanced Scorecard aims to establish some sense of equilibrium with regard to factors such as leading indicators that relate to a goal in the future; quantitative, financial hard facts and qualitative, non-financial soft facts. While such 'soft facts' are traditionally hard to come by, Bater and Cabos suggest that information systems already in place can be used by organisations to measure their performance against specific non-financial goals. To illustrate how such non-financial goals are growing in importance internationally, Bater and Cabos provide a list of existing standards to support the development of a corporate responsibility policy.

Introducing their 'road map for sustainability', the authors say that the aim of 'triple bottom line reporting' is to enable businesses to account for their performance equally according to economic, environmental and social criteria, which are the cornerstones of sustainability. They say that:

> The ultimate aim of 'triple bottom line' reporting is that businesses should account for their performance on economic, environmental and social criteria and attempt to satisfy their stakeholders on all three sets of criteria. As a result, corporate responsibility should encompass management of environmental, social and governance issues...

The authors conclude by describing the actions organisations need to take in seven domains if sustainable development is to be achieved.

Bater and Cabos's chapter provides a very valuable contribution to the literature on KM, value and intangible assets, and is something which can now very much be built on.

Part 1 concludes with my own chapter, 'Leadership in the knowledge revolution: an Open Marxist theoretical perspective and analysis'. I argue that being an effective leader in the new economy/knowledge revolution essentially involves extracting ideas, knowledge and information out of the workforce (especially their unconscious tacit knowledge). In essence, good and effective leadership is about extracting value (in an objective sense) from intellectual labour, and once this value has been created and extracted, it then becomes embedded in the commodity. Value can only ever be created by labour: in today's knowledge revolution, the latest phase of capitalism in the developed world, value is created from intellectual labour in particular. These commodities are then sold in the marketplace, and through this process, profits are derived. These profits are ultimately derived from value. Thus, through this process capitalism is sustained and perpetuated while labour is exploited, alienated and objectified. Effective leadership in the knowledge revolution is also about endeavouring to intensify the commodification of knowledge itself (such as through patents and software products), as well as about how to transform knowledge from the knowledge worker/intellectual labourer into structural capital.

A number of different areas are considered within the chapter, including the meaning of leadership itself, the role of female leadership in the new economy and the Scandinavian model of leadership development. When focusing on leadership, I consider some of the main ingredients traditionally considered necessary for an effective leader, such as vision, authority, charisma, decision making, team building and planning. With regard to female leaders, recent research indicates that female qualities are becoming increasingly valued for leadership roles in the new economy, with the focus more on democratic and diverse techniques rather than authoritarian styles of leadership. Findings from research conducted at the Hagberg Consulting Group, a California firm of psychologists specialising in leadership development and organisational effectiveness, for example, concluded that women managers were often better than their male counterparts. Thus, a flexible leadership approach is often needed in the new economy/knowledge revolution and females can play a vital role here.

Furthermore, the Scandinavian model of leadership development has been involved with developing alternative leadership qualities, and with the adoption of a more holistic, humanistic and value based approach, compared with the traditional leadership model. With the Scandinavian model, there are different stakeholders, such as public/private sectors, activist movements and trade unions. The model recommends a flatter, non-bureaucratic structure, with devolved responsibility in a more trusting and caring environment. As I say, it is interesting to note that:

> ...more socialist/social democrat-type countries in Scandinavia are producing models of leadership that can actually help more clearly focused capitalist-oriented countries to gain further competitive advantage ... Subtle approaches are needed to be able to nurture intellectual labour, and thereby extract value from it.

These alternative and more subtle forms of leadership are needed to extract value effectively from intellectual labour. Once again, the importance of a Marxist analysis, including in particular a Marxist theoretical analysis of value, becomes clear, and this is all explored further in this chapter.

Part 2 focuses on KM and practical perspectives, and there are two chapters in this section. Mandy Webster, Library and Information Services Manager at Browne Jacobson, LLP considers 'The role of the library in knowledge management', while Paul Catherall, Web Developer at North East Wales Institute of Higher Education, focuses on 'Accessibility issues for web-based information systems'.

In Chapter 4, Mandy Webster begins by saying that, 'through their traditional role of managing and organising, information libraries are ideally qualified to take on the role of managing knowledge'. She adds that librarians need to move beyond 'the traditional role of housing information, to analysing and using that information'.

This is a topic that I address elsewhere (R. Rikowski, 2000a, 2000b, 2003a). In these articles, I say that KM provides a great opportunity for librarians and information professionals in the knowledge economy, and ideally they need to seize this opportunity more than they have done so far.

Mandy Webster considers the transferability of the librarian/information professional's skills into KM work. Within this, she focuses on a number of key areas, including database selection and management (focusing, in particular, on library management systems); classification and taxonomies; current awareness; management; training and information literacy; intranets and extranets; auditing and user needs, and market research and competitive intelligence. Regarding management, for example, she says that:

> At the heart of all KM initiatives is the need to manage ... KM can be a unique path to move from managing the library to managing the organisation the library serves in creating a more public arena for the librarian's talents.

Webster, however, thinks that the biggest change needed is with regard to moving from managing explicit knowledge to facilitating and enabling the capture of tacit knowledge. She concludes by saying that, for librarians and information professionals, there are 'exceptional opportunities to become partners in creating and using knowledge not just providing a home for it and managing that home'.

Paul Catherall, author of *Delivering E-learning for Information Services in Higher Education* (2004), examines a number of important aspects regarding web accessibility and its applicability to KM, focusing in particular on some of the issues effecting disabled people. His chapter discusses web-based accessibility and the law, web standards and web accessibility standards, web-based validation and auditing techniques, web usability and the role of assistive technology. With regard to technical standards, for example, he refers to the need to try to 'ensure that web pages display as the author intended and in a consistent manner within any standard web browser'.

However,

> Conformance to web standards among modern information or knowledge management systems delivered via a web-based interface has been mixed and there is still much reliance on the web author or systems developer either to purchase a standards-compliant system or modify system 'templates' to produce a more compliant HTML output.

Catherall considers fundamental web usability issues, such as graphical user interface design, information technology literacy and the role of user education. Regarding accessibility, Catherall focuses in particular on the needs of users with disabilities. Users with visual disabilities, for example, may require a facility to increase or otherwise modify the textual display, while users with cognitive disabilities may require alternative textual content within the web document itself. Meanwhile, 'individuals with motor related disabilities, such as cerebral palsy, arthritis or repetitive strain injury (RSI), may rely on alternative input devices such as tracker-balls, soft keyboards or specially developed input devices'.

Catherall also examines various validation and auditing techniques for web accessibility and standards compliance, including use of validation software, reviewing content using a text-only display and within a variety of web browsers, using spelling and grammar checkers and reviewing the document for clarity.

Thus, many interesting and important aspects surrounding web accessibility for information management and knowledge management systems are covered throughout the chapter, with a wealth of information, and Catherall concludes by noting that:

> While the World Wide Web has contributed to the massive growth in computer usage in the home, education and industry, it can be seen that this new communications medium poses new challenges for accessibility and usability.

Part 3 focuses on KM within and across cultures. The section is divided into four chapters that I have written. The first (Chapter 6) begins by briefly considering definitions of knowledge management and related concepts, and culture itself; it then focuses on KM within and across cultures in the developed world and the developing world. It also examines cultural theories, with the focus on Hofstede's work and his five dimensions of cultural variability and how this can be applied to KM. This is also related to Bird and Metcalf's framework on negotiating behaviour.

Chapter 7 provides a brief literature overview of KM and culture (focusing largely on the developed world), a consideration of knowledge transfer/knowledge sharing across cultures and a cross-cultural case study of KM in a Japanese manufacturing subsidiary. A number of important findings from the case study are highlighted, including the fact that there were a number of knowledge blocks in existence, the most prevalent of which was the language barrier. This is followed by an examination of KM and organisational learning in the developing world, drawing on the work of Hovland. Hovland emphasises, for example, that northern non-governmental organisations (NGOs) should try to build up a better relationship with southern NGOs, to try to utilise knowledge in an endeavour to lessen poverty.

Chapter 8 focuses on internal and external cultures and KM, and KM and social culture. The main focus on internal cultures is on communities of practice, and as I say:

> 'People to people' connections and communities of practice are now generally recognised to be more important than just having efficient IT systems for KM. Knowledge cannot simply be captured and recorded in an IT system in a simplistic way. A significant shift in thinking has taken place in this regard and more and more importance is being attached to tacit knowledge (both conscious and unconscious tacit knowledge), and CoPs can help to extract this tacit knowledge.

The main focus on external cultures is on globalisation, and consideration is given to some of the terminology used in this area, such as *deterritorialisation*, *homogenisation* and *hybridisation*. However, I emphasise that we should really be referring to a 'global capitalist culture', rather than a 'global culture', in the same way as we should really be referring to 'global capitalism' rather than 'globalisation'.

In Chapter 9, I place KM and cross-culture within an Open Marxist theoretical perspective, emphasising the fact that having effective KM practices in the developed world is more important than in the developing world, in order to ensure the continued success of the knowledge revolution, this being the latest phase of capitalism. This is because capitalism is sustained by the extraction of value from labour. In the knowledge revolution in the developed world, the extraction of value from *intellectual* labour is of crucial importance. In the developing world, meanwhile, the focus is still more on manual labour, thus effective KM practices here are supportive, rather than key.

Part 4 examines wider, theoretical perspectives on KM and contains chapters by Dr Leburn Rose, Head of the Department of Mathematics, Statistics and Foundation Studies at London South Bank University, and myself.

Rose's chapter is entitled 'Thermodynamics and knowledge: principles and implications' and he focuses on thermodynamics, energy and principles as they can be applied to knowledge and knowledge management in an organisation.

Rose says that, 'the science of thermodynamics lies behind much of what we experience and take for granted in the physical world around us, and the organisations in which we work'. He continues, saying that:

> The relevance of thermodynamics rests on the notion that organisations may in general be described as systems into which resources such as intellectual capital, raw materials and energy flow, undergo transformation, and leave the system in the form of products and/or services.

He begins his chapter by referring to the three laws of thermodynamics, which are all idealised states. As he says, the first law 'establishes the principle that in a totally closed system, it is not possible to lose energy, but merely to "transform" it to another form'.

The second law suggests that even if a system is totally isolated from its surroundings, 'the energy flows that take place will, to a lesser, or greater degree be associated with losses from the totality of the system's energy'. Therefore, energy flows will cause an 'irreversible decline of the systems total energy'.

Meanwhile, the third law 'establishes an idealised physical limit at zero entropy (and zero energy) in an isolated system, which, irrespective of the number of energy flow processes that occur, can only be approached, but never actually reached'.

This means that successive energy flows will 'progressively degrade the system' and the third law emphasises the need for strategies for the renewal of energy. In order to slow down this decline of the system, 'strategies are needed for maintaining operation of the isolated system as far as possible from its equilibrium state'.

Rose then considers the relationship between matter, fuel, energy and data, information and knowledge and says that, 'there is a remarkable analogy between the physical relations of matter, fuel and energy, and the organisational relations of data, information and knowledge'.

He then relates energy, knowledge and value together, saying that, 'it follows that as energy results from the chemical combustion of fuel, likewise, knowledge could also be the psycho-social processing of information in a form that achieves *added value*' (my emphasis). He also emphasises that energy can be 'transformed into different forms and ... stored in different ways.'

Rose then moves on and considers the relationship between thermodynamics and the organisation. He asks whether thermodynamic energy can be conceptualised as 'organisational energy' and whether the concept of energy can be ascribed to the inputs and outputs of organisations. He says that:

...while all organisations to some degree lend themselves to valuation on thermodynamic grounds, the efficiency with which their mechanical and intellectual work can be valued will depend on the organisation's architecture, and the extent to which it engages in work that is predominantly mechanical or knowledge-based.

While the science of thermodynamics 'dictates that flow processes should result in a change in state, shape, or location of the object that absorbs the quantity of energy', this also has to be related to organisational structure – and means that the path does not, necessarily, run smoothly. Instead:

...factors such as structural inflexibility, and political and cultural conflict, which are a daily feature of organisational life, can undermine the continuity of flow processes, and result in further diffusion of an organisation's finite energies.

Rose goes on to say that:

...where organisations manage to achieve a good degree of alignment between their communication (human and technological) and structural architectures, predictions on the basis of thermodynamics are likely to yield results that are close to the true valuations of their flow processes.

In this way, thermodynamics can arrive at a fairly accurate approximation. Whereas 'many problems arising from weaker causality between flow processes stem from poor alignment of the architectures that make up the organisation'.

Thus, he points out that knowledge flow processes can be interrupted for a variety of reasons, such as through political and cultural conflict. Furthermore, he adds that organisations devise various methods to try to overcome this, and project management is one example of this.

Rose relates this energy to knowledge in a very innovative way, in the section entitled 'Knowledge creation as dynamic, but not necessarily spirals'. He points out that while energy can be stored in various physical media, knowledge can also be stored in a number of different repositories within the boundaries of an organisation. These include written reports, databases, rituals and stories. Furthermore, 'like energy, once knowledge is created there will be a natural tendency for it to diffuse'.

He then considers Nonaka and Takeuchi's tacit and explicit knowledge model in this regard, but argues that their model, whereby knowledge is transmitted through an organisation in upwards and downwards spirals is 'instructive, but idealised'. Instead:

> A richer interpretation of the tacit-explicit and structure-process relationships may be to conceive them as idealistic states on a spectrum, which describes knowledge states that are part tacit, part explicit, part structure, and part process.

Thus, it might be more useful to conceive of knowledge creation 'as a process that is not only behaviouristic and unimpeded, but also one that is systemic and arises from the need to reconcile the form of knowledge with the design of the organisation's architecture'. From this, what emerges 'is a more enlightened notion of knowledge as an entity that is dynamic and changing, rather than a set of bipolar states'.

In this way, knowledge can be seen to be dynamic. Lloyd highlights the need for a dynamic approach to knowledge in his chapter, just as Bater and Cabos argue that we need to recognise that an organisation is dynamic. Interesting parallels could also be drawn here with Open Marxism, which I consider in Chapter 11. Indeed, the dynamics of an Open Marxist approach become imperative.

Rose continues, saying that while Nonaka and Takeuchi would argue that a written report, for example, is a repository of explicit knowledge, a more dynamic interpretation is needed for knowledge transfer to take place. Instead, reports etc need to be internalised and interpreted, which involves various mental processes. Thus, knowledge is dynamic and 'exists in a persistent state of becoming and is neither sterile nor static'.

From here, Rose formulates an alternative thermodynamic schema for knowledge creation in an organisation, which proposes four processes through which knowledge is transferred, namely: conduction, convection, radiation and combustion. He says that each process is enveloped by a unique combination of 'knowledge form' and 'organisational architecture'.

First, there is 'knowledge creation by conduction', which reproduces explicit knowledge and 'describes the process of energy diffusion through direct physical contact between objects'.

Convection is the second process; it is in the tacit-rigid envelope of the firm and it 'fine-tunes and refines the firm's tacit knowledge resources'. Furthermore, 'convective energy transfer is where diffusion takes place by means of a buoyancy effect'.

Places such as coffee shops and accessible meeting rooms are 'likely to significantly enhance convective knowledge circulation'. Communities of practice (which I examine in Chapter 8) also enhance the circulation of convective knowledge. The third process is 'knowledge creation by radiation', which concerns the creation (and destruction) of ideas. Here, Rose says that, 'radiant modes of knowledge transfer and creation are made possible by the presence of and interaction between people, processes and physical spaces within the organisational arena'.

Knowledge creation by radiation is in the tacit-organic envelope of the firm and it is 'where energy is diffused from one object to another, but with no physical contact between objects'. Furthermore, 'training and coaching, formal and informal meetings and briefings, brainstorming and teamwork are exemplars by which the radiant transfer and creation of knowledge is made possible'. On rare occasions, this process can lead to leaps in creative energy, which can greatly benefit the firm.

Finally, combustion 'enables the creative adaptation of the organisation's scarce repositories of explicit knowledge'. It resides within the explicit-organic envelope of the firm and it 'integrates explicit knowledge into novel permutations'. However, knowledge through this process might gradually decline.

Rose also makes the point that the process of combustion differs from conduction, radiation and convection, because combustion actually creates energy, while the other three processes 'facilitate energy transfer'.

Rose argues that the firm can be represented in two dimensions – architecture and knowledge forms. The architecture can be seen to be on a continuum of organic to rigid, and knowledge forms on a continuum of tacit to explicit, and firms can be positioned along this continuum. Thus, Rose argues that the organisation can be represented as a series of four such knowledge zones: tacit-organic, tacit-rigid, explicit-organic and explicit-rigid.

In the concluding section, Rose says that:

> The science of thermodynamics offers an intriguing and fresh perspective for understanding the nature and scope of knowledge management in organisations. The discussion of the three laws of thermodynamics in relation to matter, fuel and energy, alert us to the remarkable correspondence between matter, fuel and energy, on the one hand, and data, information and knowledge on the other.

Thus, Rose's chapter gives us plenty to think about in regard to the laws of thermodynamics and how they can be related and applied to knowledge and knowledge management. In this way, he also brings science and social science together. His work is ground-breaking and hopefully, these ideas can be developed further by Rose himself and others in the future.

Continuing from this theme, in Chapter 11 I consider the concept of energy and then relate this to the concept of value, focusing on Marx's theory of value in particular, and a Marxist analysis of the 'commodity', which I then relate to KM. Thus, this chapter is about developing an Open Marxist theoretical analysis and perspective on KM. Energy as a concept needs to be considered further within the social sciences, and I believe the social scientific community can learn from the scientific community in this regard. From this, value (building on Marx's theory of value) and energy can be bought closer together and a deeper understanding of society can start to emerge, which can benefit the scientific and the social scientific community, as well as society at large.

I suggest that an Open Marxist theoretical analysis provides us with a much better grounded theory than does any other social scientific theory. It not only provides us with a far better, deeper analysis and explanation of the social, economic and political world in which we find ourselves, in general, but also provides us with a better understanding of value and KM in particular. In essence, KM practices assist with the effective extraction of value from intellectual labour. The extraction of this value ensures that companies can make profits, and that capitalism is thus sustained. It is also concerned with transforming knowledge from intellectual labourers into structural capital.

The chapter is broken down into a number of sections. First, it considers the evolutionary nature of social systems and the fact that we clearly need to realise that social, economic and political systems evolve, and that this needs to be recognised as an established fact/theory. As I say:

> A social system will go through different phases; one phase will evolve into another, as the system adapts to the changing world in which it finds itself. It will do this until the changes become so significant that it actually evolves into another system entirely. This can also be compared with the evolution of the species.

We then need to move beyond this evolutionary process and start to become proactive, so that we can start to think about how to create a better world for ourselves.

Second, it examines the commodity in some detail. Here I emphasise that, leading on from Marx, our analysis of capitalism must begin with the commodity, and furthermore, that capitalism is essentially about the commodification of all that surrounds us (even though this is impossible in reality). I consider the physical and natural form of the commodity and use value and exchange value. The physical form consists of the materials and substances that make up the physical components of a commodity, such as plastic, iron and wood. Whereas, as Marx made clear, the value form is created specifically and only through human labour, and it is the value form that is the focus of this chapter.

While commodities are useful and so have a *use value*, they are also exchanged in the market in capitalism, so they have an *exchange value*. As I say:

> ...the exchange of commodities is a fundamental part of capitalism. Exchange-value, in essence, is the way in which the value in the commodity can be quantified/measured in an objective sense, and in capitalism, this is achieved through money. Commodities can be exchanged equally (they acquire an equivalence), through the money-form. However, money is, in essence, simply another way of expressing the labour that is embedded in the commodity. It is embedded in the commodity in the form of abstract labour.

Third, I consider the fact that capitalism is based on value, and that capitalism forever needs to be creating value from labour. Furthermore, value is actually a type of energy (social energy). I then move on to focus on surplus value, added value, the valorisation process and the law of value. As I emphasise:

> Value is continually expanded and perpetuated and it becomes a dynamic force, multiplying itself time and time again in capitalism. This is accomplished through the creation of and then the continual expansion of surplus value. Surplus value becomes a 'dynamic totality', which Postone refers to as the 'valorisation of value', the 'valorisation process' or 'self-valorising value'... So, Marx developed a dynamic and transformative theory of value, the drive of which drive is towards 'ever-increasing levels of productivity' ...

The following section focuses on the fact that value is extracted from labour, and it considers the significance of intellectual labour and value.

I argue that it is impossible to determine the length of the working day for intellectual labour, because new ideas and knowledge can be formulated in minutes, or they could take months or even years. Furthermore, complex effective KM practices are required in order to extract value from intellectual labour.

I then consider the objectification of labour and relate this to alienation saying that:

> Human beings labour, but in capitalism this labour becomes objectified and then dominates the labourers themselves. People cannot really feel a part of the world that they have created; they cannot relate to it and can no longer appreciate the fact that the alien world in which they live is of their own making, constructed by their own labour. Thus, the labourer becomes dominated by their own labour, and becomes alienated. This is true, even if people do not have an appreciation of this and say that they are not alienated, and that they can relate to the world they have created. This merely demonstrates the extent of the alienation, because objectively they are alienated – their labour-power is sold for a price and generates surplus value for capitalism.

From here, I then consider traditional Marxism versus Open Marxism, and emphasise the importance of an Open Marxist dynamic approach. This is followed by a brief consideration of social scientific theory and Marxism, where I highlight that Marxism demands that social scientific theory in general needs to be more rigorous. Finally, I emphasise that we need to overthrow capitalism and abolish value as its means of sustenance, through its embedment in the commodity.

In sum, my Open Marxist theoretical analysis of KM begins with an analysis of the commodity, followed by an analysis of value (which is social energy) and the different forms and aspects of value. Value can only ever be created from labour, and this value then becomes embedded in the commodity. Commodities are sold in the marketplace, and profits are made, and profits can only be derived from value. Thus, value is essential for the continued success of capitalism. However, in the knowledge revolution there is a greater exertion of intellectual labour than manual labour. To extract this value from intellectual labour, subtle processes are required and effective KM practices become crucial. This is why KM is so important today and this is what we need to keep firmly in mind. By this process, labour becomes exploited, alienated and objectified, while capitalism continues to thrive. Furthermore, KM is also about finding mechanisms to enable knowledge from intellectual labour to be transformed into structural capital.

I therefore suggest that we should try to use our knowledge and understanding in a different way – where our labour starts to liberate us, rather than dominate us. Once society starts to understand itself more in this way, we will then be on the road to a brighter and a fairer world – indeed, we will be on the road towards a socialist/communist society.

Chapter 12 is the concluding chapter, bringing some of the main themes of the book together, and emphasising the valuable contribution that the authors have made to the KM literature in general. It also provides some critique and outlines some of the ways in which the authors' work could be, and hopefully will be developed. Thus, it is hoped that this book will appeal to a wide variety of people, while also offering an alternative and deeper thought-provoking perspective on KM.

Ruth Rikowski
June, 2006

Part 1
Social, economic, political and philosophical perspectives

Knowledge management practices obviously operate within the wider social, economic, political and philosophical framework, and this section gives some consideration to this. Although it only touches on a relatively small number of topics, it aims to provide some important and thought-provoking insights. This perspective is also developed at a deeper level in the final theoretical section of this book.

This section begins from a philosophical perspective, with a chapter by Bruce Lloyd, Professor of Strategic Management, who considers the part that wisdom plays in KM. His chapter is entitled 'Knowledge management: what has wisdom got to do with it?' Lloyd argues that the development of strategy over the last decade has moved into the importance of learning and learning organisations. But what is learning? Lloyd asks whether it is trying to do things 'better'. From here, he says that the focus on learning has now been extended into a relatively new industry called 'knowledge management'.

Lloyd considers the data, information, knowledge and wisdom paradigm, arguing that it is not a linearly related, step-by-step movement up the pyramid from data to wisdom; instead, it is a never-ending dynamic process. Furthermore, he suggests that wisdom is the integration of knowledge and values, and often moves down from wisdom to knowledge, rather than moving up. Lloyd argues that it could be useful to reverse the data/information/knowledge/wisdom progression and consider that it is our values/wisdom that define the limits of what we consider acceptable in the first place. That decision then determines our priorities, what information is required, and then what further questions need to be asked about the data required. He says that we need to understand these two pyramids/progressions, and how they relate to each other.

Furthermore, Lloyd also argues that wisdom is one thing, being wise is quite another, and that being wise is certainly more than the ability to recycle wisdom. In essence, he argues that being wise involves the ability to apply wisdom effectively in practice.

Lloyd says that as we move into the knowledge economy, we need to consider what is the core of knowledge, distilled through the experience of history into wisdom, that is critically important for us to preserve and pass on to future generations. Furthermore, he argues that wisdom consists of insights that have stood the test of time. Additionally, the topic of wisdom is very important and yet it is often ignored in futurist, strategy and KM literature.

Lloyd is of the opinion that we seem to spend more and more time focusing on learning knowledge or facts with a relatively short shelf-life, and less and less time on knowledge that overlaps with wisdom that has a long shelf-life. Why do we not spend more time to ensure that what we have learned in the past ('wisdom') can be passed on to future generations? Instead, he argues, what we really need to focus on is 'the wise economy'.

Lloyd concludes by saying that if we cannot take wisdom seriously now, we never will, and we will pay a very high price for this neglect.

This is followed with a chapter by Bob Bater, KnowPlexity Ltd and Isabelle Cabos, European Investment Bank, Luxembourg, entitled 'Intangible value at work: personal, organisational and social dimensions'. Bater and Cabos consider the fact that the spread of knowledge management practices has highlighted the role of intangible value, both within and outside the organisation, and their analysis places KM firmly within the wider social, economic and political framework. They argue that when intangible value is taken into account, the traditional 'value proposition' of the business – return on investment for shareholders – is brought seriously into question. Furthermore, they say that shareholders are only one kind of stakeholder in the business, others being employees themselves, the local economy and the environment. They say that an emphasis solely on monetary profit not only ignores the obligations the business bears to these forgotten stakeholders, but also grossly oversimplifies the psychological motivation of employees and the complex nature of their relationship with the business. Businesses are evolving, they say, to embrace a new model based upon trust and ethical behaviour – where business is not solely about 'profit' in terms of monetary value, but also about minimising environmental impact and generating social benefit.

Bater and Cabos emphasise that a number of KM practitioners have proposed ways of measuring the contribution of intangible value to a business, although to date, this has been primarily as a way of increasing a company's capitalisation. However, they argue that a different perspective is now also emerging, which attempts to link business activity to a strategy that eliminates the negative and maximises the positive impact on society and the environment. They say that inside the business too, the old, hierarchical command-and-control structures are crumbling under the recognition that a business needs its employees and their knowledge just as much as (if not more) than its shareholder capital, and that a manager's role is less to 'manage' than to lead, enable and empower employees to utilise their knowledge to best effect for the collective benefit.

Throughout their chapter, Bater and Cabos consider the kinds of value that businesses can generate, as being constructive or destructive. They argue that the rise of intangible value is reminding us of a number of forgotten stakeholders and that people perform best in communities where trust and ethics are the guiding principles. Unless steps are taken to measure performance in respect of these personal, social and environmental directions, they claim that a business will not prove sustainable.

My chapter in this section is entitled 'Leadership in the knowledge revolution: an Open Marxist theoretical perspective and analysis', and this analysis also firmly places KM within the wider economic, social and political perspective. I begin by considering what the 'new economy' or the 'knowledge economy', or more accurately, the 'knowledge revolution' is, and then the literature on what being an effective leader in the new economy entails. From here I consider the importance of female leadership in the new economy and the Scandinavian model of leadership development. Both of these approaches adopt a more democratic, diverse, holistic and flatter (less hierarchical) approach to leadership, than that of traditional models of leadership.

What needs to be fully appreciated, though, I argue, is the fact that effective leadership in the knowledge revolution ultimately rests on the ability to extract knowledge, ideas and information out of knowledge workers, or more accurately, out of intellectual labour. This involves creating and extracting value from intellectual labour, and effective KM practices aid with this process. It is also about transferring knowledge from workers/intellectual labourers into capital. Subtle leadership qualities are needed, in order to be able to use KM practices effectively and productively, so that ideas can be extracted from intellectual labour. The benefits of female leaders thus play an important part, in this regard. What needs to be kept firmly in mind though, is that this is what leadership in the new economy must of necessity, ultimately be about. All this ensures that value is continually created in the knowledge revolution, and from this, profits are derived. In this way, the knowledge revolution is sustained and perpetuated, thereby perpetuating capitalism itself, while labour continues to be exploited. This theoretical analysis is examined further in Chapter 11.

1

Knowledge management: what has wisdom got to do with it?

Bruce Lloyd

Over the past decade, in my view, the core development in strategy has been the recognition of the importance of learning and learning organisation concepts. Indeed, it is increasingly recognised by organisations, individuals and even nation states that effective learning is the only sustainable competitive advantage.

I certainly do not find it surprising that, in the past few years, this focus on learning has been extended into a whole new industry called 'knowledge management'. Obviously, if you are concerned with learning, it is natural to ask the question: what are we learning? And perhaps even more importantly: what do we *need* to learn? This development coincided with the widespread use of computers, which created massive new challenges from what is known as the 'information explosion'.

In parallel, there has been the influence of the millennium itself. That event was probably the greatest learning point in human history. Never before has so much intellectual effort been focused on reflecting on – and learning from – our history. Reflective learning should start by trying to define what has been distilled into wisdom by exploring three basic key questions:

- Where have we come from?
- What are we doing here? and
- Where are we going?

Surely H. G. Wells was right when he said that: 'Human history becomes more and more a race between Education and Catastrophe' (H. G. Wells, *The Outline of History* (1920)).

How often do we seem to be either obsessed with technology, or so focused on the experience of the here and now, that the issue of wisdom appears to be virtually ignored?

We also need to recognise that the more change that is going on in society, the more important it is that we make sure that our learning is as effective as possible. This is the only way we have any chance of being able to equate change with progress. So, if we want to have a better future, the first, and most important, thing that we have to do is to improve the quality and effectiveness of our learning.

An underlying assumption of the word 'learning' is that we are trying to do things 'better'. We are trying to improve things. We are trying to make progress. Of course, the concepts behind the words: 'improve', 'better' and 'progress' are powerfully values-driven.

I recognise there is a risk in expounding the concept of wisdom that I might be seen to be supporting the view that somehow I, or we, know all the answers. That is certainly not the intention. The prime objective is to raise some questions that, in my view, do not appear to be asked often enough.

Wisdom statements are those that appear to be useful in helping us all make the world a better place in the future. But they are only useful if they also check out with our own experience. Of course, that relatively simple objective is not quite as easy as it sounds for at least two reasons.

First, the word 'better' explicitly and implicitly means that we are involved in considering the whole complicated subject of values that are embedded in the question: what do we mean by 'better'? It should surprise no one that a critical part of the content of any wisdom statement is the extent to which it incorporates judgments about values. Indeed, in many ways, this is a critical part of the definition of what we mean by wisdom. But that does not mean that all statements that reflect values can be defined as wisdom; the extra dimension required is that they are widely accepted, and that they have stood the test of time.

Second, it is important to recognise that in trying to make the world a better place for us all, we can run into potential areas of conflict; for example, making things 'better' for some people at the expense of making it worse for others. Much of the conflict that arises in this area is because different people mean different things as they are using different time horizons when they talk about the future. Some are obsessed with tomorrow, while others are primarily concerned with what they perceive to be the needs of the next hundred years.

If learning is critical, we then have to ask ourselves:

- What is the wisdom?
- How do we learn it? and
- How can we pass it on (more) effectively?

Wisdom can be considered to be a useful truth (or knowledge) with a long shelf-life. And knowledge is useful information with a shorter shelf-life than wisdom, with information being data but with a longer shelf-life.

The traditional approach to the data/information/knowledge/wisdom link is to see the relationship as part of a pyramid that starts with data at the bottom and ends with wisdom at the top. In my view this progression has a fundamental flaw, which is that the relationship between these four items is not linearly related and that there is no step-by-step movement up the pyramid from data to wisdom. The expectation of a basically mechanistic progression is partly reflecting the Newtonian tradition, repacked through the management science of Taylorism. The reality is that the integration of all four concepts requires at least one, if not two, quantum/qualitative jumps.

Information can certainly be considered a 'higher' form of data because it provides greater context and so greater meaning. However, the transformation of information into knowledge requires the first quantum jump. A book that describes how a jet engine works is a vehicle that contains information. It is only when information is actually used that it is turned into knowledge. In essence, knowledge is information in use and, of course, it is through its use that you gain further information, which then gets turned into even more legitimate knowledge. Overall, it is a never-ending dynamic process.

But where does wisdom come in? Wisdom can be considered the way we integrate our values into our decision-making processes. It is one thing to turn information into knowledge that makes things happen, but it is quite another thing to make the 'right' (/'good'/'better') things happen. How we actually use knowledge depends on our values; instead of moving up from knowledge to wisdom, we actually move down from wisdom to knowledge – that is the way we incorporate our values into our knowledge-based decision making, as well as see the application and relevance of what we generally call wisdom. It is only justified for decisions to be reduced to a cost-benefit analysis, if it is possible to quantify all the 'values' elements within the equation in monetary terms. In the past, values had been included implicitly, whereas today that dimension need to be made much more, if not fully, explicit.

All decisions involve the integration of the economics dimensions of value, with the ethical (i.e. 'right') dimension of 'values'. Of course, this is a dynamic process and there is continual feedback from the experience of our actions into whether we need more technical information (what and how much are also value-influenced decisions) and how values are assessed both as the ends and the means of the decision/outcome itself.

To complete this picture it is useful to reverse the data → information → knowledge → wisdom progression into wisdom → knowledge → information → data, and consider that it is our values/wisdom that define the limits of what we consider acceptable in the first place; this decision then determines our priorities over what we do. This determines what information we require, before we move on to asking further detailed questions about the data we need. If we want to understand both how we incorporate values into our decision-making processes, and why wisdom plays such an important role, then we need to understand these two pyramids/progressions, and how they relate to each other in practice. The way these words and concepts have been used in the past, however, has not always helped this process. Perhaps that is one reason why wise decision making has not been as widely practised as we would have liked. Being decisive is easy; being decisive about the 'right' things is the real challenge that confronts us all.

A few years ago, I started collecting what I considered to be the important quotations that contained long shelf-life knowledge (i.e. 'wisdom') that I felt ought to be given a high priority in what we consider passing on to the next generation through learning.

In many cases, there is considerable scope for disagreement over who said what. But if we are focused on the future, rather than the past, we should give a higher priority to the message, rather than the messenger. Indeed, sometimes, even when the quotation itself is well recognised, research shows that it was based on an earlier version, with a very minor modification. For example:

1. 'If I have seen farther, it is by standing on the shoulders of giants' – Sir Isaac Newton (1642–1727);

2. 'Pygmies placed on the shoulders of giants see more than the giants themselves' – Marcus Lucan (39–65 AD); and

3. 'We are like dwarfs on the shoulders of giants, so that we can see more than they, and things at a greater distance, not by virtue of any sharpness of sight on our part, or any physical distinction, but because we are carried high and raised up by their giant size' – Bernard of Chartres (c. 1120 AD).

There are also situations where the generally accepted quotation can be different from the original version. For example, the Bible is supposedly the source of 'Money is the root of all evil', when the original version is, in fact: 'For the love of money is the root of all evil.' (1 Timothy 6:10). Even here, there is a precedent: 'Love of money is the beginning of evil, because the operation of evil is connected to love of money' (Pythagoras).

Of course, wisdom is one thing, being wise is quite another. Being wise is certainly more than the ability to recycle wisdom. In essence being wise involves the ability to apply wisdom effectively in practice. This issue is aptly reflected in the comment, 'Those who are arrogant with their wisdom are not wise' (Anon).

In theory at least, once we can agree on the important messages, it should not be too difficult to ensure that there are appropriate channels for the effective learning of these messages. In addition, it is not unreasonable to assume that, if we have learned the right things, we ought then to be in a position to do the right thing with that knowledge. Of course, that is an assumption and, perhaps, there are more issues in that jump from knowledge to action than are normally recognised. But if that is the case, then we probably need to revisit messages to ensure that we give a higher priority to those that reflect the importance of meaning and motivation in human behaviour. For example:

> Our values are revealed by what we do, not by what we say. (Anon)

and

> It is not enough to know what is good; you must be able to do it. (George Bernard Shaw, *Back to Methuselah*, Act IV, scene 1, (1921))

This is not just an academic exercise. Our future is critically dependent on what we learn, and unless this subject is given much greater attention, it is extremely unlikely that we will be involved in anything remotely like progress, however it is defined.

There is enormous scope for debate, both practical and philosophical, about the specific wisdom items identified in this chapter. It only really becomes important when we try to establish priorities which, of course, in the end, we always need to do. At this stage, however, I am just concerned with trying to encourage the debate.

I would also like to acknowledge the parallel (and overlapping) contributions of other publications, I have come across recently:

- Covey, S. R. and Merrill, A. R. (1994) 'Appendix C: The wisdom literature', in *First Things First*, London: Simon and Schuster; pp. 342–6. This explores the patterns, consistencies and themes that they consider represented the most validated database in all human experience.

- Wayne W. Dyer (1998) *The Wisdom of the Ages: Eternal Truths for Everyday Life*, London: Thorsons. This is a remarkable analysis of how we can live more meaningful lives by close study of the words of poets and philosophers throughout the ages.

- Della Costa, J. (1995) *Working Wisdom: The Ultimate Value in the New Economy*, Toronto: Stoddart Publishing Co. This strongly argues that our perceived wisdom is the driving force behind our behaviour and that the subject is a vital part of any effective knowledge management programme.

Yet in a quick survey of 18 books on knowledge management, I found only three that felt the subject of wisdom was sufficiently important to mention in the index. Apart from these three mentioned above, which were not essentially knowledge management books, none gave the subject of wisdom the importance I believe it justifies.

However, as we move through the present millennium, the 'knowledge economy' is being given more and more attention. As a result, we are, and need to be, increasingly concerned with what is the core of knowledge, distilled through the experience of history into wisdom, that is critically important for us to preserve and pass on to future generations.

History does appear to show that it is incredibly easy to ignore the learning experiences of earlier millennia:

> If we still have not learned the lessons of two thousand years of history, why should we suddenly start being able to learn it now? (Anon)

Or to put that another way:

> The only lesson we appear to be able to learn from history is that we don't learn the lessons of history. (Anon)

Many of the important messages about the state and future of the human race were made over a thousand years ago, in China, the Middle East and other early sophisticated societies. This should not surprise us, as wisdom consists of insights that have stood the test of time, precisely because they are concerned with making statements about relationships between people, either individually or in societal context, or about our relationship with the universe as a whole.

> Knowledge is a process of piling up facts; wisdom lies in their simplification. (Martin H. Fisher)

> To know how to grow old is the masterwork of wisdom, and one of the most difficult chapters in the great art of living. (Henri Frederic Amiel)

And what are some of the general wisdom messages that we might like to pass on to future generations?

> Growth for the sake of growth is the ideology of the cancer cell. (Edward Abbey)

> By doubting, we come to examine, and by examining, so we perceive the truth. (Peter Abelard)

> It is easier to fight for one's principles than to live up to them. (Alfred Adler)

> Greatness lies not in being strong, but in the right use of strength. (Henry Ward Beecher)

And a few quotations specifically related to the future:

> The farther back you look, the farther forward you see. (Winston Churchill)

> If you won't be better tomorrow than you were today then what do you need tomorrow for? (Rabbi Nahman of Bratslav)

> Depression is the inability to construct a future. (Rollo May)

> You must be the change you want to see in the world. (Mahatma Gandhi)

> Education is your passport to the future. For tomorrow belongs to the people who prepare for it today. (Malcolm X)

> I touch the future: I teach. (Christa MacAuliffe)

In recent years, we have seen efforts to move people from the idea of 'working harder' to 'working smarter'. Increasingly we need to move beyond 'working smarter' to 'working wiser'. And, as we move along that progression, we need to recognise that we are moving to a situation where the important issues primarily reflect the quality of our values, rather than the quantity of our physical effort.

Perhaps one cannot teach wisdom, but it is certainly most unlikely that it is in our genes – so, somehow, it must be learned. The question is how can we make that learning process more effective – on the assumption, of course, that we consider it an important thing to do?

If we want to manage complexity successfully, and make progress in the world today, we have to start by getting the simple things right. This needs to be based on more effective understanding, and use, of accumulated wisdom. Unfortunately, problems arise all too often precisely because we have not got the simple things right in the first place. This includes the need for a greater emphasis on sharing knowledge, rather than the more traditional concept of 'knowledge is power'. We also need to be reasonably sure that we are starting by asking the right questions.

Probably the most important of those simple things to get right is for leaders to 'walk the talk'. It is relatively easy to know the right thing to do – the hard thing is to ensure that it gets done. Indeed, why does it appear to be relatively easy to recognise wisdom, but so incredibly difficult to be wise in practice?

The wise decision inevitably includes value judgments, beliefs and feelings, as well as thoughts; it invariably involves moral choices.

In addition, it should not surprise us that statements of wisdom are relatively timeless. They help us provide meaning to the world about us. But what certainly surprised me when I started looking at this subject, was the paradoxical gap between how critically important this area was in all our lives, and yet how often it seems to be almost totally ignored in futurist, strategy, or knowledge management literature. Another paradox is that we appear to be spending more and more time focusing on learning knowledge, or more strictly, information/facts, with a relatively short shelf-life, and less and less time on knowledge that overlaps with wisdom that has a long shelf-life. Why is that? What can we do about it?

Finally I come back to the point I made at the beginning. Why are we interested in the way we appear to be spending more and more time focusing on learning knowledge, or more strictly information/facts, that have a relatively short shelf-life, and less and less time on knowledge that overlaps with wisdom that has a long shelf-life? The answer, I believe, is that we are concerned about trying to make things better. So we need to re-ask the question – why do we not spend more time to ensure that what we have learned in the past ('wisdom') can be passed on to future generations?

How do we ensure these messages are learned more effectively? These are critical strategy questions and are at the very foundation of anything we might want to call 'the knowledge economy'. And what we really need to focus on is trying to move to a state that could be defined as: 'the wise economy'.

I hope I have not given the impression that I know what this illusive concept of 'wisdom' actually is. Or how we can pass it on more effectively. All I am arguing is that we urgently need to give the whole subject of wisdom much more serious thought than has been the case in the past.

If we cannot take wisdom seriously now, we never will. And we will pay a very high price for this neglect.

Note

A slightly revised version of this paper is available at: *http://www .collectivewisdominitiative.org/papers/lloyd_wisdom.htm* (accessed June 2006); also in 'Creating Global Strategies for Humanity's Future', Papers Arising from the World Future Society Conference, Toronto, 2006.

2

Intangible value at work: personal, organisational and social dimensions
Bob Bater and Isabelle Cabos

To have failed to solve the problem of producing goods would have been to continue man in his oldest and most grievous misfortune. But to fail to see that we have solved it and to fail to proceed thence to the next task would be fully as tragic. (John Kenneth Galbraith, *The Affluent Society*, 1958)

Introduction

Knowledge management (KM) has been equally applauded as the paradigm for a new socioeconomic age and ridiculed as yet another vacuous management fad. While KM is being taken more seriously than ever before, this continuing debate tends to obscure the fact that KM is merely the economic manifestation of a much broader and more far-reaching shift in the value systems underlying our society. Although still at the incubation stage, an old and ailing culture obsessed with material wealth at any cost, is evolving into a multi-stranded polyvalent culture embracing a less tangible value system rooted in health, well-being and fulfilment. Unlike the paradigm it aims to replace, the protagonists of the new culture insist upon counting every cost – tangible or intangible.

The ascendancy of intangible value is causing the gradual replacement of the Protestant work ethic and the profit motive by more human and ecological values. This has profound implications for the memes and mores that govern our social and economic milieus. In the first part of this chapter, we examine how intangible value is likely to change how people relate to each other in work. In the second part, we describe how intangible value is demanding its rightful place in the corporate balance sheet, challenging the glib assumptions of global corporatism and changing the way corporates relate to the world around them, setting us all on a route to a more sustainable future.

Part 1: People and the business

Business: a new approach

Many critics claim that KM is an oxymoron – a contradiction in terms – insisting that if knowledge is largely tacit and intangible, then it cannot be 'managed' in the conventional sense. Such critics fail to see that the root of the problem is their assumed meaning of the term 'manage'. For 'management' as applied in business today, has its roots in the 'scientific management' school of Frederick Winslow Taylor, which exerted such great influence on the industrialists of the early twentieth century.

Scientific management took a severely impoverished view of workers, with Taylor believing that in repetitive jobs, they would work at the slowest rate they could get away with without being punished. Indicative of his outlook, he called this 'soldiering', implying that workers needed to be coerced into performing well through strong command-and-control systems.

Regarding people and processes as individual or collective value-maximisers is a valid point of view, but it certainly is not the only one. The growth of the knowledge economy has brought with it a whole new perspective. Increasingly, the notion of 'intangible value' as embodied and embedded in the diversity of corporate technologies, in corporate workflow cycles, and in governance and regulatory processes, is casting an informative light on the changes taking place. Organisational performance, once measured in terms of output and sales of widgets per quarter, is now more likely to be measured in terms of the quality of customer relationships, mitigation of environmental and social impact, and reputation. In the knowledge economy, these factors, rather than sheer quantity of production, are increasingly affecting share price.

The estimation of market value-added by corporate activity has evolved in recent years beyond the simplistic measure of 'share value' because of two major changes in the global economic environment. First, companies need networks to compete more effectively, to gain market position and to communicate. Facing increasing pressure from financial market authorities, shareholders and non-governmental organisations (NGOs), premiums are being placed upon leadership, motivation, good governance, transparency and brand value. Second, they cannot escape the emerging understanding that production and consumption patterns contribute to climate change.

The social and economic costs of climate change are generating new environmental, social and governance reputation risks for corporates. In 2003, weather related disasters cost $70 billion; a European heatwave killed 20,000 people; in 2004, a tsunami destroyed whole tracts of coastal zones in several south Asian countries at great human and economic cost. The number of natural disasters recorded by insurance companies reached an historical peak. And as if to remind us that rich and poor all share the same planet, the after-effects of the environmental pollution and human displacement resulting from Hurricane Katrina which struck the US Gulf Coast on 29 August 2005, is a story which will continue to unfold for some time.

In a 2003 report (Starovic and Marr, 2003), the Chartered Institute of Management Accountants noted that 'intangible value drivers are replacing traditional hard assets as principal value creators of a growing number of listed companies' and that 'currently there is little consistency in the way intangible assets such as people, brand and knowledge are valued, managed and reported'. The report pointed out that only about 5 per cent of the market value of businesses such as Microsoft and Coca-Cola is represented in their balance sheets, and that even for companies like BP and Honda, it is no more than 30 per cent. The discrepancy represents the intangible assets these companies are known to have – in part their brand value, but mostly the behaviours and skills required to manage intangible qualities like skill, competence and knowledge. The risk attached to these is generally higher than that of physical assets. Knowledge assets, such as new discoveries (drugs, software products, etc.), or unique organisational designs (e.g. Internet-based supply chains) are by-and-large not traded in organised markets, and the property rights over these assets are not fully secured by the company, except for patents and trademarks.

Knowledge is an asset, just as capital is an asset. It is the fundamental component (basic 'good') of the knowledge economy. Environmental, social and governance values are assets that affect transparency and reputation. Both represent a major share of an enterprise's value-added. In times of economic uncertainty, managing the factors that drive business value becomes especially significant. Ultimately, such management may lead to business success or failure. Increasing numbers of companies have been measuring customer loyalty, employee satisfaction, environmental impacts and other performance areas that are not financial, but which they believe ultimately affect profitability. By looking at indicators measuring intangibles, employees can receive better information on the specific actions needed to achieve strategic objectives. Managers can get a glimpse of the business's progress well before a financial verdict is pronounced and the soundness of their investment allocations has become open to question. Stakeholders can gain a better sense of the company's overall performance, as non-financial indicators usually reflect realms of intangible values, such as new product development and low environmental impact, which conventional accounting rules do not recognise as assets.

Intangibles metrics are important for resource allocation decisions, and for estimates of corporate value and risks, so that shareholders can understand how their capital investments, applied to intangibles, can affect future growth, e.g. by investment in employee training. Conventional approaches to return on investment, assets or equity are seriously flawed as several value measures are missing from the denominator of these indicators: knowledge assets are all about creating future growth and environmental, sanitary and social risks require the application of responsibility and precaution management because the consequences might be worldwide and irreversible.

The need to manage intangible value induced by the advent of KM is requiring significant changes not only to the conventional ways of measuring value; it is requiring equally significant changes in organisational behaviour towards stakeholders and in perceptions of the organisational sphere of influence. These changes are not new in themselves – they have been debated for decades by social thinkers and commentators – but they are now beginning to occupy the centre ground in the business strategies of many organisations. They involve a radical change from our inherited ideas of what a 'business' is about, to new, accountable, social, ethical and environmental paradigms: corporate sustainability and responsibility.

Models of business

The need to manage and measure intangible value is deepening our understanding of what business organisations are and how they need to behave. The long-established view, rooted in eighteenth-century mercantilism, regards a business purely as an instrument of its owners for making profit. This model views the business as a machine, with internal linkages as rigid as any gear train, and therefore relies upon enduring stability both within and external to the business. In such a model, predictability is a more reliable guide than adaptability for building the business, and uncertainty – an unacceptable threat to stability – is dealt with severely. Trust and ethics are not regarded as intrinsic to organisational cohesion in this model of business. Rather, they are irritating characteristics of the imperfect human machine requiring strict control lest they result in lost production through symptoms such as absenteeism and inefficiency. One of the biggest recurring threats to stability experienced by such businesses is fluctuations in the labour supply.

The co-evolution and partial convergence of systems theory and ecological science during the latter half of the twentieth century provided the first clue that organisations (businesses among them) are actually more than mere machines. This organismic model recognises the effects of interdependency and exchange among the components of an organisation, the role of feedback and the creative potential of synergy. It begins to acknowledge that such human activity systems are dynamic and potentially unstable, unless an internal balance of forces is encouraged and the whole organism is able to respond effectively to stimuli from its environment. It recognises that components respond to each other's stimuli, but persists in regarding such responses as essentially non-sentient and quasi-mechanical, little different from those within a plant cell. Thus, as the differential take-up of technological advances among competitors causes uncertainty of competitive position, the response in the organismic model tends to be a tightening of command-and-control to fortify the current position, rather than to encourage the release of human creativity and innovative solutions.

Since the turn of the millennium, increasing attention has been given to organisations as social systems. In this model, organisations are regarded as voluntary associations of individuals who come together in purposeful action in pursuit of defined and agreed objectives – a vision already far removed from the Taylorist mechanistic model. This model recognises at last, that employees are not cog-wheels in a machine, but living, sentient beings with their own agenda quite separate from that of their employer. Of course, this produces a scenario far more complex than most employers would wish for. Employees do not just have individual agendas and aspirations; these are grounded in individual value and belief systems, which may engage closely, or not at all with corporate ambition.

More recently still, some commentators have suggested that complexity theory can be applied to the modern organisation. They argue that with the right interventions, organisations can (and should) become self-organising, 'complex adaptive systems' (CAS). So, which model applies to the twenty-first century business? Well, the answer would seem to be all of them. Most businesses exhibit some characteristics of all four models: machine, organism, social system and CAS, all blended into a complex whole. While it is only realistic to expect some degree of mechanistic command-and-control to remain necessary, commentators do seem to agree that what the modern business needs in today's turbulent and fast-moving markets, is flexibility and adaptability, underpinned by innovative capacity. These, in turn, can only be generated by harnessing the full potential of the organisation's intangible value – the knowledge embodied in its people, and the capacity for value-generation arising from the creative relationships among them. In other words, it is not machines, not managers, not marketers, but people who are the key actors, and it is their knowledge that generates and sustains the flow of value among individual and groups of employees; among the business, its associate businesses and the local economy; and between the business and the environment.

Forgotten stakeholders

The recognition of intangible value as a key business driver has profound implications, both within and external to the business. Not least, it questions the traditional hegemony where the shareholder's interests are paramount. In the knowledge economy, a business requires a number of different resources in order to function, and different resources are provided by different stakeholder communities. Money from shareholders and other investors is necessary but not sufficient without labour, knowledge and skill; labour, knowledge and skill are necessary but not sufficient without money. In this sharpened perspective, the shareholder is just one stakeholder among many. A business, after all, does not stand alone; it is a node in a network of commercial, economic and social entities, all interacting voluntarily for mutual benefit. In the broadest sense, therefore, a business must include equally among its stakeholders not only shareholders and investors, but also its associated businesses like suppliers, its customers, the local economy, society at large, the environment, and last but certainly not least, its employees.

There is ample evidence to suggest that business at large has not yet evolved sufficiently to acknowledge the full range of its stakeholder communities and its responsibilities towards them. In the socioeconomic sphere, wave after wave of 'economy with the truth' and spin in government and industry alike, fat rewards for thin performance in business leadership, company value-inflation through 'creative accounting' and asset and debt hiding, not to mention pension fund raiding, do little to inspire optimism that a new paradigm is forming, a paradigm of ethical governance transparency, of corporate responsibility and new, more equitable, ethical and egalitarian relationships among business and all of its stakeholder communities. That a business has responsibilities not only towards its employees but also towards its suppliers, was amply demonstrated in April 2005 when MG Rover in the UK's West Midlands went into receivership and ceased production. Quite apart from the company's own 6,000 workers, the jobs of up to 20,000 employees of its suppliers were immediately put at risk.

It is taking an extraordinary amount of time for us to realise that people, society – even civilisation itself – are intimately tied in with the welfare of our natural environment. On a supranational basis, global warming is perhaps the biggest single issue bringing about a change of attitude. Increasingly, businesses are expected to acknowledge the intangible knock-on effects of irresponsible corporate behaviour such as pollution. Perhaps the initial impetus and enduring momentum for the charge of corporate irresponsibility arose from the Bhopal catastrophe in India in 1984, when negligent discharges of toxic chemicals from a Union Carbide plant killed 3,000 people in a single night and which has caused more than 10,000 further deaths since. It is estimated that today, 10–15 people per month still die as a result. Dow Chemical, who purchased the remains of Union Carbide, still refuse both to clean up the site and to pay compensation (Prakash, 2003).

Nor can such irresponsibility be regarded (as many do) as a symptom of reckless global capitalism. The 1986 Chernobyl disaster in Ukraine, then part of the Soviet Union, belies that claim. Unbridled, irresponsible corporatism is the culprit, whether capitalist or socialist. The trend towards global corporatism is not only unsustainable, it is unhealthy, for the economic system, for society and for the environment.

Taking responsibility

There are encouraging signs that business is at last beginning to acknowledge the intangible value it can create or destroy both internally and externally. Corporate responsibility is the buzzword that has emerged to remind corporates that profit generation should not be their sole focus and that real costs and benefits, in environmental terms, in energy terms and in terms of global social justice need to be accounted for. Gradually too – but only gradually – the message is getting across that corporate responsibility is not simply a 'feel-good' factor; it is of real strategic and financial importance to every business. Corporate responsibility is manifesting itself in both mandatory and voluntary forms. The mandatory is represented by examples such as the Sarbanes-Oxley Act 2002 in the USA, the Financial Services and Markets Act 2000 in the UK, and Basel II in Europe, as well as the growing body of environmental regulations. However, responsibility is not something that can or should be regulated entirely by statute, and the various initiatives designed to encourage businesses to honour their responsibilities voluntarily have a vital role to play.

In the UK, 700 companies, including 72 from the FTSE 100 have come together to form Business in the Community (BIC), an independent business-led charity committed to the continual improvement of its member companies' impact on society. Over 2000 UK companies now participate in its programmes and campaigns (*Sunday Times*, 2005). In 2002, BIC set up the Corporate Responsibility Index (BIC, 2005a) to provide a voluntary benchmark for responsible business practice. In mid-2005, 144 companies were using the index to assess the degree to which their corporate responsibility strategies were being implemented in all areas of their businesses. Focusing on four key areas – community, environment, marketplace and workplace – BIC claims the index has 'provided a framework to show the wider world what corporate responsibility looks like in practice'.

In another initiative, the FTSE Group – the UK financial and investment indexing company – has introduced the FTSE4Good Index Series, designed to encourage socially responsible investment (SRI). Although both the BIC and FTSE4Good initiatives are praiseworthy steps in the right direction, it is obvious that the corporate responsibility message has many ears yet to reach and that progress is likely to be slow. The 144 current participants in the BIC Corporate Responsibility Index were all that resulted from inviting an initial 500 top national and international companies to participate. And in its March 2005 review, while FTSE4Good was able to report that a further 61 companies worldwide had met its SRI criteria, another 27 were removed from the index for failing to do so.

On a more positive note, one of the most remarkable examples of the corporate responsibility message getting home, is that of flooring materials manufacturer Interface Inc. in Atlanta, Georgia, USA (Interface, year unknown). Interface's Chairman, Ray C. Anderson, has embraced the philosophy and principles of sustainability with a breadth and depth of understanding, and a commitment, difficult to parallel elsewhere. Based upon a vision that sustainability is 'a dynamic process which enables all people to realise their potential and to improve their quality of life in ways that simultaneously protect and enhance the Earth's life support systems', Interface has embarked upon an ambitious programme to make its business both responsible and sustainable.

Interface's sustainability focuses on three key domains: economic, social and environmental. Economically, Interface argues that sustainability makes perfect business sense. In the social domain, social interaction and cultural enrichment, protecting the vulnerable and respecting social diversity are the priorities. Environmentally, Interface argues that we are not only depleting the Earth's natural resources and compromising its ability to regenerate them, but that we are also putting current and future generations of humankind at risk through harmful emissions.

Interface makes a number of commitments to achieving its vision, which it states as:

> To be the first company that, by its deeds, shows the entire industrial world what sustainability is in all its dimensions: people, process, product, place and profits – by 2020 – and in doing so we will become restorative through the power of influence. (Interface year unknown)

The Interface website then lists what amount to the key performance indicators by which it will be able to measure its progress towards sustainability. This is complemented by a remarkably lucid model showing the relationships among people, processes and capital within the company, and suppliers, customers, community and the environment outside it. While Interface may not be the instigator of what is becoming known as 'industrial ecology', it must certainly be recognised as an influential thought leader.

Equity and ethics in employment

'Doing the right thing' versus 'doing the thing right' has become something of a cliché in management education circles since American business leadership evangelist Warren G. Bennis first said, in his book *On Becoming a Leader*: 'Leaders are people who do the right thing; managers are people who do things right' (Bennis, 1989). This pithy observation has been repeated, appropriated and re-interpreted innumerable times in various contexts, but for most who have heard it, 'doing the right thing' relates to effectiveness, while 'doing the thing right' relates to efficiency. And the implied message? Well, that it is a formula for failure to 'do the thing right' (efficiently) if you're not 'doing the right thing' (something effective) in the first place.

The right thing to do in the twenty-first century is for a business to manage its intangible assets and to create the conditions where they can be used to generate value for all stakeholder communities. Yet, it takes time to change entrenched paradigms, and those in executive and managerial positions who have heeded this message in the past, have often found themselves ensnared in a tightly-knit web of vested interests whose instinctive focus on the conventional 'bottom line' leaves little room or desire to see beyond the financial balance sheet.

Somehow, the business world still seems to delude itself that its employees are 'conscripts', and that they can be 'commanded' to achieve certain goals and performance criteria with no consideration of the complexity of the interactions of personal belief and value systems, collective ambition, and the key role of leadership whatsoever. This archaic attitude becomes even more ironic when one considers that employees are decidedly not conscripts. They are volunteers and are free to move on as they wish. As Charles Handy points out:

> If your real assets are truly your intelligent people, the ones who create and maintain your intellectual property, then those people are precious. Unlike other assets, however, they can walk out of the door. (Handy, 1996)

Knowledge management is a response to a situation where a business's key resources are no longer in safe deposit, under strict control and accountable for by well-defined mathematical procedures. The key source of value now is intangible and largely locked inside people's heads. You cannot command someone to think, be effective or to innovate; cooperation cannot be coerced. Such behaviour has to be facilitated, encouraged and ultimately rewarded. In twenty-first century business, it is commitment that matters, not compliance; commitment to effective action in the collective pursuit of shared outcomes, a commitment grounded in mutual respect and trust within a network of open, multi-dimensional relationships conducive to cooperation and collaboration rather than compliance.

So, by all means 'manage' intangible value in this new environment, but recognise that 'manage' no longer means what it did under the old mechanical model of business. Managers in the knowledge economy lead rather than command. They look to the longer term rather than the shorter, and address an holistic vision of outcomes, rather than isolated 'objectives'. They encourage flexibility rather than consistency, they focus on people and their skills, competences and knowledge, rather than organisation and structure; enabling rather than restraining, developing rather than maintaining, directing rather than controlling. This new breed of manager has to be equally aware of and responsive to the diverse needs of individuals and of teams and other groupings, integrating individual competences and agendas into an effective whole, ensuring knowledge and information are accessible and shared in pursuit of the collective vision.

Just as businesses are 'nodes' in a cybernetic network of industrial and commercial, economic, social and environmental causes and effects, so employees are 'nodes' in a cybernetic network of functional, operational, managerial and professional relationships, where value is exchanged and created through effective and sustainable relationships. Such organic systems cannot be 'managed' in the conventional sense, only empowered through effective leadership to become autonomous and self-organising.

In its turn, self-organisation can only flourish where people are enabled to perform effectively through access to relevant information and being competent in their roles. Just as biological organisms constantly exchange nutrients and energy among their components and with their environment, so individuals and teams exchange tangible and intangible value, sustaining the processes that determine their structure and the structure that results from their processes. Verna Allee describes this scenario as a 'value network': 'A value network is any web of relationships that generates tangible and intangible value through complex dynamic exchanges between two or more individuals, groups, or organizations' (Allee, 2002).

In Allee's value network approach, tangible exchanges involve goods, services and revenue, while intangible exchanges support the core product and service value chain but involve 'exchanges of strategic information, planning knowledge, process knowledge, technical know-how, collaborative design work, joint planning activities, and policy development' (Allee, 2002). Each 'value input' is made on a quid pro quo basis – a form of barter – where the giver expects to receive something in return, if not at the time of giving, then subsequently. If one places Allee's value network approach in the context of the relationships between employee and employer, then it is difficult to escape the observation that the conventional relationship is heavily biased in favour of the latter.

Many businesses have gone some way towards redressing this imbalance through the introduction of individual performance assessment processes. While such processes initiate a welcome dialogue between the employer (manager) and the employee, what might be called the 'terms of reference' of this dialogue remain skewed in favour of the employer. Even when a personal performance plan is linked closely to a personal development plan, the formal framework of association between employee and employer is enshrined in the contract of employment and job description – both of which overwhelmingly state what the employer expects of the employee, with scant reference (beyond grading and salary scale) to the reciprocal expectations. If businesses are to acknowledge the importance of intangible value properly – with their employees' skills, competence and knowledge at the top of the list – then the expectations and aspirations of employees need to be enshrined equally in any formal framework of association. As Charles Handy, talking of what he calls the 'new professionals', says:

> Such people want an organization that recognizes their individual talents and provides space for their individual contributions. They prefer small, autonomous work groups based on reciprocal trust between leader and led, groups responsible, as far as possible, for their own destiny. (Handy, 1996)

Such a reciprocal framework of association would not only recognise that employees, after all, are a major stakeholder community and that their economic and social well-being and their employer's sustainability are mutually interdependent; it would also provide a far more rigorous and systematic framework for linking individual and team performance into organisational performance measurement systems such as the Balanced Scorecard, as well as enabling those individuals and teams to understand their particular contribution.

In Allee's value network model, business value is generated through the exchange of both tangible and intangible value, the latter often being in the form of knowledge. But it remains unstated that this exchange occurs on the understanding that the employer will duly recognise an employee's total value input, trace it through to business results and compensate them accordingly. Yet, while the exchange of tangible value expected (by both employer and employee) may be made generally explicit in the contract of employment and job description, few such agreements currently include any reference to the intangible value to be exchanged, thereby failing to recognise the major contribution that employees' skills, competences and knowledge make to business success. This serious omission is giving rise to an interesting conundrum requiring urgent resolution for both employers' and employees' sake: who 'owns' the knowledge that sustains the knowledge-based business?

No convincing answer to this question can emerge until some clarity has been achieved regarding the respective expectations of employer and employee in terms of intangibles exchange. What is needed is some form of framework that can stand alongside that which deals with tangible value (the contract of employment and job description). Emeritus Professor at the University of Manchester, Enid Mumford, may already have provided the basis of such a framework in her remarkable book *Systems Design: Ethical Tools for Ethical Change* (Mumford, 1996). Although focused on the socio-technical design of information systems, much of Mumford's book is a discussion of the ethical aspects of design and their history in the modern age. Her ETHICS method could be described as 'systems design as if people mattered' and is based upon her postulation of five implicit contracts between employer and employee. Although one of the five – the psychological contract – was first described by others in the 1960s and has in recent years become a more acceptable adjunct to the legal contract, at least among those concerned with employee personal development, Mumford's five contracts together provide a much richer account of the employer-employee relationship. The five are:

- the knowledge contract;
- the psychological contract;
- the efficiency contract;
- the work structure contract;
- the value contract.

What follows is a brief description of Mumford's 1996 contracts with minor additions to emphasise their relevance to the current discussion.

The knowledge contract

In her/his assigned roles, the employee provides the skills, competence and knowledge required, while the employer ensures that these are utilised to the fullest possible extent and adequately remunerated, that they are supported by effective information flows and access to the knowledge of others, and that the employee is provided with opportunities to develop his/her capabilities further.

The psychological contract

While the employer is looking for its employees to be loyal, motivated and enthusiastic – for commitment – the employee seeks occupational and professional fulfilment, responsibility and recognition, and scope for applying her/his competence to the fullest.

The efficiency contract

As already noted, efficiency has tended to preoccupy employers more than any other aspect of employment. Inasmuch as this is the result of too sharp a focus on the financial bottom line, its influence will be deflated somewhat when measures concerned more with intangible value join it in the corporate performance metrics toolkit. Employers will continue to expect employees to meet customer quantity and quality requirements, but equally, employees are entitled to expect employers to maintain controls and services that support personal and team efficiency, and ensure that demands made upon employees are not excessive.

The work structure contract

Traditionally, employers' tendency towards 'accounting by numbers' has obscured the significant contribution that work satisfaction and absence of stress can make not only to productivity and quality, but also to innovation. Employees are entitled to expect work structures and processes to be designed to minimise the boring and routine elements and to make work as interesting and challenging as possible. It is also incumbent upon employers to ensure that tasks are matched to the competences of those who are to perform them and integrated smoothly with those of others. However, employees must accept that the boring and the routine cannot always be entirely eliminated. Work structures need to be designed by both employer and employee together through negotiation and cooperation, not confrontation.

The value contract

Mumford's own words cannot be bettered here:

> This last and most important contract sets out the ethical principles that each side wants or expects from the other. It covers intangibles

such as mutual loyalty and trust, shared objectives and the provision of a high quality of working life for employees. Over the years, many European firms have built their reputations on the strength of this contract. Its practical form has been shown in effective consultation, good communication, a continuing concern for the welfare of all employees, both in work and at home, and a wish to be seen as a good, caring employer, whose first responsibility is to employees rather than to shareholders. (Mumford 1996: 36).

Although Mumford's five contracts leave a lot of questions yet to be asked, it must be remembered that she was writing some ten years ago. Since then, a number of major developments in the workplace and in the business environment have tended to reinforce her vision of the business as a partnership between employee and employer. Not least among them is the recognition of knowledge and intangible value in general as key business resources and the change of emphasis in business goals from unqualified success to sustainability. There is every sign that a rapprochement between the employee and employer agendas is occurring and that corporatist self-interest will eventually give way to what Piero Formica, Dean of the International University of Entrepreneurship in Ijmuiden, Amsterdam, calls 'cooperative partnership' as the business model of the future. This, he says, is:

> ...founded on the intelligence of individuals from diverse backgrounds, their interactions in socially heterogeneous groups and concentration on complying with the tasks required to structure the process of knowledge innovation, rather than on buying influence at the political market. (Formica, 2005)

Asking 'how to fill the gap between individual and organisational knowledge', Formica answers his own question by noting that:

> There has been a shift toward a more advanced culture of co-opetition among all parties in the supply chain. The invisible hand of the market must be accompanied by an invisible handshake (i.e. connectivity and trust-led businesses). (Formica, 2005)

There will, of course, be many who will refuse to engage at all in any such handshake, and still more who will do so sceptically. But sooner or later, the fact must be faced: the key resources of the knowledge economy are in the hands – or rather, the heads – of those (obliged) to use them – employees. Knowledge and intangible value now call the tune, not capital. And for those who still harbour doubts that such a transformation is possible, there are many precedents which may be cited. These range from initiatives hatched in highly politicised circumstances to those concerned simply with the preservation of humanistic values in business.

One of the most famous examples of the former is the Mondragón experiment initiated in 1941 in Spain's Guipúzcoa province by the young priest, Father José María Arizmendiarrieta (Wikipedia, 2005). In the wake of a horrendous civil war, Arizmendiarrieta set up a school, based upon cooperative principles, dedicated to improving the economic circumstances of the town. In 1956, five young graduates of the school set up a cooperative venture to manufacture petrol-based heaters and cookers. In 1959, they inaugurated the Caja Laboral, a sort of credit union providing access to financial services for cooperative members and ultimately acting as a source of start-up funds for new cooperative schemes. Mondragón has grown into a huge network of cooperative ventures in Spain and is not without its critics and detractors, both from within and external to the cooperative movement. Yet, despite its shortcomings, it has proved sustainable for over half a century, which is more than can be said for an astronomical number of conventional businesses.

At the purely humanistic end of the spectrum, there is probably no example quite so starkly indicative of what can be done where there is a will – driven by enlightened leadership – as that of Semco, a Brazilian company that has gone further than any other documented case towards building a fully democratic, humanitarian and sustainable business agglomerate (Semler, 1993). Semco's innovations in business structure and relationships – while still achieving business success – are truly astounding. Consider a business which, when it becomes too large to properly address the real-life needs of its employees, divides like an amoeba to spawn new, autonomous businesses small enough that employees can contribute meaningfully to something they understand. Consider a business, where the advantages of openness and truthfulness are seen to outweigh the disadvantages, such that all employees have access to the company books. Consider a business that has turned its back on the facile assumption that profits belong solely to those who invest the capital, and openly espouse profit sharing. Consider a business where it is employees who assess the performance of their managers, not the other way round, where the old pyramidal hierarchical structure of command-and-control has been replaced by a strategy-coordinating innermost circle, a mid-placed second circle of 'partners' who lead the different business units, and an outermost circle including everyone else as 'associates', and coordinated by those who have demonstrated the necessary competence and leadership abilities.

Part 2: Business, society and the environment

The need to value intangibles

Traditional financial reporting methods disclose only a fraction of the information that is relevant to investors. Intangible assets have become key drivers of shareholder value in the knowledge economy, but accounting rules do not yet acknowledge this shift in the valuation of companies. The traditional reluctance of accountants and corporate executives to recognise knowledge and other intellectual capital as assets in financial reports, on a par with physical and financial assets, has generated a large information gap, which completely overlooks the value of research and development, patents, copyrights, customer lists and brand equity. To a degree, such an attitude in the accounting community concerning balance sheets may be understandable, but there is no longer any excuse for financial markets or performance measurement specialists to avoid seeking information that recognises knowledge or other intangible assets and factors, such as environmental impact, as either value or risk. The problem they need to resolve, though complex, can be stated quite simply: how to demonstrate a cause-and-effect link between improvements in non-financial areas and cash flow, profit, or stock price.

In response to this problem, many companies have adopted measurement frameworks such as Kaplan and Norton's Balanced Scorecard (BSC), Accenture's Performance Prism or Skandia's Intellectual Capital Navigator, in an attempt to capture the financial value-added of intangible assets. On this basis, the importance of intangibles in the market value of a company can be shown to vary between 33 per cent (according to Cap Gemini Ernst and Young – CGEY) and 85 per cent (Innovest). The CGEY (1999) Center for Business Innovation's Measures That Matter survey showed that over one-third of an institutional investor's valuation of a company is based on non-financial elements.

In May 2004, Innovest issued, for the Carbon Disclosure Project, a survey on the cost of climate change to FT500 Global Index companies representing roughly 13 per cent of all emissions from fossil fuel combustion worldwide. Conclusions indicate that taking climate change risks into account is now becoming a key component of smart financial management. This is likely to result in greater pressure on firms to measure and disclose the risks they face. Generally accepted carbon accounting principles at national and international levels will emerge in the near future. They are likely to attribute up to 85 per cent of a company's true market value to intangible value drivers. Such intangible value drivers cover a wide range of factors, including the notion of corporate leadership, brand value and the reaction of directors, officers and employees to climate change challenges.

Strategy maps: aligning intangibles to corporate ambition

The issue of valuing intangibles forms the core of a much more fundamental challenge: how to ensure sustainable business success. This is not simply a matter of concern for those traditionally regarded as having the greatest vested interest in the business – directors, shareholders and senior executives. As we argued in Part 1, sustainability is vital to the interests of all stakeholders. Corporates therefore need to devise a strategy for sustainability, comprising a selected set of activities in which the organisation will excel in creating a sustainable difference in the marketplace. The core of the strategy focuses on three key elements:

- *Mission*: Provides the starting point by defining why the organisation exists or how a business unit fits within a broader corporate architecture. It identifies how the organisation expects to compete and deliver value to customers;

- *Values*: Define codes of conduct to support and/or encourage sustainable business practices;

- *Vision*: Mid to long-term goals. External and market-oriented in visionary terms. Paints a picture of the future that clarifies the organisation's direction and helps individuals understand why and how they should support the organisation.

The inventors of the Balanced Scorecard – Kaplan and Norton – began collaboration in 1990 to explore new ways of measuring organisational performance, and addressed these issues first in an article (Kaplan and

Norton, 1992), and subsequently in their best-selling book *The Balanced Scorecard: Translating Strategy into Action* (Kaplan and Norton, 1996).

In the BSC, business strategy is mapped against four broad domains and seeks answers to a number of key questions:

- *Customer*: In order to satisfy customers, which operational processes must the corporate excel at? Kaplan and Norton present four generic processes of customer management: select, acquire, retain and grow relationships with customers. This implies not only the need to monitor customer relationships, but also to ensure their long-term demands are satisfied – e.g. those related to knowledge acquisition.

- *Financial*: To financially sustain its mission, what must the corporate focus on?

- *Internal*: What key internal business processes create value? Answers usually include operational management, customer management, innovation and regulatory and social processes.

- *Staff learning and growth*: How will the corporate sustain its ability to innovate, change and improve? Almost invariably, the response relates to which internal intangible assets need to be aligned and integrated to create value, and developed in order to sustain an advantage.

Kaplan and Norton subsequently developed their thinking to take account of the growing significance of intangibles in their book *Strategy Maps – Converting Intangible Assets into Tangible Outcomes* (Kaplan and Norton, 2004). The authors rightly insist that every company needs to dig deep to discover and track the activities that truly affect the BSC's broad domains. Kaplan and Norton believed that 'knowledge-based assets – primarily employees and information technology' were 'becoming increasingly important for companies' competitive success. But companies' primary measurement systems remain the financial accounting systems'. In Kaplan and Norton's taxonomy, intangibles pervade their broad domains of customer relationships, internal efficiency enhancement and staff learning and growth, but also include environmental performance. The difficult question is to identify 'what is the framework to measure intangibles that can possibly assure accurate intangible performance measurements?'

Representing intangibles in performance measurement

The BSC focuses on the fact that companies, facing modified conditions of competition in the era of information technology, need specific financial management and controlling systems in order to stay competitive. Their message was that companies need management techniques for intangible assets such as employees, infrastructures or technologies employed. The BSC is thus designed to address the challenges of the information age better and to include assets such as customer satisfaction, process quality and organisational development, alongside more traditional financial indicators. The BSC allows for the management of the demands of the company relevant to stakeholders and for the development of financial goals for the business through a systematic architecture of causal relationships.

By introducing non-financial, more qualitative 'soft facts', the potential benefit of investments in intangible assets becomes more visible, encouraging all members of the firm to adopt a long-term view looking substantially beyond the next quarterly report. The BSC tries to establish equilibrium in various respects, considering equally:

- short and long-term related goals;
- internal aspects (such as processes and organisational development) as well as external ones (i.e. customers and shareholders);
- leading indicators that relate to a goal in the future as well as results ('lagging indicators') to depict the effect of aims and measures in the past;
- quantitative, financial hard facts and qualitative non-financial soft facts.

The four objectives at the core of Kaplan and Norton's proposed matrix may therefore be re-stated as:

- *Financial objectives*: Similar to traditional systems of management and accounting.
- *Market perspective*: For the identification of relevant customer and market segments that contribute to the financial goals.
- *Internal processes*: To identify and structure efficiently the internal value-driving processes that are vital regarding the goals of the customers and the shareholders.

- *Organisational development*: To depict all staff and organisational-related aspects that are vital to the organisational re-engineering process.

Transforming the bottom line

Some schools of thought consider conventional methods of budgeting as precluding any real progress towards a 'bottom line' which properly balances Kaplan and Norton's four enterprise objectives. In the twenty-first century model of management for the knowledge economy, the focus is upon strategic performance (not just financial), generating added value and managing intangibles. This model relies heavily upon trust-based relationships among the major participants – managers, workers, customers and associate businesses – and this trust can rapidly evaporate where managers find they are not meeting largely financial performance targets set months earlier when conditions were very different. Faced with such a situation, they revert to old-style command-and-control practices – a syndrome often referred to as 'managing by numbers'.

The Beyond Budgeting Round Table (BBRT) is a collaborative think-tank committed to convincing businesses in the twenty-first century that managing by numbers – as represented by conventional budgeting – is an indicator of performance, which, in the knowledge economy, is at best misleading and at worst useless (Daum, 2004). When the operating environment of the business changes so rapidly as it does today, what the BBRT call the 'fixed performance contract' set months previously quickly becomes meaningless. As Jeremy Hope, one of the founders of the BBRT says:

> This process of engaging huge numbers of people in a protracted cycle of detailed planning, and then making them march to the drumbeat of the budget, seems to us not just a waste of time, but also an insult to their intelligence. (Quoted in Daum, 2004)

Perhaps not surprisingly, many of the pioneer examples of beyond budgeting management models occur in Scandinavia, the best-known being Svenska Handelsbanken. Of this initiative, BBRT founder Jeremy Hope says:

> The Handelsbanken management model introduced by Dr Wallander is predicated on the belief that the only sustainable

competitive advantage available to a firm in a fast-changing world, and especially in a service business, lies with its people – especially their creativity, insights, and judgments. (Quoted in Daum, 2004)

Mapping activity to business strategy

Whether or not conventional methods of budgeting are retained, clear organisational goals and a strategy for pursuing them are at the core of the sustainable business. How the strategy is communicated and translated into specific actions throughout the company can determine the successful attainment of these goals. Only a small percentage of the workforce may actually understand the overall company objectives, and an even smaller number are sure their work aligns with the corporate goals. This can lead to a disjointed and inefficient implementation of the strategy across the enterprise. In addition, teams may not see how their work affects other areas of the business. Effectively communicating and translating strategies into actions throughout the company can avoid the all-too-common conclusion: 'we had a good strategy but we failed to execute'.

Examining key business drivers, organisational values, business ethics and codes of conduct improves the alignment of business units and workgroups to corporate objectives, assigning accountability, monitoring progress and accelerating exception resolution. Strategy maps, scorecards and in-context dashboards are the traditional key tools to help the understanding of the strategy to evolve over time. To the extent that these tools must be based upon value-generating activities in the business, techniques may be used which are similar to those employed when producing functional taxonomies for records and information management (RIM) purposes.

RIM is concerned with linking information use and records generation to the activities and transactions of the organisation primarily for resource management purposes. However, the functional mapping that provides the effective foundation for RIM, can also provide a useful starting point for defining how knowledge-based assets contribute to organisational viability and sustainability. Functional mapping produces a taxonomy of business activities in terms of key business processes and their constituent activities and transactions. If details of information consumption and production (documents and records) are included, then a valuable picture emerges of how knowledge-based assets contribute to value generation. Interviews with staff involved in posts representative of the key activities of the enterprise allow individual and team objectives to be cascaded from the overall business objectives and to be linked internally and externally and to other relevant activities. This helps to effectively gauge the impact of events in other areas of the business and to identify intangible value flows in much the same way as does Allee's value network approach.

Methodologies such as DIRKS (Design and Implementation of Record-Keeping Systems – DIRKS 2003) can be used to determine what Kaplan and Norton call 'a strategic theme' and which they describe as 'the process, the intangible assets, the targets and the initiatives required to execute a piece of the strategy'. Tools such as Mind Maps® are very useful for charting the results of this analysis, and offer the particular advantage of providing a pictorial representation of the value-generation model that may easily be communicated, understood and validated by others.

A taxonomy of business activities provides the opportunity to create a clear, tangible picture of the benefits of intangibles as they relate to the goals of the organisation, and in turn supports the identification of the key elements of the sustainability balanced scorecard:

- strategic themes based on value-creating processes, activities and transactions;
- staff roles in the business process;
- internal and external information flows and needs; metadata required for each activity in a business process.

Such a taxonomy can also be used to generate further benefits:

- *Knowledge*: The taxonomy provides to all staff a general understanding of all activities.
- *Collaboration*: Collaborators are aware of the relationships within the organisational structure.
- *Transparency*: Metadata could track the degree of internal and external confidentiality of all business-vital documents and should become the backbone of a transparency policy.
- *Dialogue*: The taxonomy allows for multidimensional navigation in electronic records using semantic web technologies.

An examination of how vital documents and records and other knowledge-based assets are produced and consumed over time, provides low-level indicators that support the monitoring of performance achievement at different stages of internal business processes. This is especially important for confidential information and for corporate transparency. For instance, measuring the numbers of a specific document type deposited in an electronic archive centre would be effective to monitor:

- the reach of a specific activity undertaken by a team during a period of time;
- the degree of implementation of a transparency policy.

Record-keeping specialists and lawyers could then determine stakeholders' access to documents, monitor the storage of vital records in the repository by users and control the quality and availability of records.

Managing beyond: triple bottom line accounting

Despite its already comprehensive structure, the BSC lacks a number of elements if it is to be an instrument of corporate sustainability performance. How, for instance, might it integrate the concerns of society at large, or the impact of corporate activity on the environment and on quality of life? The answer to these questions might lie in the concept of triple bottom line accounting (TBLA), which proposes ways of extending conventional business performance reporting to include outcomes in the social and environmental dimensions as well as the financial. The concept was first introduced by sustainability consultant John Elkington in his book *Cannibals with Forks*. Elkington suggests that, rather than monitoring each bottom line separately, partial integration may be the answer:

> Some of the most interesting challenges, however, are found not within but between the areas covered by the economic, social, and environmental bottom lines ... New concepts and requirements (are) emerging at the interfaces between each of these great agendas, in the 'shear zones'. (Elkington, 1998)

By concentrating on the 'shear zones' between two dimensions, Elkington offers the opportunity for companies to think about the links between two dimensions separately. The purpose is then to understand the 'business case' for sustainability: how does environmental (or social) sustainability contribute to economic sustainability? It allows firms to pursue shareholder strategies precisely through environmental or social sustainability; their strategies would aim for 'eco-efficiency' or 'social productivity'. But we still lack a number of key elements in the analysis: what is the quality of the management? Is the corporate ready to be transparent? Will the corporate be prepared to conduct a dialogue with stakeholders about its environmental and social impacts?

Such triple bottom line performance measurement can be added to the current BSC. The question is to determine how to monitor effectively the contribution of environmental and social strategies to the bottom line, how to set, track and control clear targets for environmental management and corporate social responsibility? The purpose of such monitoring must be clearly understood to be to identify when it really pays to be sustainable through making the relation between non-financial and financial indicators explicit, and to point the way towards ethical rationality in activity management (Guinomet, 1999).

Sustainability balanced scorecards

The strategy map framework enables human, information, organisational capital and the environment to be represented as assets that are eventually converted to value. It shows the road to success. Managers need techniques to identify the intangibles, including approaches for visualising how these resources drive performance and tools to measure and value the stocks and flows of these assets. An organisation cannot assign a meaningful financial value to an intangible factor like 'attract, retain and motivate high-quality staff' because intangible value can be derived only in the context of the strategy. Specific competencies support each strategic internal process: the human capital, information and organisational capital.

Although most of the dimensions analysed have been around for a long time, it is only since the mid-1990s that companies have begun to be aware of the impact of their (lack of) social understanding in the business arena. For instance, the well-documented cases of Shell, Nike and BP have brought issues such as human rights into corporate boardrooms. To align internal and external environmental, social and governance assets in the corporate strategy, some degree of transformation of the scorecard can allow perspectives to be developed to take into account the sustainable development of the business, as expressed through the four dimensions of the BSC (Figge et al., 2002).

Transforming the customer dimension

This implies the identification of any group or individual who can affect or is affected by the achievements of the corporate strategy and objectives, the purpose being to increase mutual understanding and cooperation.

Transforming the financial dimension

Many popular products are less resource-intensive than in the past, as technological advances have made possible the development of better performing products which require fewer physical resources. The development of eco-efficiency, integrating externalities such as waste into production processes, has proven to be an excellent way to maximise resource productivity. Access to information, development of relationships, accountability and transparency strengthen licence to operate, reduce risk and boost human and intellectual capital, thus developing the strength of the corporate financial statement and its access to capital.

Transforming the internal dimension

This is certainly the dimension in which returns on investment (ROI) require patience, as investments to develop solid and consolidated information systems are subject to the quality of the business analysis and the accuracy of the solution developed. As managers prefer to have short-term ROI, gaining their support necessitates the comparison of best practices and presentation of standards to change research and development priorities within the corporate or to develop integrated information systems. The same applies to the transformation of information capital, which consists of two components: technology infrastructure (central mainframes, communication networks, managerial expertise, such as standards, disaster planning and security) and information capital applications (information, knowledge, technology, operation management and regulatory and social).

Knowledge management has a vital role to play here, as it can provide a platform for the integration of many disciplines:

- *Human resources*: Identification of strategic jobs and skills, identification of communities.

- *Information technology*: Identification of key metadata, permissions; integration of IT applications.

- *Content and information management*: Records-keeping strategy, communication flows, communities point of view mapping, transparency.

- *Strategic planning*: Identification of relevant performance measures, alignment to the policies – compliance, responsibility, communication with stakeholders, process re-design.

- *Corporate learning*: Training, sharing information sources.

Transforming the staff learning and growth dimension

This starts with transforming human capital by identifying the specific job families expected to drive performance improvements for each strategic internal process. It ensures that a sufficient number of people, within each of the strategic job families, have the right skills to support the associated internal process. Such an effort leads to two key outputs: the definition of competency profiles and the development of human capital development programmes. Organisational capital is typically built upon four components:

- *Culture*: Awareness and internalisation of the mission, visions and core values needed to execute the strategy.
- *Leadership*: Availability of qualified leaders at all levels to mobilise the organisation toward its strategy.
- *Alignment*: Individual, team and departmental goals and incentives linked to attainment of strategic objectives.
- *Teamwork*: Knowledge with strategic potential shared throughout the organisation.

In developing regulatory and social processes, corporates often seek to go beyond complying with the minimal standards established by regulations in all aspects of their business. They wish to perform better than the regulatory constraints, so that they develop a reputation for good governance practice and of being an employer of choice. Responsible practice will include standards related to human rights, workplace conditions and employee aspirations and expectations as expressed in Mumford's five contracts, and the engagement of business partners and non-business partners, for example NGOs and civil society. Good practice will also include the degree to which a company actively and constructively uses its resources to support the social and economic development of communities, through direct investments of cash, in-kind support or staff time, or through company policies that generate community capital, such as local sourcing, hiring, partnerships and education.

Addressing corporate responsibility

Corporate responsibility reporting

Corporate responsibility reporting is more than a 'feel-good' public relations exercise (BIC 2005b). Corporate responsibility – also often called corporate social responsibility (CSR) – encompasses the three pillars of sustainable development, also called the 'Three Ps': people, planet, profit. Corporate responsibility views the promotion of respect for business ethics, people and communities, and protection of the environment, as an integral strategy that increases value added and thus improves the competitive position of a firm. Indeed, the first trends in the USA were about advertising philanthropic activities.

In Europe, the word 'social' has been added and used to evolve from the purely environmental reporting to social, ethical, environmental and economic reporting. This period reflected corporate involvement in understanding the need to offer to future generations the capacity to meet their needs according to existing practices and standards. Accompanying the tenth birthday of the Rio Agenda, corporates stressed their will to support millennium development goals, publishing either sustainability or corporate social responsibility reports. Following Enron, Parmalat and other misleading financial reporting exercises, the CSR reporting practice embraced the corporate governance covered by Sarbanes-Oxley and the terminology 'corporate reporting' is now used.

The purpose of such reports is to provide a platform for the corporate view when dealing with a dilemma. Indeed, activities and financial reporting are well appreciated. But the way these are managed is up to the Board. Since the launch of the very first World Social Forum, NGOs and civil society have developed new ways of exerting influence, such as partnerships and consultation processes. Such practices are proving to be a learning exercise within corporates to understand the sensibility of civil society to certain aspects of their activity.

The development of the Internet has also provided a channel for the promotion of the agendas of NGOs. They use the Internet to launch challenges and comments on corporate practices. The corporate responsibility reporting exercise is therefore an opportunity for corporates to present their dilemmas from their viewpoint and to justify the choices they make. Such practices prove very important for industries able to benchmark against the competition and then demonstrate their best practices on the market, or for investment banking operations, which acquire the ability to demonstrate that profit is part of the overall picture, but that environmental, social and governance credit risk assessment is a new and vital element of the corporate risk profile.

Becoming accountable

Baruch Lev (1999), who devised a special intangibles scoreboard, argues that the lack of public information and disclosure on intangibles' value contributes to a higher cost of capital and affords abnormally large gains to insiders at the expense of outside investors. To level the playing field, Lev (2002) proposes that companies periodically release, in addition to the required income, balance sheet and cash flow statements, quantitative and standardised information most relevant to the company value chain or business model, such as innovation processes. Innovation processes are where economic value is created in today's knowledge-based businesses in nearly all industrial sectors.

The objective of such reporting is to make relevant information available to outsiders. The goals are clear: transparency and accountability. Following this trend, in 2005 the International Accounting Standards Board changed the rules on how firms should report intangibles. All public and very large private companies in the UK have to produce an operating and financial review (OFR). Besides traditional financial measures, the OFR requires companies to include an account of how the company's intangible assets contribute to its overall value generation and how the conflicting stakeholder interests are balanced. Several European countries now request corporates employing more than 1,000 employees and quoted on the stock exchange, to report on their triple bottom line.

The European Commission has placed corporate social responsibility at the core of Europe's competition strategy, and has issued a Green Paper on CSR and a subsequent communication outlining the Commission's definition of CSR, along with steps that companies, governments and civil society can undertake to refine their commitments to CSR. Local, national, European and international regulations on the environment, on employee health and safety, and on hiring and employment practices impose standards on corporate operations. Existing rules and standards of corporate responsibility in Europe help to identify areas of non-financial governance. These standards are tools or methods for presenting corporate responsibility information to stakeholders. Table 2.1 (overleaf) proposes a list of existing standards to support the development of a corporate responsibility policy.

A road map for sustainability

The ultimate aim of triple bottom line reporting is that businesses should account for their performance on economic, environmental and social criteria and attempt to satisfy their stakeholders on all three sets of criteria. As a result, corporate responsibility should encompass management of environmental, social and governance issues and thus requires action in seven domains.

Table 2.1	Existing standards to support the development of corporate responsibility

Anti-corruption	OECD convention on combating the bribery of foreign public officials in international business transactions The Proceeds of Crime Act 2002 UN Convention against Corruption Council of Europe Criminal and Civil Laws Convention on Corruption
Corporate governance	US Sarbanes-Oxley Act 2002 Basel II OECD Principles of Corporate Governance Caux Principles for Business Standard and Poor's Governance Services UNEP Corporate Social Responsibility Guidelines The EU Action Plan for Company Law
Corporate responsibility promotion	The Global Compact OECD Guidelines for Multilateral Enterprises The Principles for Global Corporate Responsibility Global Reporting Initiative (GRI, year unknown) Corporate social responsibility index Sustainability Integrated Guidelines for Management SIGMA (first TBL) ICC Business Charter on Sustainable Development UN Sub-commission on Human Rights Draft Norms on the Responsibilities of International Corporations and other Business Enterprises Business leaders initiative on human rights European Green paper – promoting a European Framework for corporate social responsibility Commission recommendation that member states should require companies to disclose relevant environmental information in their annual financial accounts Communication from the commission CSR: A business contribution to sustainable development – Commission strategy to promote business contribution to sustainable development CSR EMS Forum European Council of Minister's Resolution on CSR EP's report on the communication from the commission on CSR
Environment	ISO 14001 EMAS UK Environmental Guidelines Natural Step

Table 2.1	Existing standards to support the development of corporate responsibility *(cont'd)*
Social	Universal Declaration of Human Rights AccountAbility 1000 (AA 1000) Social Accountability 8000 (SA 8000)
Employment	Fundamental ILO Conventions The Framework Directive EC Directive on Information and Consultation of Employees EC Directive on The Implementation of Equal Treatment for Men and Women as Regards Access to Employment, Vocational Training and Working Conditions
Procurement	EC General Procurement Guidelines

Promoting a vision, including facilitating prosperity, competitiveness, cultural exchange and social inclusion, while minimising negative social and environmental impacts. Observing the wider picture to create a clear and tangible view of the benefits of intangibles as they relate to goals in the corporate, implies an adequate understanding of which intangibles are key to the business sector. The purpose of this first step is to understand the driving forces of the sector and to be aware of the potential of intangible assets for competitive advantage. This step will help to determine the role of intangibles and intellectual capital within the corporate and for its stakeholders.

Thinking long term and seeking to be challenged by leading experts. Innovating and presenting new products.

Developing dialogue. Pursuing a stakeholder partnership approach to the decision-making process on projects and investments affecting the wider community, listening to and understanding the concerns of stakeholders, developing practical programmes of action to address them. In order to liaise between the strategic objectives determined by the Board and the reality of everyday activities handled by staff or impacting stakeholders, consultations are an explicit requirement for good practice in corporate responsibility. The ultimate goal of such a process is certainly to give stakeholders confidence in corporate behaviour and in the legitimacy of its activities; differences among stakeholders can co-exist without disrupting the process.

The process is transparent when it brings all relevant stakeholders together in one forum and publicises activities in an understandable manner to the general public. In such a process, the corporate recognises that its stakeholders are aware of the quality of their environment and intend to defend it. Nowadays, stakeholders are aware of the implications (for health, safety and finance) of climate change and of ozone layer depletion, of the loss of natural resources and of biodiversity, of water pollution and waste management. The real challenge is in the integration of corporate responsibility into the strategy and operations of a complex organisation in an increasingly globalised economy. It is an unfolding learning journey, which passes through different phases including two major ones: the publication of a corporate responsibility report and the building of a new training and awareness programme accessible to all staff, on what sustainable development means for their activities (Van Heel et al., 2001).

Integrating strategies and systems to support internal communication, transparency, trust and straight-through processing. For knowledge managers it is crucial to identify:

- *routines and procedures*: e.g. processes, functions, activities, transactions and tacit rules;
- *human resources*: e.g. roles, skills, know-how, experience;
- *culture*: e.g. values, codes of conducts, dignity at work, gender and whistleblower policies;
- *stakeholder relationships*: e.g. NGOs, government, partner, customer, supplier and civil society relations;
- *intellectual property*: e.g. patents, trade secrets, brand.

Improving performance through objectives, value added, externally audited targets, key performance indicators and reflecting these priorities in relationships with business partners and suppliers. Measurement is undoubtedly the least developed aspect of knowledge management, human resources skills and external communication. This is not surprising given the difficulties and costs implied to define them. Learning where they are and what role they play in the organisation is the first important task along the path for all employees. However, though measurement is important, it should be performed in the context of the stakeholders and of the sector in which the corporate operates. Different steps resulting from experience and from the classification proposed by Karl-Erik Sveiby to identify the value of intangibles (Sveiby, 2005), provide results to:

- monitor performance and uncover hidden value (e.g. control through key performance indicators);
- acquire or sell a business (e.g. brand valuation);

- report to stakeholders – Triple Bottom Line, Global Reporting Initiative (GRI, year unknown);
- guide investment (corporate responsibility reporting used by environmental and social rating agencies for the creation of sustainable and responsible investment portfolios).

Communicating performance internally and externally via externally-assured reporting to become accountable. To adhere to a standard voluntarily is a step forward, but how can good management of corporate intangibles be assessed? With the recognition of the importance of intangible value comes the problem of how to identify it properly and assign it a value within the corporate. Different sorts of intangible value impact the bottom line of the business. These are grouped under four headings: governance, social, ethical and environmental impacts.

Such new ways of thinking and working should be put into practice slowly, according to a sequence of steps that will attract sponsorship by management and support in the form of a budget, which together provide the warrant to align environmental, social and governance assets to the corporate strategy. The sequence proposed below is a good example of how to proceed.

Phase 1

- Ensure the commitment of the management committee.
- Examine key business drivers, including the principal areas of sustainability risk and opportunity.
- Examine organisational values, business ethics and codes of conduct.
- Define the role and responsibilities of the management team and choose specific limited sustainability interventions with clear objectives.
- Identify environmental, social and governance performance indicators.
- Monitor and evaluate intangible performance indicators against specific sustainable development and corporate responsibility criteria and objectives.
- Undertake a progressive stakeholder engagement process.

Phase 2

- Ensure the commitment of staff and the Board.
- Analyse sustainability risks and opportunities in detail (marketing of products, customer relationship management).

- Incorporate sustainability principles in a code of practice.
- Look to integrate a sustainability framework across the organisation including an overall strategy.
- Train and build awareness in all staff.
- Integrate sustainability issues into key internal management systems.
- Communicate the sustainability strategy internally and externally.
- Undertake reporting of sustainability risk management and opportunities.
- Develop a knowledge management and learning framework.

Phase 3

- Act to inspire the whole organisational network, including suppliers and key partners.
- Benchmark and use diagnostic tools to evaluate environmental and social performance.
- Apply external standards.
- Undertake an externally-audited sustainability or CSR reporting process.
- Consider external-auditing to enhance credibility of the CSR annual report.
- Conduct an ongoing review and analysis of performance against measured targets.

Conclusion

In this twenty-first century, we are facing unprecedented challenges at all levels of our ecosystem – personal, social, economic and environmental. In this chapter, we have tried to show how the growing importance of knowledge and other forms of intangible value is changing the dynamic interplay of relationships, both within and outside the world of work. Whether the actions and attitudes, mores and methods we have described will prove sufficient to meet these challenges remains to be seen, but knowledge and information management professionals must be left in no doubt that they have a vital role to play.

3

Leadership in the knowledge revolution: an Open Marxist theoretical perspective and analysis
Ruth Rikowski

Introduction

In this chapter I will, first of all, examine what the 'new economy', or 'knowledge economy' or 'knowledge revolution' is. Consideration will be given to the definition of leadership, followed by an outline of some of the main qualities that leaders should possess. From here, I will then examine what I think being an effective leader in the new economy involves. I will emphasise the importance of extracting knowledge and ideas from people, and how this even includes tapping into people's unconscious knowledge – knowledge that people did not even realise that they had. Consideration will also be given to female leadership in the new economy and to the Scandinavian model of leadership development. I will conclude by highlighting the fact that effective leadership in the knowledge revolution essentially involves extracting value from intellectual labour, the ideas and knowledge that people have, as well as transforming knowledge from knowledge workers/intellectual labourers into structural capital.

The new economy/knowledge economy

In the developed world, we are now in what is often referred to as the 'new economy' or the 'knowledge economy', or more accurately, 'the knowledge revolution'. As I have emphasised elsewhere (e.g. see R. Rikowski, 2000a, 2000b, 2003b, 2004a, 2005a) this 'knowledge revolution', is, in essence, the latest phase of capitalism. Capitalism goes through various phases: there was the agricultural revolution, then the industrial revolution and now we are moving into the knowledge revolution, where knowledge is becoming the key to success. Many leading people have highlighted this fact. Tony Blair, for example, said 'Knowledge is the key. To succeed in this new, competitive, global economy, Britain's businesses need to be knowledge driven' (Blair, 1999).

Similarly, Leadbeater, who has often been referred to as Blair's 'favourite thinker' speaks about the knowledge economy, saying that 'Our institutions, public and private, will have to change quite fundamentally for us to release the potential of the knowledge-driven economy' (Leadbeater, 1999: 52).

Stephen Byers, the then UK Trade and Industry Secretary, described this knowledge revolution at the Confederation of British Industry, saying, 'The first industrial revolution was based in investment in capital and machinery. This revolution we are going through now requires investment in human capital – skills, learning and education' (Byers, 1999).

Meanwhile, others such as Dilts and Dilts have related this new economy to IT, commenting that 'accelerating changes in technology and the explosion in the use of the Internet have led to the establishment of a "new economy", characterized by e-commerce, virtual teams and a global marketplace' (Dilts and Dilts, year unknown: 1).

Many others have emphasised the importance of knowledge. Kim, for example, at the 65th International Federation of Library Associations (IFLA) Conference, said that 'knowledge may soon be the only source of competitive advantage for an organization' (Kim, 1999).

Similarly, Skyrme says that 'innovation through knowledge will be a key factor in business success as we enter the new millennium' (Skyrme, 1998: 6).

It would seem then that the new economy/knowledge economy/ knowledge revolution, is certainly something real and is here to stay.

Definition of leadership

It is obviously important to consider the meaning of leadership itself. However, Inger Buus, the Director of the Danish Leadership Institute argues that there is no single, commonly accepted definition of leadership. He further suggests that the definition of leadership is changing anyway. More importance is given to a softer approach, which is linked to emotional intelligence. In essence, a more holistic approach is now preferred, which integrates both the hard and soft sides of leadership. This is being driven forward by the Scandinavian model of leadership development. Buus refers to this model of leadership, saying that the:

> ...Scandinavian leadership and learning model might offer new inspiration for high impact, holistic learning and support the emerging new definition of leadership ... A holistic model of leadership requires much higher levels of customisation and much closer cooperation (in academia between functional departments and in companies between the internal and external stakeholders) and will result in new organisational models and consulting methods. (Buus, year unknown: 3)

Gushurst is also of this opinion, and says that:

> ...leadership styles are always evolving, with newer elements complementing more traditional ones. Increasingly, senior executives, even entire corporate cultures, are combining classic leadership values, such as discipline, focus, and execution, with more contemporary values, including openness, a greater emphasis on the quality of communication, and naturalness. (Gushurst, 2004: 1)

Meanwhile, Kevin Cashman has wrestled with the notion of the essence of leadership for over 20 years. He very much relates leadership to something deep within ourselves and has decided that:

> Leadership is not simply something we do. It comes from somewhere inside us. Leadership is a process, an intimate expression of who we are. It's our being in action. At its deepest level, leadership is authentic self-expression that creates value. (Cashman, 1997: 1)

Thus, the concept of leadership is changing. However, given the complexity of the term, it is probably more worthwhile and productive to consider some of the necessary ingredients for being an effective leader, rather than just aiming to focus on one simple definition. This is considered further in the next section.

Important ingredients for effective leadership

What, then, are some of the *essential ingredients* that a leader should possess? There is a wealth of literature on this, but only space to highlight a few points here. Some of the main ingredients traditionally include factors such as vision, authority, delegation, decisiveness, charisma and understanding; the ability to encourage creativity, foster a learning environment, encourage effective team building and foster independence and interdependence between workers; and being a motivator, influential, flexible, risk-taker, trust builder, good planner and listener. However, some of these attributes can be contradictory. If a leader is very flexible and good at fostering a learning environment, this might mean that they find it more difficult to be decisive. LaBarre, for example, considers this fact and makes the point that:

> Authentic leaders have absorbed the fundamental fact of existence – that you can't get around life's inherent contradictions. The leadership mind is spacious. It has ample room for the ambiguities of the world, for conflicting feelings, and for contradictory ideas. (LaBarre, 2000: 4)

Indeed, I would argue that these contradictions are embedded within the fabric of capitalism itself – capitalism is founded on an irresolvable set of contradictions, which we all have to try to make sense of, as we live in and through it.

What, then, according to the literature on leadership are some of the attributes that effective leaders should possess? Gushurst, for example, thinks that maturity and wisdom are important attributes and he says that 'leaders must demonstrate realism, maturity, knowledge, and a little wisdom' (Gushurst, 2004: 2).

Meanwhile, LaBarre emphasises the importance of being decisive:

> Tough choices are a daily requirement of leadership. Leaders have to hire and fire, to sign off on new strategies, and to risk investments – all of which can lead to stress and guilt. The presence of guilt is not a result of making the wrong choice but of choosing itself. And that is the human condition. You are a being that chooses. (LaBarre, 2000: 4)

While according to Rick Berry, CEO of ICGCCommerce.com, the most important quality that leaders must possess is the ability to build a team (referenced in Pandya, 2004). As noted, it is ironic that while a certain amount of egolessness is required for team building, leaders do also need strong egos. Meanwhile, Pandya says that leaders of e-commerce, in particular, need to be risk-takers and to 'have the ability to attract teams of talented risk-takers' (Pandya, 2004: 2).

Kevin Cashman, on the other hand, emphasises that leaders need to 'master' the external environment and that:

> In organizations, our success as leaders is measured by the degree to which we've mastered the external environment and delivered results in the form of revenue, profits, new product breakthroughs, cost savings, or market share increases. (Cashman, 1997: 1)

Cashman is of the opinion that there are three core principles to leadership. These are: how authentic we are; how deep and broad our self-expression is, and how much value we are creating. He argues that five touchstones are crucial to building the essential interpersonal bridge of leadership. These are:

- know yourself authentically;
- listen authentically;
- express authentically;
- appreciate authentically;
- serve authentically.

Meanwhile, LaBarre argues that leaders operate on four main dimensions – vision, reality, ethics and courage. The visionary leader, 'thinks big, thinks new, thinks ahead – and most important, is in touch with the deep structure of human consciousness and creative potential' (LaBarre, 2000: 5).

Whereas, reality is the polar opposite of vision, and 'The realist grapples with hard, factual, daily and numeric parameters. A master in the art of the possible, the realist has no illusions, sees limits, and has no patience for speculation' (LaBarre, 2000: 5).

On the other hand, ethics, LaBarre argues, are the basic human values of integrity, love and meaning, and these are ruled by principle. While courage 'is the realm of the will; it involves the capacity to make things happen' (LaBarre, 2000: 5).

LaBarre argues that the real challenge of leadership is to develop all four of these often-contradictory modes of thinking (so, once again, we are faced with the problem of contradiction). Leaders often only operate on two dimensions, at the most, and 'one of the gravest problems in life is self-limitation. We create defence mechanisms to protect us from the anxiety that comes with freedom. We refuse to fulfil our potential. We live only marginally' (LaBarre, 2000: 5).

Meanwhile, Peter Drucker argues that what is particularly important is 'change leadership'. This includes the need to be able to change what is already being done, as well as to do new and different things. Drucker argues that:

> ...unless an organization sees that its task is to lead change, that organization – whether a business, a university, or a hospital – will not survive. In a period of rapid structural change the only organizations that survive are the 'change leaders'. It is therefore a central 21st-century challenge for management that its organization become a change leader. (Drucker, 2001)

Goleman, Boyatzis and McKee, on the other hand, argue that a leader's ultimate responsibility is to create organisations that are 'emotionally intelligent'. They argue that:

> Emotionally intelligent leaders who use resonance-building leadership styles and create norms that foster healthy, effective working relationships (rather than using styles that breed fear and cynicism), will release a powerful force: the collective energy of the organization to pursue any business strategy. These kinds of leaders build with positives. They craft a vision with heartfelt passion, they foster an inspiring organizatonal mission that is deeply woven into the organizational fabric, and they know how to give people a sense that their work is meaningful. (Goleman, Boyatzis and McKee, 2002: 290)

Furthermore, they say there is a need to find passion for work: 'One more intellectual planning exercise is not going to get people engaged... [Instead, leaders need to find a way to get] ...executives emotionally engaged with each other and with their visions' (Goleman, Boyatzis and McKee, 2002: 309).

This brief overview, then, highlights some of the thinking about leadership in the literature. The following section considers leadership in the new economy/knowledge revolution and the extraction of ideas.

Leadership in the knowledge revolution and the extraction of ideas

Effective leadership in the new economy requires a particular set of attributes. Effective leaders in the knowledge economy/knowledge revolution have the ability to extract ideas and knowledge from workers and to transfer this knowledge into company assets. Another way of expressing this is to say that it assists with the process of transforming human labour into human capital and then into structural capital. This requires a very subtle type of leadership.

This is because in this 'new economy' or 'knowledge economy', or more accurately, the 'knowledge revolution', it is necessary to extract value from people's intellect and their ideas – i.e. from intellectual labour. Manville makes the point that 'Peter Drucker and various disciplines have shown us that, in the commoditizing global economy, the only distinctive differentiator is human knowledge and innovation' (Manville, 2002: 1).

Furthermore, Byers, speaking at the Mansion House in February 2000 said, 'the main source of value and competitive advantage in the modern economy is human and *intellectual capital*' (Byers, 2000: 1, my emphasis).

Mougayar, meanwhile, emphasises the importance of extracting value from information, saying that:

> The goal: create a business that relentlessly manipulates information to extract higher value from it, by reselling it, reusing it, repackaging it, or giving it away; either directly to end-users or indirectly via third parties. (Mougayar, 2000: 253)

Clearly, leadership under this scenario also needs to be closely linked to knowledge management. As Wick emphasises:

> Leadership in knowledge management belongs to us as much as to people of any other discipline. But to claim that leadership role, we must carefully re-think how we conceive of and present our value to the organizations we serve. And we must work to expand our value by broadening our technological knowledge base to make us more viable as leaders in an increasingly electronic world. (Wick, 2000: 24)

Effective knowledge management practices become essential to ensure the continued success of the knowledge revolution. As has been stated time and time again in the literature, much knowledge within an organisation is lost. This can be partly overcome by capturing it through effective and workable knowledge management practices.

Wick then refers to leadership in knowledge management saying that 'leadership in knowledge management requires exceptional analysis of the political landscape within the organization' (Wick, 2000: 21).

Leaders in knowledge management need to try to thoroughly understand the intrinsic workings of the organisation, it seems, and in particular to be able to encourage the recording and mapping of business, knowledge and information flows. Furthermore, leaders need to encourage people to communicate effectively, both formally and informally, as well as engendering an environment that furthers good and workable communities of practice.

Lambe also relates all this to the need to adopt a newer style of leadership, which has some similarities to the type of leadership outlined by Buus and the Danish Leadership Institute. Lambe argues that the 'old economy trained leaders' need to have a more humble and searching stance and need to be more aware of their own strengths and weaknesses, in the new economy. Lambe goes on to say that 'the wisest of pre-Net leaders are those who accept their blindness and seek out the most visionary of the new generation' (Lambe, 2002: 5).

Meanwhile, Manville emphasises that leaders need to have an 'enterprise-wide strategy', and makes the point that:

> ...the real value of a chief learning officer is not his or her expertise in learning or leadership development or even technology – it is rather the ability to link such things to an overall enterprise-wide strategy to drive business value. (Manville, 2002: 1)

Manz and Sims focus on a term they have coined – 'New SuperLeadership'. They coined this term in order to describe leadership that helps others to lead themselves. Manz and Sims argue that the SuperLeadership approach to knowledge empowerment encourages a knowledge-sharing culture, while also valuing individual employees. They say that:

> A SuperLeadership approach to knowledge management involves the implementation of a system that values each individual employee and aims to make each a knowledge leader. The system creates an environment that facilitates employees in their efforts to practice knowledge self-leadership, builds natural rewards into the

knowledge management process, and helps employees in the field to act and make key decisions without supervision from their bosses. (Manz and Sims, 2001: 120)

Andy Hickford, is a Signify Associate of a UK-based motivation and leadership development organisation. He believes that success in the new economy does not simply rest with implementing new technology. Instead, leaders of companies can ensure success by viewing their employees as volunteers and listening to what they want. Hickford says:

> To succeed in today's economy, leaders must cultivate and motivate their culture of leadership across the company. The companies that focus on their emotional capacity are the companies that do well. Ask yourself, is there a buzz among your employees about going to work? If there isn't, find out why. Discover what kind of leader your employees want to work with and you will ensure success. After all, executives may fly the plane, but leaders navigate the journey. (Hickford, year unknown)

Hickford thinks that the key to leadership in the new economy lies with talking to employees, and that the more that leaders talk to their employees, then the greater chance they have of success (Oram, 2001).

Meanwhile, Amidon and Macnamara argue that there are 'seven C's of knowledge leadership': context, competence, conversations and common language, communications, coaching, culture and communities. They say that:

> Modern leaders do not fear the speed of change; they embrace an agenda of learning. They know that effective management is not a matter of having the most knowledge; it is knowing how to use it. It is not enough to know modern management concepts. How do they get implemented (i.e. put into action)? Leadership is more an art than a science, but that doesn't excuse us for searching for appropriate metrics for a return-on-leadership (ROL). We must develop an innovation competence and how to measure the performance thereof. (Amidon and Macnamara, 2001: 1)

With regard to knowledge leadership as a matter of context, for example, they say that effective knowledge leadership is also a function of vision, but this includes uncertainty, something leaders often find difficult to deal with. While, in regard to knowledge leadership as a matter of competence, they argue that it is virtually impossible to be taught leadership, but that instead you have to learn it and experience it.

In conclusion, this section has emphasised how effective leadership in the new economy involves how to extract ideas, knowledge and information out of the workforce effectively. Creating value from knowledge becomes key. This is actually a two-fold process. First, there is the need to extract value from intellectual labour, which then becomes embedded in the commodity. Second, there is a need to transfer knowledge from the knowledge worker/intellectual labourer into structural capital. Various leadership qualities will come into play here, and the leader in the knowledge economy/revolution will have to decide which of these leadership qualities they consider to be most appropriate and important. Good and workable knowledge management practices will certainly assist with this process, as will effective knowledge leaders, to drive through these knowledge management programmes.

Female leadership in the new economy/knowledge revolution

Another interesting angle concerns female leadership in the new economy. Some argue that, in many ways, females are better able than men to be effective leaders in the knowledge revolution. The effective extraction of information and ideas from people is a subtle process, often involving more democratic and diverse techniques, and perhaps, is something that can be better achieved by women than men. Mary Van der Boon makes the point that:

> Women's focus on relationships, comfort with direct communication and diversity, refusal to compartmentalise skills, talents and lives, innate scepticism of hierarchy and, most importantly, desire to lead from the middle (not from the top) are all key attributes required by tomorrow's leaders. (Van der Boon, year unknown: 1)

Furthermore, according to Sally Helgesen, best-selling author of *The Female Advantage: Women's Ways of Leadership*, the talents, experiences, attitudes and skills that women have are just what is needed in the post-industrial economy.

Findings from research conducted at the Hagberg Consulting Group, a California firm of psychologists specialising in leadership development and organisational effectiveness, concluded that women managers were often better than their male counterparts. The research involved 396 women and 1,600 men and included feedback from supervisors and self-assessment data. In one part of the survey, research was undertaken with 425 high-level executives, and each was evaluated by about 25 people. The women executives won higher ratings on 42 of the 52 skills measured. In general, the research found that women were better at keeping people informed, using influence rather than authority, creating and articulating a vision, taking charge, being an inspirational role model, setting high standards of performance, assuming responsibility and managing a diverse workforce than their male counterparts (see Collison, 1998; Patterson, year unknown; Sharpe, 2000; Van der Boon, year unknown). Richard Hagberg says that 'what emerged [from the survey] was the picture of women executives as having a more appropriate style for managing in the new millennium. It's a much more team-oriented style' (Hagberg, 2003).

Other studies have produced similar findings. The Personnel Decisions International study, a consulting firm in Minneapolis, MN, examined 58,000 managers. It gave women the advantage in 20 out of 23 areas. Similarly, the company Lawrence A. Pfeffand Associates conducted a study, and examined evaluations from 2,482 executives and it was found that women outperformed men on 20 measures. Meanwhile, the Management Research Group study compared male and female managers at the same firms, at the same management level and with the same amount of supervisory experience. Robert Kabacoff, the Vice-President examined 1,800 supervisors in 22 management skills. The women outranked the men on half the measures (Collison, 1998).

Furthermore, according to Mary Van der Boon (year unknown), studies have found that women ranked higher than men on 28 of 31 diverse management and leadership criteria, which included intellectual areas such as producing high-quality work, recognising trends and generating new ideas and acting on them.

In conclusion, it seems that females can be, and indeed are, very effective leaders in the knowledge economy/new economy. Why do females make such successful leaders in this way, one might ask? One of the reasons for this, I think, is because it is impossible for women to create as much value as men in capitalism. This is because women spend more of their time than men in creating the next lot of labour-power – i.e. they spend more time nurturing and nourishing their offspring!

Marx speaks about the nurturing of labour-power, saying that:

> Labour-power exists only as a capacity, or power of the living individual. Its production consequently pre-supposes his existence. Given the individual, the production of labour-power consists in his reproduction of himself or his maintenance. For his maintenance he requires a given quantity of the means of subsistence ... in other words, the value of labour-power is the value of the means of subsistence necessary for the maintenance of the labourer ... His means of subsistence must therefore be sufficient to maintain him in his normal state as a labouring individual. (Marx, 1867: 168)

While females are nurturing the next lot of labour-power, they cannot be adding to the value of their own labour-power. But capitalism must always be seeking new ways to create value, so it now needs to try to tap into some of this unrealised value potential in women, and in particular, in regard to women that have the potential to become leaders. The nurturing of female intellectual labour-power is becomingly increasingly important in the knowledge economy/ knowledge revolution. Therefore, this is all starting to happen today, in various ways. Indeed, it is essential that this happens – the new economy requires quite different management and leadership techniques, compared with the old economy, and females can make a valuable contribution. In my future works, I plan to develop gender and value issues further, through an Open Marxist approach, with Glenn Rikowski.

Scandinavian model of leadership development

The Scandinavian model of leadership development adopts an holistic approach to leadership, and integrates the hard and soft sides of leadership. This holistic approach has been developed over the last 20 years and is now being adopted in various organisations around the world. Although Scandinavians have not really tried to promote their views on leadership to others, many people have been interested in the model, and it has formed the basis of many case studies. The Scandinavian leadership style includes factors such as showing respect for the individual as well as adopting an holistic, humanistic and value-based approach. With this approach, there are different stakeholders, such as public/private sectors, activist movements and trade unions. The Scandinavian leadership style recommends flat, non-bureaucratic structures with devolved responsibility within a trusting and caring environment.

The Danish Leadership Institute carried out a major study into challenges and best practices in leadership development in various European organisations, resulting in some interesting findings. One of the participants in the study, who used to send hundreds of managers on these traditional leadership development programmes, cancelled all their classic programmes, for example, so it was a major change in policy. Instead, leadership training was replaced with just-in-time, highly-related consultancy programmes, and a creative and motivating workplace was engendered and encouraged. Thus, this new leadership style was considered to be a more effective leadership style here.

It seems that the Scandinavian leadership style is very suited to the post-industrial knowledge economy, where change and innovation become increasingly important. Buus says that:

> Scandinavian countries already come high on the leadership related elements in international rankings, e.g. Sweden, Denmark and Finland are the three highest ranking countries on 'willingness to delegate responsibility' in the Global Competitiveness Report from the World Economic Forum. (Buus, year unknown: 2)

Birkinshaw and Crainer (2002) say that the success of Scandinavian corporations globally shows the 'transferability' of the model. Indeed, many that have successfully implemented the model have actually operated outside of Scandinavia. Meanwhile, Steve Covey argues that while traditional hierarchical leadership structure might have been useful in the industrial age, this model is outmoded today. Instead, the flat, democratic, open model that has been adopted by Denmark and its Nordic neighbours provides the way forward.

How though, does this leadership model convert into meaningful and effective leadership development practices? The Danish Leadership Institute defined a number of learning principles as guidelines for more effective executive learning:

- *Reality*: All development should be focused on real-time challenges.

- *Reflection*: Learning occurs when actions, experiences and reactions are put into perspective by a process of reflection.

- *Challenges*: There is need for an element of risk.

- *Dialogues*: Teasing out tacit knowledge in interactive format.

The 'Real Life Leadership Labs' at the Danish Leadership Institute are an example of how these learning principles are applied in practice. The laboratories included experiential and action learning techniques, reflective and dialogue practices, including peer feedback and coaching, as well as Socratic questioning techniques. In the laboratories people worked in groups – there were 5–6 executives in each group and they were guided by an experienced facilitator, who was often a business psychologist. While the laboratory facilitators provided the framework for reflection and experimentation, the executives brought the contents through their own experiences. In this way, an holistic approach was adopted.

As Buus says:

> The Real Life Leadership Labs are an example of complete integration of the business and the people aspects of leadership. The method demonstrates how the Scandinavian leadership and learning model might offer new inspiration for high impact, holistic learning and support the emerging new definition of leadership ... A holistic model of leadership requires much higher levels of customisation and much closer cooperation (in academia between functional departments and in companies between the internal and external stakeholders) and will result in new organisational models and consulting methods. (Buus, year unknown: 3)

In conclusion, it is particularly interesting to note that more socialist/social-democrat-type countries in Scandinavia are producing models of leadership that can actually help more clearly focused capitalist-oriented countries to gain further competitive advantage. Obviously, Scandinavian countries are still part of the global capitalist economy, but they are not driving it forward as enthusiastically as other countries, such as the USA and the UK. On initial consideration, this might then seem a rather strange irony. Yet, if one reflects further, then it becomes clearer. Capitalism needs to find different ways in order to extract value from labour effectively. The authoritarian leadership approach simply will not always work. Indeed, it can even have the opposite effect, and could discourage intellectual workers from producing new ideas etc, particularly given the fact that this is such a subtle process. It is far more difficult to get people to come up with new ideas, than it is to get them to dig up the next lot of coal, for example. More socialist/social-democrat-type countries are likely to use and adopt more democratic and inclusive styles. Yet, these techniques can also be used for the advantage of advanced capitalism. Subtle approaches are needed in order to be able to nurture intellectual labour, and thereby extract value from it. Thus, the Scandinavian model of leadership development, with its holistic approach, is a model that can be, and is being adopted by leadership globally.

Extracting tacit and unconscious knowledge from intellectual labour

LaBarre says that the visionary leader, 'thinks big, thinks new, thinks ahead – and most important, is in touch with the deep structure of human consciousness and creative potential' (LaBarre, 2000: 5).

However, when it comes to extracting knowledge from the workforce, another very important area is the extraction of people's tacit and unconscious knowledge, as well as their conscious knowledge. The important point is to extract as much value out of intellectual labour as possible, and this needs to be achieved by looking at all forms of knowledge – i.e. both conscious and unconscious knowledge. The extraction of value from labour is considered in far more depth, at a theoretical level, in Chapter 11 of this book and also briefly in Chapter 9, particularly in regard to the extraction of value from manual and intellectual labour.

What also becomes necessary is to get the knowledge out of people's heads and into the organisation, so that knowledge workers do not just take their knowledge and ideas home with them at the end of the day. As CMS Wikki says regarding knowledge management:

> Knowledge Management describes an organization strategy to get the knowledge of its workers out of their heads and into an information storage and retrieval system where it can be used and reused. When workers leave an enterprise, their knowledge, (information in their heads) goes with them. KM captures their knowledge in a form that can be shared with other workers and especially future workers. (CMS Wikki, 2004)

Furthermore, it emphasises that KM aims to externalise institutional memory and to optimise knowledge transfer.

Extracting tacit, let alone, unconscious knowledge can be difficult, for a number of reasons. With regard to tacit knowledge, there is the fear of giving away secrets, for example. There might also be an inadequate language structure and a lack of trust. Endeavouring to capture both these types of knowledge is important for the success of an organisation, in today's new economy. As David Skyrme says:

> Very often the most valuable knowledge that an organisation has is in the heads of its people, and those of its stakeholders, especially customers. However, 'people walk', so forward looking companies continue to seek ways of locking it in to their organisations. (Skyrme, 1998: 3)

Skyrme suggests that a knowledge strategy should be developed, and he outlines two complementary approaches. First, to convert the tacit knowledge into a more explicit form, by converting it into documents, databases, processes etc. He says that this is often referred to as 'decanting the human capital into the structural capital of an organization'. Second, to enhance tacit knowledge flow through better human interaction, 'such that the knowledge is diffused around the organisation and not held in the heads of a few' (Skyrme, 1998: 3).

He goes on to say:

> Add some basic elements of good human resource management, including a stimulating environment, personal development plans, motivation and suitable reward and recognition systems (such as knowledge sharing awards and stock options), then there is less chance of your best knowledge workers wanting to leave. (Skyrme, 1998: 3)

With regard to unconscious knowledge, specifically, Milton (2000) describes various ways in which organisations try to tap into people's unconscious knowledge. He says that two types of tacit knowledge can be distinguished – conscious (what you know that you know) and unconscious (what you do not know you know). He suggests undertaking brain mining to extract the unconscious tacit knowledge from people's minds. As Knowledge Manager for BP Amoco, Milton described the brain mining techniques he has used for the extraction of this unconscious knowledge, including 'after action reviews' where small teams undertake a brief action and are then questioned to extract their knowledge. It was found that superficial questions produced shallow answers but harder questions extracted the deeper knowledge. Thus, by such measures unconscious knowledge can be extracted from workers, knowledge that they are not imparting freely and willingly.

Milton also makes the point that the capturing of tacit knowledge is made more difficult by the fact that both conscious and unconscious knowledge can often reside in teams rather than in isolated individuals. There are a number of tools for capturing unconscious tacit knowledge and for making this knowledge conscious. Apart from the after action reviews, there are also, for example, the comparisons of a team's expectations of events with the actuality, and the need to find reasons for the differences between the two. There are also hard questioning techniques and learning-history studies.

Furthermore, some companies today offer brain mining techniques to other companies, in order to help them to extract both tacit, and unconscious knowledge from the workforce, to tap into new ideas and to 'unlock the genius'. One such company is the Merritt-Gentry Group (see *www.merritt-gentry.com*), which makes the point that most organisations have untapped talent and staff expertise in their organisations. Furthermore, they stress that organisations need to consider factors such as:

- how to take advantage of knowledge, skills and experience that teams possess;
- how to capture existing processes to safeguard the organisation;
- how to generate 'outside-the-box' thinking.

They refer specifically to their brain mining methods, saying that:

> Using our unique BrainMining method of group dynamics, and roll-up-your-sleeves and grind out the answers techniques, Merritt-Gentry will help your best minds come to the best answers designed specifically for you – in your business. Effective consultants understand that ultimate success depends on your organization's own resources ... Our job at the Merritt-Gentry Group is to help unlock the genius already there and help identify the unique focus for your operation. (Merritt-Gentry Group: 2)

Bonac (2001) has, meanwhile, written an important article, 'The forbidden knowledge of the unconscious'. Here, Bonac examines 'communicative psychoanalysis' and says that:

> ...therapists are able to reach the very depths of the unconsciously held information of another human being and to connect this information with the details of the lives of patients and of themselves in a concrete and practical manner. (Bonac, 2001: 1)

He goes on to say that 'this knowledge can be acquired without the need for consent and, alarmingly, without the conscious awareness by the patient that the information was ever communicated' (Bonac, 2001: 1).

So, now we can extract information and knowledge from the depths of people's unconsciousness, by therapy. Techniques such as this are very powerful, and will become more so as we become more advanced in the new economy, and the need to extract new ideas from the workforce becomes more and more urgent. Yet, the implications of all this are really very scary, and will upset many people's notion of morality. As Bonac says, the unconscious meaning of certain communications can create a body of knowledge that can 'endanger the moral, intellectual and emotional environment of therapy and must remain taboo' (Bonac, 2001: 1).

In conclusion, in order to ensure the continued success of the knowledge revolution, extracting tacit knowledge in general and unconscious tacit knowledge in particular from the workforce and more specifically, from intellectual labour, all becomes very important. Thus, this even includes extracting the knowledge from people's heads that they did not know they had – their unconscious knowledge. Various techniques have been devised to try to capture this tacit and unconscious knowledge. These include converting the knowledge into a more explicit form, such as converting it into documents and databases and improving the flow of communication. Other methods include after action reviews, hard questioning techniques and various brain mining techniques as well as communicative psychoanalysis techniques. Effective leadership can help to ensure that these techniques are performed well and efficiently, in order to maximise output. Once again, the particular leadership qualities considered most important to achieve this (such as the quality of being decisive, and/or a good listener, and/or authoritative and/or flexible) will have to be left to the discretion of any individual leaders and organisations, I would suggest. *How* to achieve the result – that is the main aim, as far as the leader in capitalism is concerned.

An Open Marxist analysis of leadership in the knowledge revolution

In this final section, I will place leadership in the new economy or, more precisely, the knowledge revolution, within an Open Marxist theoretical analysis. In essence, I am arguing that the labourer is still exploited in the new economy, and the knowledge worker is not empowered, as some people would have us believe. Effective leadership assists with this process.

Marx began his analysis of capitalism, or the capitalist mode of production, with the commodity, and indeed, this is where our analysis must begin, in order to be able to effectively understand, explain and critique capitalism. In *Das Capital*, Vol. 1, Marx says that:

> The wealth of those societies in which the capitalist mode of production prevails, presents itself as an 'immense accumulation of commodities', its unit being a single commodity. Our investigation must therefore begin with the analysis of a commodity. (Marx, 1867: 43)

Many writers refer to the commodity in various ways today, and realise the importance of it. An article entitled 'Leadership' refers to the knowledge economy and the commodity in a very interesting way, saying that 'the knowledge economy flows from handling the unspecified. The specified will be increasingly commodified' (Challenge Forum, year unknown: 1).

Thus, the knowledge economy endeavours to handle knowledge that is floating around, to capture it and then to commodify it. However, there will always be another idea on the horizon, which has not been commodified, and must then be chased. As such, it will never be possible to specify and commodify everything. Yet, this is capitalism's aim.

Meanwhile, Stuart Hamilton considers, in particular, how information is being transformed into a commodity through the Internet, in particular. He says that:

> ...it is possible to suggest that the Internet, and the flow of information on it, will eventually revert to an 'advanced capitalist' model – that a combination of information as a commodity, class inequalities in the distribution and access of information, and the priorities of the large corporations will transform the Internet from a tool of democracy and a voice of the disenfranchised into an extension of the High Street, where all information costs money. (Hamilton, 2002: 192)

As Marx says, commodities have a physical natural form and a value form, and it is the latter that interests us here – i.e. the focus is on *value*. There are different forms and aspects of value, including use value, exchange value, surplus value and added value. All this is considered in more depth in Chapter 11 of this book. However, what is important to fully appreciate here is the fact that labour, and only labour, can create value. As Marx says, 'human labour creates value' (Marx, 1867: 57). Furthermore, 'the value of a commodity ... is determined by the quantity of labour contained in it' (Marx, 1867: 203).

So, it is workers' sweat and labour that creates value, and sustains capitalism. Yet, although labour creates value, it has no value in itself. As Marx says, 'human labour creates value, but is not itself value. It becomes value only in its congealed state, when embedded in the form of some object' (Marx, 1867: 57).

Workers undertake two types of labour: manual labour and intellectual labour. However, the balance has changed. Whereas in the industrial revolution, more of the labourers' energy was exerted by undertaking manual labour, in the knowledge revolution there is a greater exertion of intellectual labour. The making of physical commodities, such as cars and boats, requires a large exertion of manual labour, whereas intangible commodities require a large exertion of intellectual labour. So, in the knowledge revolution the emphasis is on both the commodification of knowledge itself, and various other intangibles, and also on the extraction of value from intellectual labour (as opposed to manual labour), in particular, which then becomes embedded in these commodities. Boyett and Boyett speak very clearly and frighteningly about the extension of this commodification in what they term the new 'post-knowledge economy', saying:

> A new post-knowledge economy may be emerging that is based not on the exploitation of information, but on stories. This market for feelings may gradually eclipse the market for tangible products. Six such emotional markets can be discerned now: adventures for sale, the market for togetherness, friendship, and love, the market for care, the who-am-I-market, the market for peace of mind, and the market for convictions. (Boyett and Boyett, 2001: 47)

Here, then, Boyett and Boyett refer to the possible selling of emotions such as friendship, love and caring – all qualities that have largely been seen to operate outside of the market. They go on to say that:

> Ultimately, we may see the development of an even newer post-knowledge economy in which the chief value that companies deliver won't be food, material things, information, connectivity, emotional satisfaction, or experiences but individual or personal transformations. (Boyett and Boyett, 2001: 47)

Let us return to the need to begin our analysis of capitalism with the commodity. In capitalism, the aim is to commodify more and more areas of life, into the infinite – i.e. its ultimate aim is the commodification of all that surrounds us. We witness privatisation of the beaches and water, etc. – why not the air we breathe? In reality, this is impossible, but this is because capitalism is, in essence, a madhouse and is based on irresolvable contradictions. It is a system that has evolved from other systems and it is not a system that we have worked out by using our intellect. This is considered further in Chapter 11 of this book. Yet, we have to live in and through this madhouse, and try to make some sort of sense of it.

Value that is created from labour is embedded in these commodities, and then these commodities are sold in the marketplace. Profits are derived from this process; these profits can only ever be derived from value, and this value can only ever be created by labour. All this is necessary in order to sustain capitalism.

Therefore, being an effective leader in the new economy/knowledge revolution involves finding the most effective way in which value can be created and extracted from intellectual labour. This is why the different methods to tap into unconscious knowledge, such as through brain mining techniques, become so important.

Three separate parts to being an effective leader in the knowledge revolution can be discerned. First, the extraction of value from intellectual labour, and this value then becomes embedded in the commodity. Second, there is the commodificiation of knowledge itself, through the creation of commodities such as patents and software packages. Third, there is the transferring of knowledge from the knowledge worker/intellectual labourer, into structural capital within an organisation.

All this sounds really unpleasant and unpalatable, but we need to face up to the stark reality – the horror of capitalism. It might be necessary to employ some appealing and attractive techniques as a leader, such as being more democratic, flexible and understanding, but being kind and understanding to the workforce is not the ultimate aim. This is not to say that individual leaders might not operate in this humane way, but it must be stressed that were this the ultimate goal of leaders in the new economy, then these people would become poor leaders (by which I mean that they would not help to perpetuate the success of the knowledge revolution, and thus, capitalism itself). Instead, the more attractive techniques that a leader might use can only be tolerated and encouraged if this encourages intellectual labourers to be more productive – i.e. to come up with more ideas and more innovative thinking. Then, from these ideas, value can be created and extracted. So, these more attractive techniques are used to extract knowledge, information and ideas from the workforce more effectively. From this knowledge, value can be derived, and the importance of creating this value from knowledge has been indicated clearly by many thinkers and writers. From this process, profits can be made, companies can thrive, and capitalism is sustained.

Therefore, while some of the techniques that leaders will use in this new economy will appear to be quite attractive, others will also be far less palatable – such as Milton's after action techniques and various communicative psychoanalysis techniques.

So, the importance of value-creation through knowledge is emphasised in much of the current business and information literature. Meyer says, for example, that '*value* is in the intangibles like knowledge, information, services, software, and entertainment' (Meyer, 2000: 193, my emphasis).

Furthermore, Potter notes that 'the main source of *value* and competitive advantage in the modern economy is human and intellectual capital' (Potter, 1999: 7, my emphasis).

Thus, by this process, capitalism is sustained but labour continues to be alienated, exploited and objectified. The objectification of labour is considered further in Chapter 11 of this book. All this is far removed from moral and humane concerns. As Marx says, 'capital cares nothing for the length of life of labour-power' (Marx, 1867: 253).

Neither does it care about the length of the life of the labourer. Instead, it encourages and perpetuates a system that exacerbates inequalities, misery, suffering, death and destruction – this, is global capitalism. All this is done in order to exacerbate the never-ending drive to push up profit margins. We need to be fully aware of the reality of the world that we live in. Whether we want to be effective leaders in this global capitalist world is then something that each of us will have to decide for ourselves.

Summary

This chapter has considered a number of aspects regarding leadership in the knowledge economy, or, more precisely, the knowledge revolution. First, it considered the new economy/knowledge economy or the knowledge revolution itself (this being the latest phase of capitalism), as well as the definition of leadership and some of the important ingredients needed for being an effective leader. It then examined leadership in the knowledge revolution and how, in essence, this leadership is fundamentally concerned with the extraction of ideas from the workforce. It then considered the particular role and attributes of the female leader in the knowledge economy and the alternative, Scandinavian model of leadership development. From here, it then considered the fact that effective leadership in the new economy also includes extracting people's tacit knowledge and even their unconscious knowledge – knowledge that they did not even realise that they had. It then placed all this within an Open Marxist theoretical analysis, emphasising the fact that the essence of capitalism is about the extension of the commodification process. Value is created and extracted from labour (and largely from intellectual labour in the knowledge revolution) and this value then becomes embedded in the commodity. From this process, profits are derived, and capitalism is sustained, while labour is alienated, exploited and objectified. Furthermore, knowledge itself is being commodified (such as through patents, software products and branding), and knowledge from the knowledge worker/intellectual labourer is being transformed into structural capital. Being an effective leader in this new economy, therefore, involves leaders finding new and effective ways of extracting knowledge, ideas, information and the elements of genius out of the workforce. Whether we want to be part of that process is something that each of us needs to decide for ourselves.

Note

This chapter was originally a paper that was prepared for, and presented to, Masters in Business Administration students at London South Bank University, at the request of George Bell, MBA Course Director, in April 2005, in the Faculty of Business, Computing and Information Management.

Part 2
Practical perspectives

Many areas address the practical implementation of knowledge management (KM). This section focuses on two of these areas, namely, libraries and information resource centres, and web accessibility.

The first chapter is by Mandy Webster, Library and Information Services Manager at Browne Jacobson, LLP, on the topic of 'The role of libraries in knowledge management'. Webster makes the point that although managing information is different from managing knowledge, there are many transferable skills. She considers how existing skills/procedures in information management are transferable to a KM context. She sees some of the main skills/procedures in this regard as being:

- creating, maintaining, evaluating and selecting databases;
- training and training materials, and information literacy;
- abstracting;
- current awareness;
- classification, taxonomies and metadata;
- encouraging sharing of materials and making them accessible;
- intranets – managing, selecting, evaluating, publishing and giving context;
- internal/external expertise capture and knowledge mapping;
- auditing;
- market research, e.g. clients/potential clients;
- management skills and diverse and dispersed teams.

Webster argues that through their traditional role of managing and organising information, libraries are ideally placed to take on the role of managing knowledge.

The following chapter is by Paul Catherall, web developer at North East Wales Institute of Higher Education, and is entitled 'Accessibility issues for web-based information systems'. Catherall begins by considering the emergence of web-based systems in parallel with the development of web standards, providing an insight into the technical challenges of delivering web content in a form effectively usable both by humans and machine agents. Web usability and accessibility are introduced as complementary requirements for the effective delivery of content for disabled users and also for the general audience of the World Wide Web. Various web technologies are discussed in this context, from basic HTML documents to complex web-based systems. Catherall introduces several core standards developed by the World Wide Web Consortium (W3C) which provide a practical basis for accessible HTML authorship and web design. Various forms of disability are considered in the context of web accessibility, including potential barriers to users with motor, visual or cognitive disabilities; brief examples are given of how general difficulties using the Web can be lessened or overcome by implementing content inherently compliant with the W3C standards.

In the second part of the chapter, legal issues are considered for web accessibility, including implications arising from the Disability Discrimination Act and Special Educational Needs and Disability Act. A clear legal argument is made for compliance with W3C standards and guidelines, citing excerpts from legislation, the recommendations of statutory bodies and statistics indicating levels of disability in the UK. The impact of the World Wide Web as an increasingly pervasive information medium is discussed in this context.

Later sections in the chapter deal with formal standards, focusing on technical and subjective W3C guidelines; these include standards for mark-up (e.g. HTML code used to write web documents) and the Web Content Accessibility Guidelines, a partly technical and partly subjective list of recommendations for developing accessible web-based resources. Methods for validating web content are also discussed, including automatic or software-based tools and manual or review-based approaches, such as auditing content using a text-only web browser.

Another section in the chapter expands on the issue of web usability, including a wide range of core issues affecting the delivery, effectiveness and quality of resources. Issues covered include the design of navigation menus, file size and bandwidth issues. Other considerations include comprehension and clarity of the web document as a text, and barriers to content availability due to file format issues, such as use of commercial or proprietary document formats as opposed to freely downloadable viewers.

Finally, the chapter considers the role of assistive technology, that is, additional software and hardware available to support disabled users in viewing or reading web-based documents. Assistive technology hardware such as Braille readers or screen readers are introduced, and features to support accessibility within popular software such as Word and Netscape Navigator are also discussed.

Thus, Catherall covers this whole topic of accessibility issue for web-based information/knowledge management systems in some considerable breadth and depth, and provides the reader with a wealth of valuable information.

4

The role of the library in knowledge management

Mandy Webster

Through their traditional role of managing and organising information, libraries are ideally qualified to take on the role of managing knowledge. Although managing information is different from managing knowledge, there are a lot of transferable skills involved in the management of both and this is recognised in the increasing numbers of appointments being advertised for librarians taking a knowledge management (KM) role, especially in the legal and health sectors. This chapter examines those transferable skills as part of the librarian's role in KM.

The greatest challenge facing librarians moving into KM is moving from the traditional role of housing information to analysing and using that information. Information can be viewed as the explicit form of knowledge and KM as management of the tacit knowledge inside people's heads to make it as accessible to others as possible. Orna (2005) suggests KM is making what individuals gain by experience available to others in a constant cycle of transfer and further development. Managing such a process strategically involves collaborative working with a wide range of teams, such as human resources, IT and marketing; an extension of possibly more ad hoc project-based collaborations and a shift from providing a service to producing information, e.g. in the form of expertise databases on the intranet or gathering together the people needed to produce information.

Database selection and management

For many years, librarians have taken a central role in evaluating, selecting and negotiating the licensing agreements for commercially available databases. Being a specialist in a particular subject area places the librarian in a unique position to identify the needs of users and evaluate databases to match those information needs and ease of use to match their users' known capabilities. It would be pointless to purchase any system users could not or would not use. In addition, librarians have created or selected and maintained library management systems (LMS). Preparing detailed specifications for purchasing LMS is ideal preparation for drafting specifications for KM systems, and evaluating and giving weight to the different criteria is a central part of this process. The delicate compromise between desirable and essential elements of any system and the pivotal decision of whether to buy an off-the-shelf or customised version of the package has to be made by most librarians at some point in their professional lives, and sometimes more than once, as new generations of systems evolve. These library systems have become more sophisticated and capable of a wider range of functions than the original bibliographic databases.

Some LMS are now capable of storing full-text documents, such as precedents and seminar presentations, as well as abstracts and the more traditional bibliographic details, which can be searched by multiple fields in the same ways as other items on the system, and full-text searching. This takes LMS into territory overlapping with KM systems. The ability to search specific fields, such as author, piece of legislation, case name and keyword as well as full text will be important to users of both types of system. Librarians should know how their users prefer results to be organised, whether ranked by relevance or date etc. The latest versions of some LMS already allow searching across internally held resources and external commercial databases through a single search query and integrate the results in the way KM systems allow searching of multiple resources. Librarians are ideally placed to evaluate how well the results are organised and whether the origins of those results are provided clearly enough for end users. The difficult issue of whether Boolean searching works adequately under a single search of multiple databases is best left to the librarians' expertise. For evaluation purposes, issues of how search results are best displayed are also appropriate for librarians to consider, such as seeing results in context with words around the search terms or extracts organised into practice groups.

Both KM and LMS usually incorporate some form of push technology, such as acquisition lists or notification of new additions e-mailed to users on selected topics at specified intervals. User expectations are much higher now that so many are familiar with customised Internet services, where services like Amazon check which resources have been viewed and suggest similar items that may be of interest. Similarly, templates can be created for when items are to be weeded or reassessed for relevance on each type of system. Other professionals may not be familiar with the capabilities of LMS and therefore do not appreciate the overlap with some KM system functions.

Librarians have of necessity developed experience of negotiating concurrent or named end-user licences as appropriate from commercial database suppliers and the budgetary management skills appropriate to renewals and support contracts, which equates to the negotiation process for KM system licensing and ensuring reliable information is delivered by reliable software.

Experience of using a wide variety of externally created databases and directories of experts helps librarians to identify which criteria make such resources good or bad examples, and to formulate ideas of how such resources could be improved if developed from scratch. Some directories are organised in ways that are unhelpful for the end user to search. For example, some are arranged by geographical area without any cross-referencing to search by individual names, making it impossible to locate a named individual unless their geographical location is also known; alternatively, searching might be limited to only one field, instead of simultaneously across several fields to narrow the resulting hits. Librarians have had to select appropriate formats to make resources available to users, e.g. print/online/both, and from experience of users' capabilities and needs have developed the expertise necessary to assess the merits of systems and how best to format newly created internal information. Internally generated knowledge needs to be well formatted and organised or the effort of collecting it will be wasted if it cannot be located or it is in a format that cannot easily be reused. For example, for regularly used precedents, Word may be the most appropriate format to store such documents to allow easy amending for future use, however much more attractive other formats, such as PDF, may look.

The type of management information and statistics generated by LMS and used by librarians could be adapted to aid KM. Simple statistics like usage of particular resources helps librarians decide whether to buy the next edition of that resource if it has been heavily used. Some LMS track searches that fail as part of their information management, helping to identify training issues which users may feel inhibited to mention for various reasons. Deciding whether the same capacity in a KM system would be of benefit could be reached on the same criteria. The same type of monitoring could be developed to check which precedents are most heavily used and who is contributing useful adaptations to precedents ahead of appraisals and reward systems.

Classification and taxonomies

All materials added to the LMS are catalogued and classified to enable users to locate all relevant items subsequently as part of the librarian's routine functions. Librarians are familiar with the standard established classification schemes and may have developed their own schemes for specialised collections, based on pragmatic considerations of ease of use for their end users. This level of expertise is an invaluable foundation for creating and utilising proprietary taxonomies in KM systems. The expertise of a subject specialist is also the perfect basis for creating and maintaining customised taxonomies. If a commercial version is purchased, this expertise is vital in evaluating its relevance for the purchasing organisation. At their most basic levels, LMS and KM systems are mapping tools identifying what information or knowledge is available and where it is kept, whether as a physical entity, such as a book, or tacitly, such as a named individual within the organisation being an acknowledged expert in a particular field.

Knowledge management systems founded on taxonomies are superior to simple free-text search capabilities as the taxonomy works like library classification schemes to give relational structure to place concepts into a framework of relevance to avoid time wasted on irrelevant search results. A fundamental function of KM is to share relevant expertise and save reinvention of the wheel, which will fail if the taxonomy is inadequate or inconsistent. Consistency of classification is a fundamental aspect of inputting to databases as it ensures the maximum retrieval of relevant items. An understanding of field structures improves the input of data and subsequent retrieval of any database. Some form of editorial control avoids duplicated efforts from several departments using different language to describe the same topics. The structure and indexing development that aid such navigation is already within the professional capabilities of librarians. Building around a taxonomy has the important advantage of facilitating browsing from drop-down lists or menus to discover all relevant materials that inexperienced keyword searchers may not always achieve consistently. Serendipity in seeing nearby alternative terms is often helpful in putting a topic into context where bald data can be open to misinterpretation, just like browsing bookshelves and finding related subjects at nearby classmarks.

Marking up data with meta-tags equates to cataloguing bibliographic information into relevant fields and maintaining authority files for those fields for the sake of consistently full results. After deciding which items are worthy of being stored in a KM system for future use, the cataloguing and classification are the most important tasks associated with KM. If knowledge is stored in such a way that no one can locate it for future use, it is a wasted effort.

For organisations without KM systems, librarians have much to offer in terms of organising shared directories and drives into appropriate subjects and subcategories, or making documents available through the organisation's intranet in organised hierarchies. LMS usually offer an intranet or Internet option to allow end users to search catalogues, which has enabled librarians to develop expertise in intranet and portal development. Librarians have already moved into adding a great deal of value through recommending and listing useful, reliable websites with annotations and grouping these in appropriate categories to facilitate the delivery of current awareness services.

Current awareness

For many years, librarians have taken responsibility for the selective dissemination of information or current awareness services in printed and electronic versions. The skills involved in creating a detailed profile of users and their information needs are the same skills needed to create profiles for push technologies in KM to enable the right information to be delivered to the right people at the right time, and not to overload users or send irrelevant items outside the scope of their interest. This profile development is also the essence of building communities of expertise, so fundamental to any KM programme.

A particular talent required in current awareness is the ability to write abstracts of often detailed and complex documents. Abstracts help the users to scan quickly through search results to identify items worth reading in full. Such abstracts are important in KM databases and portal structures in the informing of what new materials have been added, and as part of the lists of results to speed scanning to find relevant results in valuable context while avoiding information overload. Such almost journalistic competence could also be used to capture the essentials of deals after completion, what has or has not gone well and any crucial information gleaned from secondments to clients based loosely around a similar format to the reference interview as a means of eliciting information. Current awareness is ripe for evolution into many formats such as text messaging, CDs and short video clips to run on intranets with acknowledged experts speaking about a topic or demonstrating how something is done. The practicalities of making such audio visual resources available without distracting colleagues has already been faced by academic and public libraries through headphone provision and separate rooms.

Management

Librarians in all sectors, from public and academic to special, are often based across several sites with a wide variety of professional and para-professional staff to manage. Librarians have needed to develop management skills to handle these diverse and dispersed teams effectively. A key advantage of KM is often seen as its ability to connect teams working across several branches and maintain communication between them.

At the heart of all KM initiatives is the need to manage. This need focuses on managing communication facilitating the sharing of knowledge. A broad overview of the skills and expertise within an organisation and which relevant expertise should be shared is pivotal. Libraries have a long tradition of encouraging the sharing of resources. Donations form the backbone of many famous collections to encourage the preservation and accessibility of information. The ethos of KM is to make knowledge accessible in whatever format. The most complicated aspect is that knowledge exists in the heads of organisation members. To manage this requires facilitating an organised communication network, for example, through feedback sessions after training and seminars to share new knowledge with colleagues who did not attend, or mapping the acknowledged experts in particular subjects and making their expertise available to colleagues as required. Librarians often take on the role of mapping internal or external expertise, such as maintaining lists of expert witnesses or recommended barristers, in the same way they evaluate and recommend new resources to colleagues. The criteria by which librarians evaluate external resources can be used to develop such internal resources. The reason an external directory or database of experts is authoritative, current and accessible via many different index points translates well into developing an internal database of experts. An internal directory of staff identifying their areas of expertise and experience is easy to create and make accessible on an intranet for everyone to search, but can be an invaluable means of encouraging staff to see the tangible benefits of KM. Librarians already catalogue images, maps, music and seminar presentations, so cataloguing people seems a logical next step. In the same way KM includes people as resources, there is a need to manage their skills collection to identify new skills that ought to be developed. Managers of all teams have to know the capabilities of the members of their teams, but KM systems take this a stage further by making those talents more tangible to a wider audience within the organisation. The entries on any directory will need to be updated as people acquire new skills or increase expertise and work on new projects. Many humans will always prefer to ask a question of another person rather than search a database for the quickness, interaction and difficulties of some search phrasing. Such people will readily appreciate a simple directory to identify approachable experts and the beneficial connections created between people, particularly where work becomes more specialised and organisations ever larger and dispersed, so increasing the difficulties of otherwise locating experts. Internal expertise directories could identify how the experts prefer to be contacted for advice – possibly a link to their diaries if they are happy to be contacted in person to check when they are available – and give details of membership of any internal committees or groups to help clarify their responsibilities and areas of interest.

Management of library services has always included collection development – the identification of gaps in provision and procuring the best resources to satisfy those gaps. This also includes the converse aspect of weeding out items that are outdated or no longer relevant to the organisation's needs. Librarians could extend this role to weed online databases or assist others in setting up best practices for regular review procedures for checking continued relevance. The risks of using outdated precedents are very high and potentially extremely costly in such a litigious society, making the early establishment of best practice of fundamental importance. Librarians have evolved competencies to compare and assess the relative merits of constantly developing new resources.

It is important to remember IT is only an enabler, not a solution. Some organisations function well without a formal KM system by exploiting existing IT, such as intranets. The whole culture of an organisation needs to change to a sharing, nurturing and learning atmosphere via schemes such as mentoring and adopting KM development as part of appraisals. Knowledge management can be a unique path to move from managing the library to managing the organisation the library serves in creating a more public arena for the librarian's talents.

Training and information literacy

For a number of years, librarians have been developing a role in preparing and delivering training to users both formally and informally. In particular, academic and special libraries usually take part in induction training with sessions covering how to conduct research and the use of databases available within the parent organisation. This sharing of knowledge about which resources to use in particular circumstances and how best to use those resources goes to the very heart of what KM is about: the sharing of best practice or wisdom. It presupposes a great deal of knowledge about the type of work or research users will be required to undertake and the abilities they will need to develop to complete this. Some programmes will also include training in how best to present research findings as appropriate to the organisation.

Much training activity also takes place on a more informal ad hoc basis for small groups or individuals at the point of need. Some of the most frequently asked help issues could easily be used as a basis for training sessions or frequently asked questions pages on the intranet. Librarians usually serve a large number of users, making it impossible to deliver one-to-one training or at times to cover everyone in group training sessions, and have therefore of necessity developed the ability to produce training packages through e-learning or more traditional handouts and questions for self-testing. Users often contact librarians for their advice on navigating information resources and selecting the best sources to use based on a great deal of trust in their knowledge of those sources. Libraries have adopted an essential role at the centre of learning organisations in preserving and making accessible information with the added value of a context.

Training materials in the form of guides to using databases and learning packages including e-learning with detailed questions and worksheets illustrate the capabilities librarians have developed in teaching and educating their users. The thought involved in producing such packages and training sessions is only a small step away from helping others to develop training sessions and materials, and helping to identify the types of training that work well for users in various situations.

There is a growing recognition of the value of information literacy – i.e. the knowledge of information sources, how to use these in problem solving, how to present information and the need to verify reliable resources, which fits perfectly with KM ideals as part of a learning organisation. Training needs to evolve from simply how to use databases, to how to solve information problems, and include guidance on when to use resources and preselect reliable authoritative versions in the same way as the best resources are selected for library collections generally. Librarians have a lot of valuable expertise available to advise on when to use resources. Simple flow charts could be added to intranets or included as handouts at training sessions or with e-learning packages, directing when a particular resource is useful, with yes and no options to questions such as whether users need full text or summary items and the date ranges, as some databases may only cover recent articles.

Intranets/extranets

Librarians have readily taken on the role of evaluating, selecting and managing information held on intranets and developed technical skills to publish on and maintain these. They fully understand the value of publishing information within a context and arranging it to make it more useable as part of the ongoing cycle of creating more knowledge. A collection of precedents or client advice letters benefits from brief scope notes of commentary indicating in what circumstances they are suitable for use and any adaptations that may be necessary. Each clause could have a note of when it should be used and circumstances in which it can be deleted. This helps identify the authors of such scope notes as experts within the organisation and generates further collective expertise whenever they are used and updated or adapted. The scope notes can be similar to the abstracts librarians often create for items on LMS and current awareness services. The intranet particularly lends itself to checklist type documents and 'how to do it' pages, which form important features of KM.

Intranets could be viewed as an online library or portal directing users to relevant resources. In effect, the orientation librarians usually provide to resources becomes available 24/7 and accessible from remote locations or branches. This role of portal is central to ensuring all resources are well organised in a way which is simple to locate later on and fully linked to other relevant resources cited. Again, librarians are ideally placed to assess software for automatically adding hypertext links to documents, the links being to internally and externally held information, including subscription databases. The format and where the resource is held becomes irrelevant if it can be accessed from a central point. The lack of interaction with a help/enquiry desk makes training and ease of use of paramount importance. The wide variety of databases available generates problems of remembering different passwords for each one. The intranet can be developed to allow silent authentication directing users into each database without a password once the system has verified their IP address. Beside the lists of databases, it is a simple but valuable addition to include a link to a quick user guide, a more detailed guide, and a scope note of the sort of information the database includes, and, if significant, the date range it covers. All of this is very similar to the type of bibliographic information librarians regularly add to LMS.

Organising top-level headings to enable drilling down to relevant sections with a minimum number of clicks fits well with the development of taxonomies discussed earlier. Experience of proprietary databases develops ideas of push technologies for alerts and news feeds and how users wish to receive these to be kept fully informed without feeling overwhelmed.

There are discussion boards where questions can be asked of colleagues in secure environments with answers generated and added to avoid problems of isolation across different sites and duplicated efforts where colleagues are working on similar issues. Best practice can be continually evolving through such a process, and, providing the supporting environment is there, there is an opportunity to learn from failures as well as successes and to save time and money in not repeating them.

The type of information stored could include (copyright permitting) items like counsels' opinions where they have a general application beyond the particular case for which they were provided; for other sectors similar specialist advice from external consultants could also be stored. Seminar notes and PowerPoint presentations from seminars either given internally to update colleagues or externally for clients can be an excellent foundation for future seminars with a minimum of updating research. These may also be included on the LMS and linked from there to the full text on the intranet to preserve formatting and embedded links to other documents cited within them. There can be directories of recommended external experts with a note of who within the organisation is recommending them and the type of work for which they are recommended. There may be several different directories of external experts divided by functions, e.g. barristers, expert witnesses and foreign lawyers. Precedents usually form a useful backbone, but this may depend on integration with other systems already in place, e.g. document management or case management systems unless there is a need for confidentiality, so others can access copies of precedents without names and addresses of clients. The use of such systems will also depend on their search facilities. Manuals or guides of how to progress through a process are valuable along with links to financial information from the finance system. Protocols of how particular clients wish to be contacted or billed, or formats for their reports are useful additional elements to maintain the best possible relationship with clients. A transaction index would allow users to check quickly if a similar type of transaction has been previously carried out.

Some clients may drive the demand for standard precedents or information about their deals and cases to be made available by a secure extranet. This raises difficult issues of copyright, confidentiality and charging, as well as training these new external users and organising the system in such a way that it is intuitive for them to navigate or search. Greater collaboration with clients requires clear audit trails for documents to see who amended an item and when. Librarians can raise awareness of these potential issues and take an active role in training clients or developing e-learning packages.

Standard forms for submitting new information to be published on the intranet could be easily adapted from reference interview forms and the fields used to enter data onto LMS. Standardised templates for various intranet pages themselves also help users to navigate around different parts of the site. The editorial type overview of presentation style and content is a fitting one for librarians to adopt.

Auditing/user needs

Information auditing is usually used as a precursor to a KM initiative to establish what information is currently being used; why it is being used (there may be preferable alternatives currently unknown to users); how it is being used and shared with colleagues and clients; preferred formats; what is not being used and why not; and to identify any gaps in provision. The resulting information will help in budgeting for new services, economies in abandoning unused services if appropriate and planning training or marketing campaigns to encourage more use of underexploited existing services. If an organisation does not know what it already knows, it will be impossible to manage that knowledge, rather like trying to locate books in a library without a catalogue or classification scheme. Librarians are usually involved in information audits because of their familiarity with information resources held by their organisations and the overlap with more general work in collections development and how to arrange these to make them more accessible. Results of audits may also raise issues of training or raising awareness of resources. For example, an audit may identify a problem of staff regularly requiring information about the language skills of other staff, such as an ability to translate a document from French to English. This need to identify who can translate from French may result in e-mails across the whole organisation wasting everyone's time. If a staff directory already exists, e.g. on the intranet, it should be possible to add an additional field specifying each individual's language skills and their level of expertise in terms of written or spoken languages. This is something librarians could easily become involved in developing. If such a directory with the relevant field already exists, there may be issues of training users how to search, where to find the directory or how to update it. The training role readily fits with the librarian's role of training users how to use other resources; if the database has been developed or is updated by the library it should be promoted by the library. In organisations where nobody within the organisation has the relevant skills, librarians are ideally placed to signpost where to find relevant external expertise or to begin to create a simple database, even in the form of a spreadsheet of external experts recommended by staff within the organisation, to maintain the quality of expertise being bought in or exploit existing partnership arrangements.

Auditing helps to identify how the information provided by resources already held measures up against what is actually needed. Librarians already play a vital part in assessing and evaluating which products fill gaps in their collections. Auditing provides a useful first step in user involvement as developments do not add value if the users are not interested or wanted other things. To progress to examining internally held resources seems a small step further. An understanding of how information is created and flows around the organisation is the basis of developing a strategy to train users to overcome known barriers and fully exploit what already exists. A full KM audit should also assess the skills/knowledge an organisation currently needs or will shortly need to measure against known existing skills. Only by discovering the disparity can plans be implemented for efficient training programmes. Auditing needs to be carried out on a regular basis to be most effective in ensuring the organisation has everything it needs and resources are being used to utmost effect.

Librarians also update themselves on their users' profiles to produce current awareness services. The methods used to identify current awareness needs can be adapted to identify wider information needs. Auditing is a useful exercise in publicising the debate about information and knowledge within organisations, but a lot can be learnt from regular contact with users, from their research requests and simply walking around the building, which often attracts questions from people who have not ventured to the library. People can find it very difficult to articulate what they need to know or sometimes do not realise what they would like to know. Most organisations will already have some informal methods of sharing knowledge, e.g. by team e-mails or meetings, but the relevant items of information can be difficult to recover at the time of need. Becoming part of the informal sharing network or setting up people or systems to filter the informal sharing and extract those few elements of potential future reuse is a fundamental factor in the success of any KM initiative. Librarians can then examine how best to capture such informal sharing, e.g. by encouraging the development of discussion boards on the intranet and short practice notes to add to the intranet or KM system.

Market research/competitor intelligence

Many special librarians are becoming more involved in marketing-type activities in researching potential clients and competitor activity, either for one-off reports, or as part of ongoing monitoring fed into a client relationship management (CRM) database. Such databases are only effective if timely, reliable and relevant information is added: the work librarians already perform using LMS and intranets. Less familiar may be the skills required for prospecting new business opportunities and product development, but involvement will encourage recognition of the importance of information in product development. It offers a perfect opportunity to market the library service as a proactive agent to assist in generating income rather than simply an overhead.

Clients look for firms that understand the business sector in which they operate and know about the challenges faced by their business. The CRM database is a valuable extension of current awareness services. It looks beyond the issues affecting the organisation employing the library to those of its own clients and enables agility in identifying needs or potential new products those clients will require.

Physical space/meeting place

Libraries are moving away from the image of silent places to study books to become much more focused on their new role as meeting places and as electronic rather than physical entities. Public, academic and special libraries are increasingly including coffee bars within or close by them. This develops the serendipitous meeting of colleagues browsing shelves and exchanging news about whatever they are researching and information on problem solving or recommending resources to use. If KM is about exchanging and connecting knowledge within people's heads, then the physical meeting is one of the most important elements. Libraries play a vital part in centralising where users are likely to gather to find information. This role is best achieved if the library is in a central, easily accessible position.

Public libraries have developed this idea by hosting gatherings such as book groups. However, it could also work well for exchanges of work-related knowledge or debriefings by people who have attended courses their colleagues did not attend, where their own handouts or PowerPoint presentations might be added to the intranet for future reference. Knowledge management benefits greatly from storytelling to share and illustrate experiences/best practice, a system that could be borrowed directly from children's libraries. Provided the library continues to offer a quiet place to work, it can be utilised as a place for seminars, training sessions and team briefings for staff, e.g. at lunchtimes in a location with resources close by, including librarians' expertise.

In terms of becoming an electronic or hybrid library, as discussed previously in this chapter, the library intranet extends the library's accessibility beyond its physical location so that the role of making information accessible adopts greater importance. The library therefore becomes a knowledge management centre or hub.

Conclusions

Librarians are ideal custodians of corporate memory/corporate intelligence; to record and share experiences is a role libraries have adopted for many centuries. There has never been such a huge challenge in selecting and controlling the vast resources available and guiding users towards the best quality. The Internet and the multitude of databases available directly to users' desktops has created an information overload for end users, who do not use appropriate search strategies and either retrieve too much or too little information and abandon their search. This generates an unprecedented demand for timely user education and information literacy skills development exactly within librarians' expertise. Users have appreciated the expertise of librarians in information management to provide access to reliable, up-to-date resources, and that same trustworthiness is a secure foundation for KM initiatives.

The biggest change will be to move from managing explicit knowledge to facilitating the capture of tacit knowledge through becoming commercially aware of how managing information and knowledge fits in with business strategy. The basis of this is achieved from information auditing to analyse the organisation's information needs. Existing skills used in reference interviews are a perfect foundation for information auditing skills. The type of explicit knowledge has a wider context than traditional externally purchased resources by including files, precedents and contacts, but the principles of guiding and educating users about the best sources are broadly similar to those of managing information. Significant areas of change include moving into collaborative long-term relationships across a number of other departments and fitting together an overall structure for a wide variety of resources, such as case management systems, CRMs and documents relating to internally generated expertise. There is no reason why the particular competencies of librarians should not equip them to take a central role in coordinating such diverse teams of expertise. There are exceptional opportunities to become partners in creating and using knowledge not just providing a home for it and managing that home.

5

Accessibility issues for web-based information systems
Paul Catherall

The importance of web standards, usability and accessibility

Introduction

Recent years have witnessed the rapid growth of the World Wide Web as the most popular form of technology used on the Internet – in the areas of education, leisure and commercial activity. While it is generally accepted that the popular web browser application has broken down the barriers of technical complexity seen in early Internet technologies, the popularisation of the World Wide Web has itself given rise to further debate on its usability and accessibility as a medium of information and communications.

While there are many facets to the debate on the growing prevalence of the World Wide Web, including issues of ethics, authority and ownership, this chapter will attempt to define and explore web-based usability and accessibility issues from a technical and practical perspective – with particular emphasis on the accessibility of web browser software as an interface to information for disabled users. It is hoped that the chapter will provide an insight into universal access problems posed for the broad range of complex web-based systems, including knowledge management systems described elsewhere in this text.

The emergence of web-based systems

The availability of network technology and emergence of the Internet from the late 1970s, saw the early adoption of networked information systems, particularly within higher education and the information sector. These early systems were often text-based and driven by textual command input (usually via a terminal or telnet-type interface), requiring significant training in use of syntax that differed from system to system. In recent years, the web browser application has provided a more accessible alternative to these older, less intuitive Internet technologies. Furthermore, the growth of the World Wide Web as a medium for commerce and leisure has resulted in the prevalence of web browsing skills across society, allowing organisations to provide networked services with significantly fewer training considerations than in the past.

It is in this context that web-based information/knowledge management systems have recently been deployed across the public, educational and commercial sectors, including a wide range of 'enterprise level' (i.e. organisation-wide) systems, including systems used for library records, student and course records, staff and human resources data, information-querying and user-support systems, finance systems and learning and teaching systems. Many of these systems still rely on traditional relational database management systems (RDBMS) such as Oracle and SQL. However, the user interface for these systems is increasingly web-based and may usually be accessed via any computer connected to the Internet.

Practical examples illustrating the use of a web front-end for information or knowledge management systems could include the following:

- Use of a human resources management system by personnel staff and other administrative staff across an organisation or within a partner organisation located elsewhere in the country.

- Use of a university e-learning system providing course material and communication functions. Course material and collaboration features could be accessed by students within the university or from home. Lecturers could similarly upload new course notes or participate in student discussions from any computer connected to the Internet.

- Use of a content management system to provide a secure staff intranet – including features such as e-mail, discussion tools, online document publishing, knowledge querying or data repository functions from any networked computer.

Definition of web technologies

To understand the World Wide Web and the importance of accessibility for information/knowledge management systems, it is perhaps useful to have a basic knowledge of the Internet (upon which the Web runs). The Internet has been around a long time, developed during the 1960s by the US military's ARPA or Advanced Research Project Agency (FOLDOC, 2005a). This technology quickly spread to the US academic community and saw the development of the civilian Internet we know today. The early Internet was largely limited to academic and research institutions, with communications software such as e-mail running on complex UNIX-based terminals, which required significant technical skills to operate.

Two major advances allowed for the development of today's World Wide Web. These included the widespread adoption of graphical user interfaces (GUI), such as Microsoft Windows, which provided mouse-based interaction, rather than relying on typed input. In addition, the emergence of the web browser software application (and related technical specifications), developed by Tim Berners-Lee around 1993, revolutionised the way an ordinary computer user could interact with the Internet.

It may be worth mentioning that typical web pages are just simple text files (along with associated files such as images) located on a powerful computer linked to the Internet (called a server, and in this case a web server). In the process of browsing to a web page, the user simply downloads the web page via a web browser application onto their own computer (the client). It may be worth considering certain aspects of the World Wide Web in more detail.

Web pages are more properly known as HTML (Hyper Text Mark-up Language) documents. An HTML file usually ends in '.htm' or '.html' (e.g. mypage.htm) and can be opened in Notepad or any other text editing software. In addition to describing the file type, HTML also describes the language or script comprising the document. This script determines how the document content is displayed and is used to 'mark-up' ordinary text, for example, the HTML 'tag' for a heading is shown below:

<h1>Welcome to my web page!</h1>

As can be seen above, most HTML tags (or elements) require an 'opening' and 'closing' tag. HTML script can be viewed using Notepad or a similar text editor. However, a web browser application is needed to actually interpret the HTML and display the page content properly; the above example would display as follows in a web browser:

Welcome to my web page!

You can view the HTML for any web page by running your web browser, such as Internet Explorer – browse to a website, then using the pull-down toolbar at the top of the screen to select View/Source.

There are several structural features of HTML essential to the web page, these include the following:

- \<html> ... \</html>: This tag is used to enclose the entire HTML code.

- \<head> ... \</head>: All content in this tag is invisible to the user and occurs at the top of the document, containing the document title tag, descriptive information about the document and document style information.

- \<title> ... \</title>: This is actually inserted inside the \<head> area and defines a title for the web page which is not displayed by the web browser, but is used by search engines and for other indexing functions, for example:

    \<title>John's Web Page\</title>

- \<body> ... \</body>: This tag is used to contain all the content the user will actually see in the web browser, it could include tables, paragraphs, headings and hyperlinks to other resources.

A very basic web page could look as follows in HTML (note the \<h1> and \<p> tags used for a heading and paragraph respectively):

```
<html>
<head>
<title>John's Web Page</title>
</head>
<body>
<h1>Welcome to John's web page</h1>
<p>This page is all about John...</p>
</body>
</html>
```

Another aspect of the web browser is the use of the URL (uniform resource locator) address to request and retrieve HTML documents. This is shown in the address bar found at the top of the web browser screen, e.g. *http://www.draigweb.co.uk.*

Recent web browsers include Internet Explorer, Netscape Navigator and Opera; they are all based on the original browser developed by Tim Berners-Lee.

Recent years have seen the development of HTML into a more strictly defined mark-up language (XHTML or Extensible Hyper Text Mark-up Language), separating document display properties (such as colour and font face) from document structure (such as headings, paragraphs and other descriptive content). Some of the most widely used versions of HTML (W3C, 2005a) include:

- *HTML 4.01*: The original format for web pages, still a recognised standard.

- *XHTML 1.0*: An early version of Extensible Hyper Text Mark-up Language, permitting some features of HTML while enforcing a stricter document structure.

- *XHTML 1.1*: The most recent HTML standard providing the most highly structured form of HTML.

The main difference between HTML and XHTML concerns 'well-formedness' – i.e. providing appropriate 'closing' tags to maintain integral mark-up and 'nesting' these correctly within the document structure. For example, with <p><b>Hello</b></p> the 'bold' tag is closed and 'nested' within a paragraph tag.

XHTML emphasises the removal of display-focused tags, such as <font> and relies on an external style sheet (a file containing style information) to separate display aspects from document structure. The result is a 'vanilla' HTML document composed of purely structural and descriptive information, without the clutter of style instructions embedded in the page itself. The importance of this factor for accessibility will be discussed at later stages in the chapter.

What are web standards?

Central to the discussion of web accessibility and usability is the issue of technical standards – i.e. how to ensure that web pages display as the author intended and in a consistent manner within any standard web browser.

In the early days of the World Wide Web, a number of popular web browsers emerged, each one adhering to varying degrees with the official specifications for HTML. However, many of these early browsers also included their own proprietary HTML features or interpretations.

If the web author used browser-specific (i.e. non-standard HTML) code in their web page (e.g. special code for Netscape Navigator), they could rely on the page displaying correctly in the corresponding web browser. However, when the web page was viewed in a different browser, unintended behaviour could result.

The answer to this lack of consistency in HTML code was basically twofold: to improve the conformance of web browser software to the standard HTML model – the 'Document Object Model' (W3C, 2005b) and to ensure the corresponding HTML (the document code or script used to create web pages) was also regulated by standards. The organisation responsible for these standards is the World Wide Web Consortium or W3C (*http://www.w3c.org*), founded by the inventor of the web browser, Tim Berners-Lee.

There are several key standards integral to web resources, these include:

- *Mark-up languages*: Including the specifications for HTML, XHTML and related versions.

- *Cascading style sheets (CSS)*: Also called 'style sheets' these allow the web author to create a text file containing instructions for the web browser on how to display HTML elements; CSS files end in *.css and are referenced in the <head> area of the HTML document, for example:

  <link rel=stylesheet href="stylesheet.css" type="text/css">

There are currently two CSS specifications – Levels 1 and 2 (W3C, 2005c), either may be used by modern web browsers; version 2 – the most recent version, provides greater scope for stylising document display.

CSS allows the web author to control the visual style of an entire website using a single CSS file, allowing style consistency across all pages. Importantly, CSS allows for separation of HTML display instructions from textual content and structure. Effectively this means the HTML document can be read in a range of agents or web browsing software without the clutter of traditional HTML style tags, such as <font face="arial">. An example CSS instruction to format paragraph text using the colour black, in Arial font at size 10 could appear as follows in the CSS file:

```
p {
font-family: Arial;
font-size: 10pt;
color: #000000;
}
```

The issue of developing standard web browsers is still in process today, but has come very far indeed, with levels of conformance much improved across browsers such as Opera, Netscape Navigator, Mozilla and Internet Explorer. The issue of regulating or standardising HTML document creation is more problematic and relies mostly on the skill, awareness and conscientiousness of IT professionals responsible for HTML authoring. Additionally, web documents can be created in a number of ways, either coding the page 'by hand' to 'mark up' content using HTML tags, or using an automated method such as web editor software (e.g. Dreamweaver) which provides a 'word-processor' style interface for authoring HTML.

While it is impossible to force individual developers to adhere to HTML standards, it is perhaps more achievable to improve the standards compliance of web editor software such as FrontPage and Dreamweaver and also the automated web 'output' of recent web-based information or knowledge management systems. In recent years, web editors such as Dreamweaver have conformed more strictly to HTML specifications, including features to allow the author to audit and correct non-standard HTML or XHTML.

However, it should also be noted that organisations are increasingly moving away from traditional web page development using web editing software (such as Dreamweaver) and are instead adopting systems managed via a web-based interface. These systems, utilising technology such as RDBMS are allowing non-technical staff themselves to input and manage digital resources via the web interface, without the need to work through skilled web developers. However, the proliferation of web-based systems for a wide range of functions has itself prompted a greater focus on the capacity of these systems to provide an accessible and usable interface.

Conformance to web standards among modern information or knowledge management systems delivered via a web-based interface has been mixed and there is still much reliance on the web author or systems developer either to purchase a standards-compliant system or modify system templates to produce a more compliant HTML interface.

Examples of information systems that allow for development of web standards-compliant HTML include the open source (non-commercial) content management systems Plone (*http://www.plone.org*) and Zope (*http://www.zope.org*), which include a templates-based system, effectively allowing these systems to conform easily to web standards.

What is usability?

Usability and accessibility are related but distinct requirements for web-based resources. While usability is of general importance for the entire audience viewing web content, the latter is of particular importance for users with disabilities.

There have been many definitions of web usability, inevitably related to aspects of wider information technology and computer software. The development of GUIs through the Microsoft Windows and Apple Macintosh operating systems has increased the general usability of computing, an area which had previously been the reserve of those familiar with command line interfaces such as UNIX and DOS. The graphical interface used by Windows and similar systems is sometimes described as WIMP (windows, icons, menus and pointers).

While the graphical interface has widened the usability of a wide range of computer applications, including Internet software, such as the web browser, the transformation of computing from textual input to graphical interfaces has itself posed challenges for usability. A good example illustrating this is the change from command line programming (to develop computer software) to visual programming, which involves use of forms, icons and other graphical representations to construct computer software. Visual programming languages such as Visual C++ have posed difficulties for blind programmers familiar with older text-based programming interfaces. The FOLDOC Online Dictionary of Computing comments:

> A visually transformed language is a non-visual language with a superimposed visual representation. Naturally visual languages have an inherent visual expression for which there is no obvious textual equivalent. (FOLDOC, 2005b).

The shift from text to graphical interfaces may appear to suggest an obvious improvement in usability, but the above example illustrates the kind of difficulty presented by GUI systems for some visually impaired users.

Other aspects of usability include basic issues of information technology literacy and assumptions concerning users' technical skills. While the number of households possessing home computers and having private Internet access has increased in recent years – at 37 million Internet users in the UK (Internet World Stats, 2005), there is still debate and concern for a 'digital divide' between this IT literate section of society and certain groups who possess little or no IT skills. This group typically includes the elderly and less affluent members of society.

Usability and training are also inseparable in this regard, as an awareness of a user audience can enable anticipation of training needs while also ensuring appropriate IT resources are provided.

Basic issues of usability for the Web include aspects of page layout and design, legibility of text, appropriate contrast between textual information and background colours and conformance with web standards to enable user customisation within the web browser (e.g. to increase text size or set a preferred colour scheme).

The terms *usability* and *accessibility* are frequently used interchangeably and there is some debate on how far the two strands should be distinguished at all when implementing standards-based systems (i.e. the concept of web standards as a baseline encompassing usability for all users, regardless of particular needs or disabilities). Certainly, an integrated perspective has been adopted by the World Wide Web Consortium – particularly emphasised through the Web Accessibility Initiative or WAI (*http://www.w3c.org/WAI/*), and the Web Content Accessibility Guidelines 1.0 or WCAG (W3C, 1999a), which incorporate aspects of HTML/XHTML compliance, general usability considerations and support for specific forms of disability.

While later sections will consider general usability issues, it should be noted that the current ethos of accessibility is based firmly on core web standards, which provide a basis for delivering usable information for the entire spectrum of society.

What is accessibility?

Accessibility in a general sense is defined by the *Pocket Oxford Dictionary* (1994) as: 'reachable or obtainable; readily available ... easy to understand'. Web accessibility concerns the delivery of online information and services in a context that is universally usable for society, regardless of age, disability or culture. This definition is echoed in the TechDis introduction to accessibility: 'Accessibility is about removing barriers to participation and engagement' (TechDis, 2005).

It may be useful to consider some of the general implications of disability for web browsing and how accessibility can offset access difficulties.

Users with low or no usable vision will rely either on a facility to increase or otherwise modify the textual display, or on an alternative form of output, such as a 'screen reader' to read content via computer speakers. Display customisation (e.g. to increase text size) is possible in most web browsers and via accessibility features in the Windows operating system (e.g. use of 'Magnifier'). However, some visually impaired users may rely on additional 'assistive technology' in the form of software or equipment to fulfil their requirements. Examples of this kind of software include the Dolphin suite of applications – including a screen reader and Braille output software for use with a Braille reader (an additional peripheral connected to the PC which can output a Braille surface).

Users with cognitive disabilities may require alternative textual information within the web document itself, or use of assistive technology to improve text clarity or size. Individuals with motor-related disabilities, such as cerebral palsy, arthritis or repetitive strain injury (RSI) may rely on alternative input devices such as tracker-balls, soft keyboards or specially developed input devices. Of course, some users may require a combination of these solutions; a more detailed description of issues associated with disabilities is provided in the second part of this chapter.

In terms of the Web and HTML documents, a wide range of techniques and approaches exist to ensure web pages are constructed in a standards-compliant, logical and generally considerate manner that is usable for both general users and those with disabilities, most notably using the W3C's Web Content Accessibility Guidelines 1.0 (W3C, 1999a) for implementing accessible web resources. While it is impossible to develop web output that is optimal for every disability or circumstance, it is indeed possible via web standards to ensure content is usable within a broad range of user 'agents', thus ensuring some degree of accessibility.

Problems associated with web documents

The web browser application is a very forgiving and flexible tool – aspects of the web page such as layout, style, navigation menus, decorative images and the 'hidden' code comprising the web page itself are design factors limited only by the imagination of the web author.

In recent years, it has almost become the norm for web developers to furnish their web pages with special effects, breaking out of the limitations of the basic HTML document to include Flash animations, JavaScript menu systems or other features designed to add a sense of interaction or originality. Furthermore, web designers have traditionally used HTML in a purely pragmatic manner, often using inaccurate or non-standard HTML on the basis that their page 'works' in whatever web browser they designed it. The possibility that their inaccurate HTML will cause the page to function improperly in a different web browser has only recently become a focus among web authors.

Web browser software and the pages they are used to 'read' (i.e. HTML based documents) present a number of inherent problems particularly relevant to issues of usability and accessibility, these include:

- A wide range of web browsers exist produced by many different companies and not-for profit consortiums (e.g. Netscape, Internet Explorer, Mozilla).

- A wide range of HTML formats exists and are used across the World Wide web (e.g. HTML 4.01, XHTML 1.0, XHTML 1.1).

- A wide range of approaches exist to developing web content (e.g. development via hand coding using a text editor such as Notepad, development using a web editor application such as FrontPage or production of web pages via an automated process within a content management or similar system).

- While web and accessibility standards have been in existence for several years, it has historically been difficult to impose these on any of the above.

- Web browsers are permissive – even a very poorly coded page with HTML errors may 'work' on any particular web browser.

- There is no inherent structure or rule-set to ensure web pages provide logical, consistent or standard forms of site navigation (aside from W3C recommendations). Almost every web page is different and requires the user learn the unique navigation method (if present) and other conventions within each site; the same principle applies to layout, style, hyperlink conventions etc.

- Web browsers interpret web standards differently, i.e. while greater standardisation across web browsers now exists, discrepancies still exist in the interpretation of HTML, CSS, JavaScript etc., forcing vigilant developers to test pages in a wide range of browsers.

- Web browsers use different usability/accessibility conventions, e.g. access key functions are provided to operate the web browser via the keyboard. However, different key-combinations are used for the same functions across different browsers (e.g. Opera, Mozilla), forcing disabled users to learn dozens of new access keys within each browser used (the same problem applies to software applications such as Adobe Acrobat, Word etc.); other discrepancies include methods for using a local, user-defined style sheet and for setting local text colour, font size and browser magnification.

Mapping W3C standards

Table 5.1 illustrates some of the web and accessibility standards introduced previously, divided into three columns: aspect, specific standards and how assessed. The first aspect, 'web standards', lists the technical and structural specifications used to create web resources, including the various forms of

Table 5.1 Overview of web standards, usability and accessibility

Aspect	Specific standards	How assessed?
Web standards	Mark-up languages (e.g. HTML 4.01, XHTML 1.0), cascading style sheets (CSS 1 and 2).	Manual auditing possible (i.e. intensive review of code), but applications exist to audit entirely automatically, generate reports etc.
Usability	Usability and accessibility are reflected in both web and accessibility standards, however, subjective issues also include: ■ clarity of style, layout, font-size, use of colour and contrast; ■ use of consistent, logical and meaningful site navigation options; ■ use of written style, language and conten appropriate for the audience; ■ working hyperlinks (i.e. links not broken).	Mostly manual/subjective auditing.
Accessibility	Web Content Accessibility Guidelines (WCAG 1.0); Section 508 of the US Rehabilitation Act.	Automatic auditing possible for WCAG/US 508, but manual/ subjective auditing is still necessary for some specific aspects of these guidelines.

HTML and CSS (style sheets); the second aspect considers issues of usability and subjective issues for web auditing, the last aspect considers methods used to assess formal accessibility standards.

Web-based accessibility and the law

Disability in the UK – facts and figures

There are currently around ten million registered people disabled in the UK (around one in seven of the population), including around seven million disabled people in the workplace:

> There are approximately 10 million disabled adults in the UK covered by the Disability Discrimination Act, which represents around 18 per cent of the population ... Over 6.8 million disabled people are of working age, which represents 19 per cent of the working population. (Employers' Forum on Disability, 2005).

The forms of disability vary from visual and cognitive to motor and mobility disabilities, for a brief breakdown of disability in the UK see the figures below from The Economic and Social Research Council (2005):

- 750,000 wheelchair users registered in the UK;
- 19 per cent of men and 13 per cent of women reported having hearing difficulties;
- 55,000 people registered as deaf;
- 157,000 people registered as blind;
- 1.8 million diabetics in the UK;
- 350,000 people with epilepsy.

Implications of IT and web browsing for disabled users

As the World Wide Web becomes an increasingly prevalent information medium, it is necessary to consider the implications of web browsing for various forms of disability (Table 5.2). In this context it may be worth

Table 5.2   Overview of disabilities and conditions affecting web browsing

Disability/condition	General issues for web browsing
Speech and language impairments	Language difficulties may arise due to cerebral palsy, autism or as a result of injury; language difficulties could pose a problem for speech recognition software working via a web interface; similarly, users with difficulties comprehending language may experience problems when listening to multimedia content containing speech. Alternative textual content or use of screen readers (i.e. reading text aloud) may offset some problems faced by users with speech or language impairments.
Visual impairments	Individuals with low vision as opposed to total blindness or unusable vision may require some method to improve the clarity, size or contrast of textual or graphical information. It is important to build web-based resources with some means of resizing HTML output relative to the user's screen resolution or browser settings. This can often be achieved by using relative values for tables, text and other elements (e.g. 50 per cent width as opposed to a fixed size such as 10 pixels). Colour blindness is another issue to consider when designing resources; sufficient contrast between fonts and background colours should be used, although most web browsers allow the user to customise their own display preferences. Blind users should also be considered who may rely on screen-reader software, Braille displays or other assistive technology; these users include individuals legally blind (i.e. having less than 20/200 vision) and those with total blindness – e.g. caused by conditions such as glaucoma or cataracts; depending on the level of blindness, a combination of customised style (e.g. within the browser) or provision of alternative text (i.e. in the place of images) can offset some of the limitations for these users. Additionally, CSS now provides the ability to interact with speech readers (aural CSS), adding stress, changing the speed at which text is read and other means of suggesting an auditory equivalent to the visual features of text, such as bold or italic (see *http://www.w3.org/TR/REC-CSS2/aural.html*).

Table 5.2   Overview of disabilities and conditions affecting web browsing (*Cont'd*)

Disability/condition	General issues for web browsing
Mobility/motor limitations	Mobility or motor impairment concerns difficulties involving interaction between the user and input devices such as the mouse or keyboard. Arthritis, muscular dystrophy or repetitive strain injury (RSI) are just a few conditions where the user may not be able to use the mouse or keyboard in a typical manner. A range of methods exists to improve access for these users. For those with severe motor impairments, head or mouth sticks are used as pointing devices, while keyboard shortcuts can assist users with RSI or other conditions affecting the ability to type or use the mouse easily.
Hearing impairments	Any user who is deaf to some degree may encounter difficulties when using multimedia content (e.g. where music or speech is present). Alternative textual content is usually possible for most multimedia formats such as Flash.
Cognitive disabilities	Cognitive disabilities are neurological conditions such as dyslexia (affecting the underlying skills that are needed for learning to read, write and spell), dyspraxia (an impairment or immaturity of the organisation of movement in the way that the brain processes information) and Irlen's syndrome (a problem with how the nervous system encodes and decodes visual information).* Users with cognitive or neurological disabilities such as dyslexia or dyspraxia may have difficulties internalising or comprehending textual content in a typical manner and may require either customisation tools to improve text size, clarity and contrast, or may require alternative textual content. Epilepsy should also be considered when creating web resources, as this condition can involve seizures which can be triggered by flashing or blinking images, these type of animations should generally be avoided (see *http://www.w3.org/TR/WCAG10-CORE-TECHS/#flicker*).

*For further information on these conditions see British Dyslexia Association (2005), Dyspraxia Foundation (2005), Irlen Institute (2005).

defining these disabilities with some of the issues encountered by disabled users (technical solutions for the issues mentioned in the table are listed in the section on the WCAG Guidelines by priority level).

UK legislation

Disability Discrimination Act 1995 and amendments (DDA)

The Act describes the legal status of disability and the responsibilities of organisations to provide equality of provision for users with access difficulties (Home Office, 1995; OPSI, 1995). Core aspects of the legislation are as follows:

- A person is categorised as disabled 'if (they have) a physical or mental impairment which has a substantial and long term adverse effect on (their) ability to carry out normal day-to-day activities' (part 1.1).

- Since 1999, organisations are required to use 'reasonable adjustment' for disabled users in the provision of goods, facilities or services (including non-charging services). Examples include 'access to and use of any place which members of the public are permitted to enter', 'access to and use of means of communication' and 'access to and use of information services'.

- Employers are required to make 'reasonable' adjustment for employees having disabilities. This could include provision of assistive technology or special training.

- Educational organisations (higher and further education) were required to provide a 'disability statement', outlining 'the provision of facilities for education and research made by the institution in respect of persons who are disabled persons'.

Further information on the Act may be obtained at Disability.gov (*http://www.disability.gov.uk/*).

An amendment to the Act was introduced on 1 October 2004 – Rights of Access Goods, Facilities, Services and Premises (OPSI, 2002). This amendment requires that services and facilities provide additional 'reasonable adjustment' for disabled users, such as more accessible building layout. The Disability Rights Commission (*http://www .drc-gb.org*) has issued guidelines for the amendment, citing web-based services as examples (Disability Rights Commission, 2004a).

Special Educational Needs and Disabilities Act (SENDA) 2001

The Act requires educational organisations to employ 'reasonable adjustment' to deliver educational services for disabled users (Home Office, 2001; OPSI, 2001). Core aspects include the following:

- To make provision for disabled users without 'substantial disadvantage in comparison with persons who are not disabled'.

- Institutions must provide 'anticipatory' adjustment for disabled students, i.e. to prepare policies, procedures and resources to support learning and teaching for disabled users as a standard feature of course delivery, i.e. not simply as a response to disabled applicants.

- A range of alternative formats are required for the provision of information, such as alternative colour schemes for colour-blind users.

- 'Reasonable adjustment' is exempt where this undermines academic standards, causes excessive financial difficulty, conflicts with health and safety legislation or adversely affects the education of other students.

- Assistive technology should be made available where appropriate (e.g. screen readers, Braille readers).

- Facilities/staff resources should exist to support disabled users in the use of assistive technology (e.g. disability support team).

- Electronic resources such as web pages and other digital information should be accessible for disabled users.

It can be seen that the above legislation does cite electronic resources and that there is a corresponding legal case to ensure web-based resources are generally accessible. Furthermore, SENDA has required the education sector to apply many aspects of the DDA previously exempt for education. The specific means of implementing accessibility for the Web may at times appear arbitrary to actual W3C standards. However, web standards are mentioned in the recommendations of the Disability Rights Commission for implementing DDA and related laws, particularly in a recent report, *The Web Access and Inclusion for Disabled People* (2004):

> It is important that those who train website developers include standard training modules on disability awareness and the techniques required to translate that awareness into practice. Corresponding modules should be incorporated into any

continuing professional development prescribed. (Disability Rights Commission. 2004b: 39)

Web standards and web accessibility standards

Overview of core standards

Traditionally, a range of proprietary technologies were seen on the World Wide Web, with leading web browsers developing their own proprietary HTML standards. However, in recent years, the W3C has improved cooperation with a wide range of information technology organisations to implement web standards. Core standards developed by the W3C include:

- *CSS (cascading style sheets)*: Traditional HTML provided tags to display textual content (e.g. <p>hello</p>), to control colour and layout (e.g. <font color="000000">). CSS may be used to separate HTML structure and content from appearance. The use of a CSS file means that the web browser or assistive technology agent may parse or understand HTML without the clutter of embedded style. CSS files have a .css extension and the CSS code refers to HTML elements, e.g. the following CSS rule is used to display paragraph text using the colour blue:

  P: {color: #0000ff};

  There are two types of CSS: level 1 and level 2. The latter offers more complex display options. CSS files are linked to HTML-based documents in the HEAD region of the mark-up file, for example:

  <link rel="style sheet" href="mystyle.css" type="text/css"/>

  The specifications defining CSS are available at the W3C site (*http://www.w3.org/Style/CSS/*).

- *HTML*: The basic standard for web pages is HTML. Several versions of HTML have been defined, XHTML being the latest version. The main differences between traditional HTML and XHTML includes the requirement for 'well formed' document structure (the rules defining how HTML elements can be used within the document hierarchy), use of lower-case tags and the need to properly 'nest' all elements (e.g. a correctly 'nested' paragraph which is also bold:

<p><b>example</b></p>). HTML standards defined by the W3C include HTML 4.01, XHTML 1.0. and XHTML 1.1. Compliance with standards such as XHTML 1.1 should ensure that web resources may be viewed or accessed by any standard web browser, such as Internet Explorer, or assistive technology. The full HTML and related specifications may be obtained at: *http://www.w3.org/MarkUp/*.

Web Content Accessibility Guidelines 1.0

The W3C's Web Content Accessibility Guidelines (WCAG) 1.0 have become the industry standard for developing accessible web-based resources. Three levels of compliance exist: A (Priority 1 compliance) is the minimal level of compliance required; AA (Priority 1 and 2 compliance) provides increased accessibility; and AAA (Priorities 1, 2 and 3) indicates the highest level of compliance.

The guidelines in s. 508 of the US Rehabilitation Act 1998 (*http://www.section508.gov*) provide another major standard for web resources. Although this standard is US-specific, the 508 guidelines are actually based on the WCAG aspects of standards compliance:

- *Use of TITLE*: The title tag is one of the most important tags in the HTML or XHTML document. This is used by a large number of web browsers to store a 'bookmark' about the web page for later viewing. The title tag is also used by search engines such as Google and other systems for user searching and listing results, e.g. <title>University of Somewhere</title>.

- *ALT tags*: Where images occur in web documents, an alternative textual description could be provided for non-visual users. This alternative text may be 'spoken' by a screen reader or displayed in any text-only context, for example:

  <img src="john.jpg" alt="A picture of John" />

  A similar descriptive attribute 'longdesc' can also be used to provide a hyperlink to a web page containing further details of the image, e.g.

  <img src="john.jpg" alt="A picture of John" longdesc= "john.htm" />

  In addition to the above, the 'title' attribute can provide alt-style text for almost any HTML element, e.g. a hyperlink:

  <a href="john.htm" title="A picture of John">John's Page</a>

- *Tables*: Tables in HTML should be defined to indicate the presence of tabular data; table headers (i.e. the row across the top) should contain a 'TH' tag to define each column; tables used for layout should be avoided where possible. Additionally, a SUMMARY tag may be used to define the purpose of tables, e.g. <table summary="This table contains useful information">.

- *Captions*: Similar to ALT tags, these consist of a textual alternative for more complex multimedia presentations, such as Macromedia Flash MX. Typically, a caption will provide a short text description for audio or video files, which may be displayed onscreen for users with hearing problems.

- *Alternative style sheets*: Several alternative CSS (style sheets) may be available within a web resource, allowing the user to select from a range of available styles to display the document. Not all current browsers support selection of alternative style sheets.

- *Interactive features*: Web forms, check boxes, drop-down menus and other interactive features may present difficulties for disabled users and assistive technology, such as screen readers. Interactive features (e.g. a selection menu) may sometimes be replaced by simple hyperlinks. However, a range of methods exist to ensure interactive features are accessible – e.g. defining a 'tabindex' (to cycle through pull-down options using the tab key), or 'access keys' to use web features without the need for a mouse.

Validation and auditing techniques for web-based systems

Automatic mark-up validation

Systems may be tested using either software installed on a computer or some web-based services. Auditing web resources should be carried out using official W3C tools or software recommended by the W3C:

- *W3C HTML Validator*: The W3C site provides a range of tools for checking the core standards compliance of HTML/XHTML web resources. Web pages containing HTML or XHTML errors may present problems for either standard web browsers or third-party equipment, such as screen readers. There are several validator tools available at the W3C site, including the W3C MarkUp Validation Service (*http://validator.w3.org*) and the Web Development Group Validator (*http://www.htmlhelp.com/tools/validator*); see also 'A Real Validator': *http://arealvalidator.com/*).

- *W3C CSS Validator* (*http://jigsaw.w3.org/css-validator*): CSS used to control colours and layout may be checked using this tool.

Automatic WCAG validation

- *Bobby*: The Bobby accessibility validator is the most popular tool for auditing WCAG compliance, and also allows for checking US 508 support. Bobby is available as a commercial software application (*http://www.watchfire.com*) and a similar free online tool called WebXact is also available (*http://webxact.watchfire.com*). The Bobby/WebXact tool provides a detailed report of WCAG or US 508 compliance for a given web page.

- *LIFT for Dreamweaver or FrontPage* (*http://www.useablenet.com*): This plug-in for the FrontPage or Dreamweaver web editors provides detailed reports, interactive prompts and other features for developing accessible HTML/XHTML.

Web Content Accessibility Guidelines in detail

WCAG 1.0, defines standards for delivering accessible web resources (see the full WCAG document at *http://www.w3.org/TR/WAI-WEBCONTENT/*).

There are three 'priority' levels of compliance (levels 1, 2 and 3) described on the WCAG site (1999a):

- Conformance Level 'A': all priority 1 checkpoints are satisfied.
- Conformance Level 'Double-A': all priority 1 and 2 checkpoints are satisfied.
- Conformance Level 'Triple-A': all priority 1, 2 and 3 checkpoints are satisfied.

The WCAG site (1999a) defines the priorities as follows:

- *Priority 1*: A web content developer must satisfy this checkpoint. Otherwise, one or more groups will find it impossible to access information in the document. Satisfying this checkpoint is a basic requirement for some groups to be able to use web documents.

- *Priority 2*: A web content developer should satisfy this checkpoint. Otherwise, one or more groups will find it difficult to access information in the document. Satisfying this checkpoint will remove significant barriers to accessing web documents.

- *Priority 3*: A web content developer may address this checkpoint. Otherwise, one or more groups will find it somewhat difficult to access information in the document. Satisfying this checkpoint will improve access to web documents.

There are 14 WCAG guidelines, each guideline contains several 'checkpoints'; these are also defined according to priority level – e.g. checkpoint '3.3 Use style sheets to control layout and presentation' is also defined as 'priority 2'. Some checkpoints also apply to several priorities under certain circumstances (for a breakdown of checkpoints where these circumstances are cited, see W3C, 1996b).

The WCAG guidelines are grouped under general headings, each one contains a number of detailed subsections; however, the following list provides a useful précis of the guidelines (W3C, 1999a):

1. Provide equivalent alternatives to auditory and visual content.
2. Do not rely on colour alone.
3. Use mark-up and style sheets and do so properly.
4. Clarify natural language usage.
5. Create tables that transform gracefully.
6. Ensure that pages featuring new technologies transform gracefully.
7. Ensure user control of time-sensitive content changes.
8. Ensure direct accessibility of embedded user interfaces.
9. Design for device-independence.
10. Use interim solutions.
11. Use W3C technologies and guidelines.
12. Provide context and orientation information.
13. Provide clear navigation mechanisms.
14. Ensure that documents are clear and simple.

While it is possible to review HTML in detail for WCAG compliance, there are a range of options available for auditing web resources, such as using Bobby or similar automated methods (as previously described).

In addition, W3C (2000) provides detailed examples illustrating the checkpoints. To discover further examples of how the guidelines are implemented, search for examples on the W3C site (*http://www.w3c.org*) using the site search box to look up the required mark-up element name (e.g. 'alt').

Table 5.3 illustrates the WCAG in some detail. Further examples may be found by following the URLs provided in the second column.

Table 5.3   WCAG guidelines by priority level

Checklist item	Checkpoint notes
Priority 1	
1.1 Provide a text equivalent for every non-text element (e.g. via 'alt', 'longdesc', or in element content). This includes images, graphical representations of text (including symbols), image map regions, animations (e.g. animated GIFs), applets and programmatic objects, ASCII art, frames, scripts, images used as list bullets, spacers, graphical buttons, sounds (played with or without user interaction), stand-alone audio files, audio tracks of video, and video.	For example, in HTML: Use 'alt' for the IMG, INPUT, and APPLET elements, or provide a text equivalent in the content of the OBJECT and APPLET elements. For complex content (e.g. a chart) where the 'alt' text does not provide a complete text equivalent, provide an additional description using, for example, 'longdesc' with IMG or FRAME, a link inside an OBJECT element, or a description link. For image maps, either use the 'alt' attribute with AREA, or use the MAP element with A elements (and other text) as content. Refer also to checkpoint 9.1 and checkpoint 13.10.
1.2 Provide redundant text links for each active region of a server-side image map.	Refer also to checkpoint 1.5 and checkpoint 9.1. * See Section: '7.4.4 Server-side image maps' in the WCAG techniques at: *http://www.w3-.org/TR/WCAG10-HTML-TECHS/*
1.3 Until user agents can automatically read aloud the text equivalent of a visual track, provide an auditory description of the important information of the visual track of a multimedia presentation.	Synchronize the auditory description with the audio track as per checkpoint 1.4. Refer to checkpoint 1.1 for information about textual equivalents for visual information.

Table 5.3   WCAG guidelines by priority level (*Cont'd*)

Checklist item	Checkpoint notes
1.4 For any time-based multimedia presentation (e.g. a movie or animation), synchronize equivalent alternatives (e.g. captions or auditory descriptions of the visual track) with the presentation.	* Multimedia files such as Flash allow for 'captions' to display text alternatives when displaying audio or video, these captions may be useful for deaf/hard of hearing users.
2.1 Ensure that all information conveyed with color is also available without color, for example from context or mark-up.	* It is unwise to rely on colour to convey information. For example, an important notice displayed in red will not convey importance for blind users, this should be indicated in <B> (bold) or <strong>, or should be indicated in plain language in the context of the text.
4.1 Clearly identify changes in the natural language of a document's text and any text equivalents (e.g. captions).	For example, in HTML use the 'lang' attribute. In XML, use 'xml:lang'.
5.1 For data tables, identify row and column headers.	For example, in HTML, use TD to identify data cells and TH to identify headers.
5.2 For data tables that have two or more logical levels of row or column headers, use mark-up to associate data cells and header cells.	For example, in HTML, use THEAD, TFOOT, and TBODY to group rows, COL and COLGROUP to group columns, and the 'axis', 'scope', and 'headers' attributes, to describe more complex relationships among data.
6.1 Organize documents so they may be read without style sheets. For example, when an HTML document is rendered without associated style sheets, it must still be possible to read the document.	When content is organized logically, it will be rendered in a meaningful order when style sheets are turned off or not supported.
6.2 Ensure that equivalents for dynamic content are updated when the dynamic content changes.	* See Section: '8.1' in the WCAG techniques at: *http://www.w3-.org/TR/WCAG10-HTML-TECHS/*

| Table 5.3 | WCAG guidelines by priority level (*Cont'd*) |

Checklist item	Checkpoint notes
6.3 Ensure that pages are usable when scripts, applets, or other programmatic objects are turned off or not supported. If this is not possible, provide equivalent information on an alternative accessible page.	For example, ensure that links that trigger scripts work when scripts are turned off or not supported (e.g. do not use 'javascript:' as the link target). If it is not possible to make the page usable without scripts, provide a text equivalent with the NOSCRIPT element, or use a server-side script instead of a client-side script, or provide an alternative accessible page as per checkpoint 11.4. Refer also to guideline 1.
7.1 Until user agents allow users to control flickering, avoid causing the screen to flicker.	Note. People with photosensitive epilepsy can have seizures triggered by flickering or flashing in the 4–59 flashes per second (Hertz) range with a peak sensitivity at 20 flashes per second as well as quick changes from dark to light (like strobe lights).
8.1 Make programmatic elements such as scripts and applets directly accessible or compatible with assistive technologies	Refer also to guideline 6. * See Section: '8.2' in the WCAG techniques at: *http://www.w3-.org/TR/WCAG10-HTML-TECHS/*
9.1 Provide client-side image maps instead of server-side image maps except where the regions cannot be defined with an available geometric shape.	Refer also to checkpoint 1.1, checkpoint 1.2, and checkpoint 1.5. * See Section: '7.4.3' in the WCAG techniques at: *http://www.w3-.org/TR/WCAG10-HTML-TECHS/*
11.4 If, after best efforts, you cannot create an accessible page, provide a link to an alternative page that uses W3C technologies, is accessible, has equivalent information (or functionality), and is updated as often as the inaccessible (original) page.	* For example, provide a static HTML alternative if you cannot make a script generated page accessible. It may be necessary to update the alternative page manually to ensure content is complementary to the script generated page.
12.1 Title each frame to facilitate frame identification and navigation.	For example, in HTML use the 'title' attribute on FRAME elements.
14.1 Use the clearest and simplest language appropriate for a site's content.	* Use concise language for navigation/ menus, with hyperlink labels describing the content of actual resources as closely as possible.

Table 5.3   WCAG guidelines by priority level (*Cont'd*)

Checklist item	Checkpoint notes
Priority 2	
2.2 Ensure that foreground and background color combinations provide sufficient contrast when viewed by someone having color deficits or when viewed on a black and white screen.	* See Section: '7.5' in the WCAG techniques at: *http://www.w3-.org/TR/WCAG10-HTML-TECHS/*
3.1 When an appropriate mark-up language exists, use mark-up rather than images to convey information.	For example, use MathML to mark up mathematical equations, and style sheets to format text and control layout. Also, avoid using images to represent text – use text and style sheets instead. Refer also to guideline 6 and guideline 11.
3.2 Create documents that validate to published formal grammars.	For example, include a document type declaration at the beginning of a document that refers to a published DTD (e.g. the strict HTML 4.0 DTD).
3.3 Use style sheets to control layout and presentation.	For example, use the CSS 'font' property instead of the HTML FONT element to control font styles.
3.4 Use relative rather than absolute units in mark-up language attribute values and style sheet property values.	For example, in CSS, use 'em' or percentage lengths rather than 'pt' or 'cm', which are absolute units. If absolute units are used, validate that the rendered content is usable (refer to the section on validation).
3.5 Use header elements to convey document structure and use them according to specification.	For example, in HTML, use H2 to indicate a subsection of H1. Do not use headers for font effects.
3.6 Mark up lists and list items properly.	For example, in HTML, nest OL, UL, and DL lists properly.
3.7 Mark up quotations. Do not use quotation markup for formatting effects such as indentation.	For example, in HTML, use the Q and BLOCKQUOTE elements to markup short and longer quotations, respectively.

Table 5.3 WCAG guidelines by priority level (*Cont'd*)

Checklist item	Checkpoint notes
5.3 Do not use tables for layout unless the table makes sense when linearized. Otherwise, if the table does not make sense, provide an alternative equivalent (which may be a linearized version).	Note. Once user agents support style sheet positioning, tables should not be used for layout. Refer also to checkpoint 3.3.
5.4 If a table is used for layout, do not use any structural markup for the purpose of visual formatting.	For example, in HTML do not use the TH element to cause the content of a (non-table header) cell to be displayed centred and in bold.
6.4 For scripts and applets, ensure that event handlers are input device-independent.	* See Section: '8.2' in the WCAG techniques at: *http://www.w3-.org/TR/WCAG10-HTML-TECHS/*
6.5 Ensure that dynamic content is accessible or provide an alternative presentation or page.	For example, in HTML, use NOFRAMES at the end of each frameset. For some applications, server-side scripts may be more accessible than client-side scripts.
7.2 Until user agents allow users to control blinking, avoid causing content to blink (i.e. change presentation at a regular rate, such as turning on and off).	* See Section: '8.2' in the WCAG techniques at: *http://www.w3-.org/TR/WCAG10-HTML-TECHS/*
7.3 Until user agents allow users to freeze moving content, avoid movement in pages.	When a page includes moving content, provide a mechanism within a script or applet to allow users to freeze motion or updates. Using style sheets with scripting to create movement allows users to turn off or override the effect more easily. Refer also to guideline 8.
7.4 Until user agents provide the ability to stop the refresh, do not create periodically auto-refreshing pages.	For example, in HTML, do not cause pages to auto-refresh with 'HTTP-EQUIV=refresh' until user agents allow users to turn off the feature.
7.5 Until user agents provide the ability to stop auto-redirect, do not use markup to redirect pages automatically. Instead, configure the server to perform redirects.	* See Section: '12.6' in the WCAG techniques at: *http://www.w3-.org/TR/WCAG10-HTML-TECHS/*

Table 5.3 WCAG guidelines by priority level (*Cont'd*)

Checklist item	Checkpoint notes
8.1 Make programmatic elements such as scripts and applets directly accessible or compatible with assistive technologies	Refer also to guideline 6. * See Section: '12.4' in the WCAG techniques at: *http://www.w3-.org/TR/WCAG10-HTML-TECHS/*
9.2 Ensure that any element that has its own interface can be operated in a device-independent manner.	Refer also to guideline 8. * See Section: '8.2' in the WCAG techniques at: *http://www.w3-.org/TR/WCAG10-HTML-TECHS/*
9.3 For scripts, specify logical event handlers rather than device-dependent event handlers.	* See Section: '12.4' in the WCAG techniques at: *http://www.w3-.org/TR/WCAG10-HTML-TECHS/*
10.1 Until user agents allow users to turn off spawned windows, do not cause pop-ups or other windows to appear and do not change the current window without informing the user.	For example, in HTML, avoid using a frame whose target is a new window.
10.2 Until user agents support explicit associations between labels and form controls, for all form controls with implicitly associated labels, ensure that the label is properly positioned.	The label must immediately precede its control on the same line (allowing more than one control/label per line) or be in the line preceding the control (with only one label and one control per line). Refer also to checkpoint 12.4.
11.1 Use W3C technologies when they are available and appropriate for a task and use the latest versions when supported.	* For general accessibility information and related standards, see the Web Accessibility Initiative (WAI): *http://www.w3c.org/WAI/*
11.2 Avoid deprecated features of W3C technologies.	For example, in HTML, don't use the deprecated FONT element; use style sheets instead (e.g. the 'font' property in CSS).
12.2 Describe the purpose of frames and how frames relate to each other if it is not obvious by frame titles alone.	For example, in HTML, use 'longdesc,' or a description link.
12.3 Divide large blocks of information into more manageable groups where natural and appropriate.	For example, in HTML, use OPTGROUP to group OPTION elements inside a SELECT; group form controls with FIELDSET and LEGEND; use nested lists where appropriate; use headings to structure documents, etc. Refer also to guideline 3.

Table 5.3   WCAG guidelines by priority level (*Cont'd*)

Checklist item	Checkpoint notes
12.4 Associate labels explicitly with their controls.	For example, in HTML use LABEL and its 'for' attribute.
13.1 Clearly identify the target of each link.	Link text should be meaningful enough to make sense when read out of context – either on its own or as part of a sequence of links. Link text should also be terse. For example, in HTML, write 'Information about version 4.3' instead of 'click here'. In addition to clear link text, content developers may further clarify the target of a link with an informative link title (e.g. in HTML, the 'title' attribute).
13.2 Provide metadata to add semantic information to pages and sites.	For example, use RDF to indicate the document's author, the type of content, etc. Note. Some HTML user agents can build navigation tools from document relations described by the HTML LINK element and 'rel' or 'rev' attributes (e.g. rel="next", rel="previous", rel="index", etc.). Refer also to checkpoint 13.5.
13.3 Provide information about the general layout of a site (e.g. a site map or table of contents).	In describing site layout, highlight and explain available accessibility features.
13.4 Use navigation mechanisms in a consistent manner.	* Top-level navigation options (i.e. main categories as opposed to sub-categories) should ideally remain the same across all documents, providing a consistent method to navigate.
Priority 3	
1.5 Until user agents render text equivalents for client-side image map links, provide redundant text links for each active region of a client-side image map.	Refer also to checkpoint 1.2 and checkpoint 9.1. * See Section: '7.4.2' in the WCAG techniques at: *http://www.w3.org/-TR/WCAG10-HTML-TECHS/*
2.2 Ensure that foreground and background color combinations provide sufficient contrast when viewed by someone having color deficits or when viewed on a black and white screen.	Refer also to checkpoint 1.2 and checkpoint 9.1. * See Section: '7.5' in the WCAG techniques at: *http://www.w3-.org/TR/WCAG10-HTML-TECHS/*

Table 5.3   WCAG guidelines by priority level (*Cont'd*)

Checklist item	Checkpoint notes
4.2 Specify the expansion of each abbreviation or acronym in a document where it first occurs.	For example, in HTML, use the 'title' attribute of the ABBR and ACRONYM elements. Providing the expansion in the main body of the document also helps document usability.
4.3 Identify the primary natural language of a document.	For example, in HTML set the 'lang' attribute on the HTML element. In XML, use 'xml:lang'. Server operators should configure servers to take advantage of HTTP content negotiation mechanisms.
5.5 Provide summaries for tables.	For example, in HTML, use the 'summary' attribute of the TABLE element.
5.6 Provide abbreviations for header labels.	For example, in HTML, use the 'abbr' attribute on the TH element.
9.4 Create a logical tab order through links, form controls, and objects.	For example, in HTML, specify tab order via the 'tabindex' attribute or ensure a logical page design.
9.5 Provide keyboard shortcuts to important links (including those in client-side image maps), form controls, and groups of form controls.	For example, in HTML, specify shortcuts via the 'accesskey' attribute.
10.3 Until user agents (including assistive technologies) render side-by-side text correctly, provide a linear text alternative (on the current page or some other) for all tables that lay out text in parallel, word-wrapped columns.	Note. Please consult the definition of linearized table. This checkpoint benefits people with user agents (such as some screen readers) that are unable to handle blocks of text presented side-by-side; the checkpoint should not discourage content developers from using tables to represent tabular information.
10.4 Until user agents handle empty controls correctly, include default, place-holding characters in edit boxes and text areas.	For example, in HTML, do this for TEXTAREA and INPUT.
10.5 Until user agents (including assistive technologies) render adjacent links distinctly, include non-link, printable characters (surrounded by spaces) between adjacent links.	* See Section: '6.2' in the WCAG techniques at: *http://www.w3-.org/TR/WCAG10-HTML-TECHS/*

| Table 5.3 | WCAG guidelines by priority level (*Cont'd*) |

Checklist item	Checkpoint notes
11.3 Provide information so that users may receive documents according to their preferences (e.g. language, content type, etc.)	* Provide alternative formats, e.g. where a Word file is used, also provide an alternative HTML version.
13.5 Provide navigation bars to highlight and give access to the navigation mechanism.	Provide information so that users may receive documents * Use a menu of links to provide consistent navigation across all pages.
13.6 Group related links, identify the group (for user agents), and, until user agents do so, provide a way to bypass the group.	* See Section: '6.2' in the WCAG techniques at: *http://www.w3-.org/TR/WCAG10-HTML-TECHS/*
13.7 If search functions are provided, enable different types of searches for different skill levels and preferences.	* For example, provide an 'advanced' option for website search engines.
13.8 Place distinguishing information at the beginning of headings, paragraphs, lists, etc.	Note. This is commonly referred to as 'front-loading' and is especially helpful for people accessing information with serial devices such as speech synthesizers.
13.9 Provide information about document collections (i.e. documents comprising multiple pages.).	For example, in HTML specify document collections with the LINK element and the 'rel' and 'rev' attributes. Another way to create a collection is by building an archive (e.g. with zip, tar and gzip, stuffit, etc.) of the multiple pages. Note. The performance improvement gained by offline processing can make browsing much less expensive for people with disabilities who may be browsing slowly.
13.10 Provide a means to skip over multi-line ASCII art.	* See Section: '7.3' in the WCAG techniques at: *http://www.w3-.org/TR/WCAG10-HTML-TECHS/*

Table 5.3   WCAG guidelines by priority level (*Cont'd*)

Checklist item	Checkpoint notes
14.2 Supplement text with graphic or auditory presentations where they will facilitate comprehension of the page.	Refer also to guideline 1.
14.3 Create a style of presentation that is consistent across pages.	* Do not change the font size or layout style across a website but ensure style is consistent across all pages (i.e. using CSS.).

Source: The table is derived from the Guidelines on the W3C site (*http://www.w3 .org/TR/WCAG10/full-checklist.html*), with additional notes from the author indicated with an asterisk.
Note: this table also appeared in Catherall (2004).

Further possibilities for auditing web resources

A range of additional methods exist to audit pages for accessibility – ideally, web documents should function using a wide variety of web browsers and using alternative input devices (e.g. keyboard only); suggestions provided by the W3C (1999a) include:

- Use a text-only browser or emulator (e.g. Lynx: *http://lynx.browser .org/*). It is important to note that most screen-reader software relies heavily on the actual text comprising the HTML document; if your page functions in a text-only browser such as Lynx, there is a good chance it will function successfully using assistive technology.
- Use multiple graphic browsers, with:
  - sounds and graphics loaded,
  - graphics not loaded,
  - sounds not loaded,
  - no mouse,
  - frames, scripts, style sheets and applets not loaded.
- Use several browsers, old and new.
- Use a self-voicing browser, a screen reader, magnification software, a small display (including a range of screen resolution settings, including 800 × 600 pixels per inch and higher resolutions), etc.

- Use spell and grammar checkers. A person reading a page with a speech synthesiser may not be able to decipher the synthesiser's best guess for a word with a spelling error. Eliminating grammar problems increases comprehension.

- Review the document for clarity and simplicity. Readability statistics, such as those generated by some word processors, may be useful indicators of clarity and simplicity. Better still, ask an experienced (human) editor to review written content for clarity. Editors can also improve the usability of documents by identifying potentially sensitive cultural issues that might arise due to language or icon usage.

- Invite people with disabilities to review documents. Expert and novice users with disabilities will provide valuable feedback about accessibility or usability problems and their severity.

Further accessibility tools are listed at the W3C accessibility resources site (*http://www.w3.org/WAI/ER/existingtools.html*).

Usability and the Web

Basic usability issues

Usability is a term used widely and interchangeably with 'accessibility', but perhaps the best definition of usability for web-based systems concerns how intuitive these systems are in terms of navigation and the user interface.

The interface used to access web resources should be designed for ease of access, with a clearly defined navigation menu that provides a persistent route to areas within the resource (i.e. links to core pages or functions persistently onscreen). Links within the interface should be defined using concise and relevant language (i.e. the name of menu items should relate to the content that will be accessed).

The computer 'platform' or system specifications are also an important consideration for delivering web resources. These include the operating system used to run software, such as Microsoft Windows 2000 or Windows XP, the web browser used, e.g. Netscape Navigator 7, and the display resolution available to view web resources. A controlled and standardised platform environment is possible on computers within a defined organisation – e.g. delivering a web-based staff intranet on computers with Windows XP using Internet Explorer and a screen resolution of 1024 × 768 pixels. However, where home Internet access is required, it may be difficult to ensure a standard platform, because not all home users will possess computers capable of running the latest operating system or web browser.

While it is possible to issue guidelines for users accessing a particular web resource, care should be taken to ensure the resource is functional across a range of environments (e.g. non-Windows operating systems such as Apple Macintosh and a range of web browsers).

The W3C site provides detailed statistics on the kind of platforms used to access web resources. Currently, the most widely used web browser is Internet Explorer version 6 (with around 70 per cent using this browser), with other leading browsers including Internet Explorer 5, Opera 7 and Netscape variants. According to W3C (2005d), 'Internet Explorer 6 is the dominating browser, XP is the most popular operating system, and most users are using a display with 800 × 600 pixels or more, with a color depth of at least 65K colors'.

Navigation and content structure

The navigation menu or links provided by web resources should consist of simple hyperlinks rather than complex script-generated buttons or roll-over images. Text rather than images should be used for interface navigation. Images or icons used to access information should be clearly defined, as the meaning of icons can be ambiguous.

Bandwidth and file size considerations

Bandwidth is the capacity of a network to transfer data at particular speeds. All web pages and supporting files such as image files must be downloaded onto the user's computer for viewing. The larger the file size (e.g. in kilobytes), the longer it takes to download. For organisations with high-speed Internet access, file size is not usually a problem, but Internet connection speed may be a problem for home users connecting to the Internet via a 56k modem. Use of high-resolution images or content-rich documents such as PowerPoint presentations should be carefully considered.

Scripts and client-side issues

It is important to consider the impact of extensive use of JavaScript or other 'inline' code within the normal HTML or XHTML document. Use of JavaScript listed within the actual HTML document can clutter or seriously impair the interpretation of HTML by screen readers and other assistive technology. Alternatives to the traditional method of listing scripts within the HEAD of the HTML document include use of a JavaScript 'include' to refer to a script contained in an external file or by providing an alternative <noscript> tag to provide alternative content for agents unable to render the script, for example:

> <noscript>Follow this <a href="link.htm">link</a> for an alternative page</noscript>

While there has been a proliferation of scripts such as use of 'roll-over' buttons for navigation, it is important to consider the impact of graphical or script-based elements for users of assistive technology or text-based browsers unable to use JavaScript.

Navigation links should consist of basic HTML hyperlinks with clearly defined labels (i.e. the text the user clicks on, e.g. <a href="link.htm">Link</a>).

Use of JavaScript actions such as 'onclick' to activate hyperlinks should be avoided or alternative simple hyperlinks should be made available. However, it is possible to construct highly accessible navigation menus using relatively simple hyperlinks, while incorporating graphical effects via CSS, thus avoiding the use of JavaScript or other complex methods. (*On a slightly technical note:* the use of 'display: block' in an external CSS file can produce a roll-over effect when applied to a div containing a hyperlink, this method can be elaborated to include the border colour of the hyperlink to produce a virtual button effect – the link itself remains a simple hyperlink.)

Application formats and alternative file types

It is often useful to consider providing web resources via a range of different file formats, e.g. in both HTML and Word. Free viewers are available for the Microsoft Office Suite (containing Word, Excel, PowerPoint etc.) and for Adobe Acrobat (the PDF or Portable Document Format reader). However, the file size of these viewers are fairly large for downloading over a slow modem connection, with the result that some users may have difficulty viewing application-specific documents such as PDF or Word. Provision of any document in an alternative HTML format should overcome accessibility difficulties associated with application specific document formats.

The role of assistive technology

General concepts and system features

A range of software exists to facilitate access to web resources for disabled users; in many cases, ordinary web browsers may be used as an accessibility aid, where standard browser features may enhance the user experience. Additionally, specialist web browsers exist to provide added accessibility features (e.g. speech functions to 'read' the web page).

Where a conventional web browser is not sufficient, third-party equipment may be required, such as a Braille display machine for blind users. In addition to the above, the core operating system (such as Microsoft Windows XP) also provides useful tools for accessing digital or online resources such as the screen reader Narrator and Magnifier tools.

Overview of assistive technology software, operating systems and web browsers

Microsoft Windows XP

The XP operating system provides a range of accessibility tools, including Magnifier, an onscreen keyboard to access keys via an alternative input control (such as a joystick or mouse) and the Narrator tool to 'read' documents. Other access features include 'sticky keys' to access Windows features using key combinations pressed incrementally. Additionally, Windows colours may be customised to provide high contrast or custom colour schemes.

Microsoft Internet Explorer 6

Internet Explorer allows the user to disable style sheets provided with remotely accessed web pages and apply their own custom style sheet to the browser (e.g. to set font colour, typeface, background colour). A range of 'access keys' are also provided for users with motor/mobility problems, e.g. pressing the 'backspace' key takes the user back to the previous location (URL), whereas 'tab' moves to the next element onscreen.

Netscape Navigator 7

Netscape provides a 'text zoom' feature to increase text size; fonts and colours may also be set within browser preferences. Netscape supports selection of multiple style sheets if available within the web page (e.g. a 'text only' style sheet disabling colour or images) – these styles may be selected using a basic pull-down menu. A range of keyboard shortcuts is also provided.

Screen readers

Screen reader software such as JAWS and HAL provides additional access for users with vision problems to 'read' web resources. The latest version of JAWS provides support for a range of languages and integrates with Internet Explorer.

Screen magnifiers

Screen magnifiers provide screen or text magnification software to increase the appearance of the display, including images and text; examples include Supernova and Lunar.

Refreshable Braille readers

These systems are third-party components that work alongside a typical computer, providing a dynamically generated Braille document (e.g. using raised pins beneath a flexible surface). Both HAL and Supernova support refreshable Braille displays.

Conclusion

This chapter has sought to offer an insight into the problems posed by web-based systems for users with access difficulties and for the general usability of web resources. While the World Wide Web has contributed to the massive growth in computer usage in the home, education and industry, it can be seen that this new communications medium poses new challenges for accessibility and usability.

The guidelines established by the W3C have provided an effective approach to auditing and developing accessible web content, facilitated by automatic and manual validation methods. In recent years, these standards have been supported by leading disability organisations such as the Disability Rights Commission (*http://www.drc-gb.org*) and the Royal National Institute for the Blind (*http://www.rnib*).

It is hoped that this chapter has illustrated some of the broad issues in addressing general web usability and accessibility for disabled users. However, it should be noted that the primary goal of web development should be to develop standards compliant HTML, as valid HTML or XHTML is essential for web agents such as web browsers or assistive technology to correctly interpret and render web content. The ultimate goal, increasingly required under UK law and the statutes of other countries requires compliance with the Web Content Accessibility Guidelines at the minimum of level 1, but ideally at higher levels such as 2 or 3.

At the time of writing this document, responsibility for delivery of standards-compliant web resources (or selection of pre-developed web-based systems meeting these criteria) rests largely with individual web developers or other IT professionals. However, the onus is increasingly on companies or organisations concerned with the development of information/knowledge management systems to embrace web and accessibility standards, as organisations move increasingly away from incidental website development to use of enterprise-level systems delivered via the web browser.

To conclude, consider the words of Tim Berners-Lee, the inventor of the World Wide Web, speaking at Cambridge, Massachusetts in 1997:

> Worldwide, there are more than 750 million people with disabilities. As we move towards a highly connected world, it is critical that the Web be usable by anyone, regardless of individual capabilities and disabilities... (W3C, 1997)

Part 3
Cultural perspectives

How do knowledge management (KM) and culture relate to each other? The literature on KM and cross-cultural issues is somewhat sparse. However, to the extent that management literature does focus on the topic, the assumption seems to be that while there are a great variety of different cultures, all requiring different KM practices in order to help these cultures to prosper in capitalism, with adequate thought and planning, KM can operate effectively both within and across various cultures. Furthermore, embracing different subcultures can enhance the effectiveness of KM practices. Knowledge management teams can have members from a variety of backgrounds and cultures, for example, such as from different age groups, class, religions and gender, and these members can all contribute to knowledge sharing. To my mind, however, the literature, such as it is, can also sometimes make the topic unnecessarily complicated.

In general, though, while the literature recognises that there are problems and difficulties in regard to the implementation of KM in different cultures, it tends to argue that these problems can be overcome. As Holden says, for example:

> The task of cross-cultural management is to devise, support and implement activities which sustain articulate interanimation for knowledge-sharing. Firms use all manner of techniques to achieve these ends ... Organizations are daily creating, changing and experimenting with cross-cultural collectivities. All these activities involve forms of interactive translation to create cross-cultural synergies, new outlooks and behaviours, not to mention new organizational structures. The time has come to consider the

implications of these ideas from a knowledge management perspective. (Holden, 2002: 240)

However, I would argue that this is the wrong starting point. While all of the above is clearly true, it is not KM systems or different cultures that are driving change forward, but that instead, it is global capitalism itself. Thus, while cultures do vary greatly, and different types of KM practices are required for different cultures, and an examination and embracing of different cross-cultural perspectives can lead to an improvement in effective KM systems, it is wrong and unfounded to place the emphasis on culture. Instead, the starting point must be with an analysis of global capitalism itself. An examination of cross-culture and KM is subservient to this wider agenda. Once again, in order to effectively understand, explain and analyse capitalism, we need to return to Marx. We need to apply Marxist concepts to the global capitalist world that we find ourselves in today and to understand the topic of KM and cultures within this. Viewed from this perspective, the KM/cross-cultural debate can be more easily understood.

As I have already indicated elsewhere, I am developing a whole body of theory on globalisation and KM. My focus is on an Open Marxist theoretical analysis on globalisation, the knowledge revolution and knowledge management, and also on how IT fits into this (e.g. see R. Rikowski, 2003b, 2003c, 2004a, 2004b, 2005a, 2005b). Capitalism is sustained by value, and this value can only ever be created and extracted from labour – this includes both manual and intellectual labour. As Marx said, 'human labour creates value, but is not itself value. It becomes value only in its congealed state, when embodied in the form of some object' (Marx, 1867: 57).

In the industrial revolution, the emphasis was on the exertion of manual labour, but in the modern knowledge revolution, in the west, the emphasis is on the exertion of intellectual labour. Meanwhile, basic manufacturing is taking place more in the developing world, where manual labour is key. Thus, in order for KM to work effectively, it must respond to this situation. So, KM practices in the developed world need to focus on how to extract value from intellectual labour, whereas in the developing world, a far simpler KM method needs to be adopted, as the primary emphasis is on how to extract value from manual labour. Knowledge, on its own, is not such an important factor. The utilisation of knowledge is still necessary for economies where the emphasis is on manual labour (e.g. the knowledge needed to make a car), and in this regard, effective KM practices are still needed. But it is not knowledge itself that is being commodified, and knowledge is not key in the same way that it is in the knowledge revolution in the developed world. Cultural differences obviously have to be taken into consideration, but we need to remember that it is the capitalist agenda that is driving change forward, and not any one particular culture. This Open Marxist theoretical analysis will be explored further in Chapter 9 and again in more detail, in Chapter 11.

However, while we need to move on to a Marxist analysis in order to have a deeper understanding of the subject, Chapters 6–8 will provide a detailed examination of KM within and across cultures in its own right, covering a number of different subject areas, including internal cultures and KM, external cultures and KM and social culture. We need to have a grasp of the topic before we can move on to a Marxist analysis, but the problem is that, if we are not careful, we can find ourselves spending too much time operating at this more practical level and not enough time developing theory. Hopefully, though, further progress can be made in regard to further developing Marxist theory on this, and other related topics in due course. That is certainly my intention in the future anyway!

There are four chapters in this section. The first provides an introduction and considers definitions of knowledge management and culture, and some related terms. From here, it considers KM within and across cultures in both the developed and the developing world, and cultural theories. The main focus on cultural theories is on the work of Hofstede and on Hofstede's five dimensions of cultural variability and how this can be applied to KM. Chapter 7 includes an examination of KM and cross-culture issues in general, focusing largely on KM practices in the developed world, in this regard. There is the integration versus fragmentation perspective, for example. The integration perspective argues that workers' value systems can be adjusted to fit in with the dominant culture of the firm, and that effective knowledge flows can take place within this framework. Whereas the fragmentation perspective argues that culture can only be loosely structured and that managers need to adopt a more flexible approach and should be facilitators of knowledge flows rather than endeavouring to dominate the process. With regard to the latter point, Grant (1996) and Lowendahl (1997) argue that there is a need for diversity across the workforce for innovation. Chapter 6 also considers knowledge transfer across cultures and KM in the developing world. It examines, in particular, a case study that looks at the relationships between cross-cultural differences and knowledge transfer within an international subsidiary (Ford and Chan, 2002). The section on KM in the developing world draws on the work of Ingie Hovland (2003), who has provided a valuable annotated bibliography on the subject of KM and organisational learning in the developing world. Chapter 9 considers internal cultures (particularly on communities of practice) and KM, external cultures and KM (focusing in particular on globalisation) and KM and social culture. Chapter 9 develops an Open Marxist theoretical analysis of KM within and across cultures, focusing in particular on differences between KM in the developed and the developing world.

Knowledge management within and across cultures and cultural theories

Ruth Rikowski

Knowledge management and related concepts

Any meaningful analysis of knowledge management (KM) needs to start with definitions. This chapter will provide only a brief consideration of these definitions, as I have explored this in some depth elsewhere (R. Rikowski 2000a, 2000b).

I would suggest that one very significant difference between knowledge and information is that knowledge is about understanding. As Charles Leadbeater says:

> Information can be transferred in great torrents, without any understanding or knowledge being generated. Knowledge cannot be transferred; it can only be enacted, through a process of understanding through which people interpret information and make judgments on the basis of it ... We do not need more information; we need more understanding. Creating knowledge is a human process, not a technological one. More information is not better information ... We are deluged by useless information. (Leadbeater, 1999: 29)

Lloyd, meanwhile in his chapter in this book, says that 'knowledge is information in use'. Through this process, he says, we get more information, which is then converted into more knowledge, which is a 'never-ending dynamic process.'

Furthermore, the concept of 'knowledge' has a vast historical and philosophical background to it. As McFarlane says, 'Knowledge is a complex and elusive concept. There is an entire brand of philosophy, epistemology, which is devoted to its study' (McFarlane, 1998).

Meanwhile, Nonaka and Takeuchi ask 'What is knowledge?', emphasising the need to return to the philosophers, saying that:

> The history of philosophy since the ancient Greek period can be seen as the process of searching for an answer to the question, 'What is knowledge?' ... Western philosophers have generally agreed that knowledge is justified true belief, a concept that was first introduced by Plato in his Memo, Phaedo and Theaetetus. (Nonaka and Takeuchi, 1995: 21)

Others argue that knowledge will always have an element of subjectivity about it, as each person will interpret a piece of knowledge somewhat differently.

There is also the need to differentiate between knowledge management and information management (IM), as well as considering where data and wisdom fit into this whole picture. Wisdom is considered further in Bruce Lloyd's chapter in this book, in Chapter 1. Broadbent considers the difference between KM and IM, saying that 'knowledge management is about enhancing the use of organizational knowledge through sound practices of information management and organizational learning' (Broadbent, 1998: 24).

There is not the space to consider all the complexities here, but it is important to have an awareness of the different concepts that are used. There is also a need for greater standardisation of terms, I would suggest.

Definitions of culture

It is also very important to consider the definition of 'culture'. Leeds says that culture can be understood, 'as an expression of all the experiences of a particular people or group over time which help shape their personality and manner of perceiving' (Leeds, year unknown: 1).

Meanwhile, Huntington (1993: 22, 27) interestingly argues that it is more difficult to resolve cultural differences than political and economic issues – especially if religion plays a part in the culture.

Individualism–collectivism is often seen as being one of the most important dimensions in regard to cultural differences. In particular, individualism is likely to be more dominant in developed countries, while collectivism is likely to be more dominant in developing countries. Leeds says in regard to individualism versus collectivism that:

> In individualistic societies, identity is based on the individual, ties are loose and individuals are expected to look after themselves and immediate family. In collective societies identity is based more on the social network to which one belongs, people being integrated from birth in strong groups which provide protection in return for loyalty. (Leeds, year unknown: 3–4)

Furthermore, much of the empirical evidence suggests that morality in collective societies is viewed differently from that in individualistic cultures (see, for example, Triandis, 1989). This is obviously connected to different religious beliefs as well. In many developing countries, for example, their traditional knowledge is seen as belonging to God and therefore cannot be transformed into any form of intellectual property right, such as copyright or a patent. As I say in *Globalisation, Information and Libraries*:

> Many people in the developing world see indigenous knowledge as being part of Nature itself, and there are also many strong affinities with religion. Thus many people would be against any notion of people owning, or seeming to own, any of this knowledge, or turning it into any form of intellectual property right. (R. Rikowski, 2005a: 240)

There are likely to be elements of both individualism and collectivism in all countries and societies.

Meanwhile, Fukuyama (1995) argues that countries that are strong in 'familial communitarianism' tend to be weak in 'societal communitarianism'. Societal communitarianism involves a lot of trust between family and kin groups, on the one hand, and the State on the other. Fukuyama lists southern Europe, China and Taiwan as examples of familial communitarianism.

Ford and Chan (2002) argue that culture can refer to professional culture, an organisation's culture and national culture. Furthermore, they note that the KM literature largely focuses on organisational culture, although national culture is the primary focus of their research. Hofstede defines national culture as 'the collective programming of the mind which distinguishes the members of one human group from another' (Hofstede, 1980: 25).

Thus, there are a variety of different definitions and perspectives on culture, a few of which have been considered here.

KM in the developed and the developing world: manual and intellectual labour

The knowledge revolution is being driven forward in the developed world. This is because capitalism must be forever finding new commodities and new markets in which to sell these commodities, as will be examined further in Chapter 11 of this book. The production of tangible goods has reached a certain saturation point, so now there is a move towards the commodification of non-tangible areas of life. Obviously, we still need tangible goods and a basic manufacturing industry, but this is taking place more and more in the developing world. As Will Hutton (2000) emphasised in his article 'The murder of manufacturing', manufacturing has little place in the post-industrial, knowledge-driven economy. Thus, in the developed world the emphasis is now much more on commodifying areas such as services, intangible assets, intellectual property rights, knowledge, information and ideas. Within this, it becomes important to extract value from intellectual labour, and this value then becomes embedded in intangible goods/commodities. This is necessary in order to ensure the success of the knowledge revolution, this being the latest phase of capitalism, and for the furtherance and continued success of global capitalism in general. I explore this further in a variety of my works (e.g. see R. Rikowski, 2003b, 2003c, 2004a, 2004b, 2005a, 2005b).

Given that basic manufacturing is taking place more in the developed world, with the emphasis being more on manual labour rather than intellectual labour, good and effective KM practices are not so necessary in the developing world. This needs to be kept firmly in mind when undertaking any cross-cultural analysis of KM. The importance of KM in the developing world will increase gradually, but it will not, and indeed, cannot be as important as KM in the developed world – or at least, not until the market for tangible assets is exhausted – but that is surely impossible. When capitalism moves on to find yet another new market (perhaps moving in to space – who know, perhaps Mars will be commodified one day!), then, and only then, is KM likely to become crucial for the whole of this planet. This is considered further in Chapter 9.

Many writers have emphasised the importance of knowledge and the knowledge economy (or more accurately, the knowledge revolution). However, many are implicitly (rather than explicitly) referring to knowledge and the knowledge revolution in the developed world, but not to knowledge in the developing world. As Oxbrow says in *The Knowledge Proposition*, for example:

> The Knowledge Economy has become a reality for many organisations and nation states. The wealth of a nation no longer depends on its ability to convert raw materials into tangible goods, but rather on its ability to develop and harness the abilities and knowledge of its citizens. The success of organisations in this economy depends on the ability of their leaders to create a culture and style where knowledge is valued, nurtured and used. (Oxbrow in TFPL, 2003: 1)

It is also interesting to note that Oxbrow emphasises the need to create a culture where the importance of knowledge can be recognised and nurtured. Meanwhile, Michailova and Husted note that 'many observers have proclaimed the dawning of a new age – known as the new economy or the knowledge economy – in which society itself is on the verge of transformation through the use of knowledge' (Michailova and Husted, 2002: 2).

However, when Oxbrow refers to the 'wealth of a nation' he is essentially referring to the wealth of nations in the developed, industrialised world. Similarly, when Michailova and Husted refer to 'society' they are focusing on societies in the developed world.

So, much that has been written about KM refers implicitly to KM in the developed world, while KM in the developing world has not been considered in such depth. I will be considering the literature on KM in the developed world, but more attention will be given to the literature on KM in the developing world, in order to redress the balance a little. This will also help to illustrate why effective KM practices are more important in the developed world, and how the KM agenda in the developing world has to fit in with the needs of the developed world, and with capitalism itself.

Cultural theories and applying Hofstede

Introduction

Examining cultural theories is very necessary for any analysis of KM and culture. How then can cultural theories assist with the implementation of effective KM systems? How can the two work together? Indeed, can cultural theories be effectively applied to KM? There is a wealth of literature on cultural theories – and they certainly cannot all be explored in this chapter. Hofstede's work on cultural theories is particularly important and therefore the focus in this section will primarily be on his work and on how it can be applied to KM. It will examine Bird and Metcalf's work in this regard, and how they applied Hofstede's theory to negotiating behaviour. It will then consider some of the ways in which this theoretical framework can be applied to KM. It will also look very briefly at Trompenars' work on cultural theory.

Hofstede

Hofstede has undertaken a substantial amount of work on culture (see, for example, Hofstede 1980, 2001, 2003). Hofstede argues that people carry different layers of mental programming and that these correspond to different culture levels. He highlights five dimensions of cultural variability – namely, power distance, individualism, masculinity, uncertainty avoidance and long-term orientation.

Hofstede's taxonomy/dimension is based on a survey that he conducted with IBM in the 1970s. Questionnaires were sent to employees of IBM on a worldwide basis. Hofstede's theory says that organisational culture is not independent of the wider culture. Four factors were highlighted in the research: individualism/collectivism; uncertainty avoidance; power distance; and masculinity/femininity. Hofstede and Bond (1988) later developed a fifth dimension – long-term orientation. After identifying the dimensions, Hofstede then rated each country in relation to these dimensions, and measured this by using an index. Japan in the 1970s, for example, was found to be high in power distance, low in individualism and very high in uncertainty avoidance. The USA, meanwhile, was found to be low in power distance, high in individualism and low in uncertainty avoidance. According to Hofstede's dimensions, Japan and USA are culturally very different but Canada and USA are very similar.

What then do these dimensions actually mean, and how was the index applied? The five dimensions are considered further below:

- *Power distance* is the extent to which less powerful members of an organisation accept that power is distributed unequally and the extent to which they are content/discontent with this inequality of power. Hofstede measured power distance in a power distance index (PDI). Values and attitudes found at national level contrast 'low-PDI countries' with 'high-PDI countries' and some countries in between. Examples of high PDI countries were Malaysia and Mexico, while examples of low PDI countries were Austria and Denmark.

- *Uncertainty avoidance* is the extent to which a culture encourages its members to feel comfortable/uncomfortable in unstructured situations. How much does a society try to control the uncontrollable? Does a society celebrate uncertainty or feel daunted by it? Hofstede formulated an uncertainty avoidance index (UAI) with a range of questions on rule orientation, employment stability and stress. Countries that scored highest on the UAI were Greece, Portugal, Guatemala, while countries that scored lowest were Singapore, Jamaica and Denmark.

- *Individualism versus collectivism* considers the extent to which a culture is individually-based or collectivist-based. National differences in individualism were calculated on an individualism index (IDV). Countries that had the highest IDV scores were USA, Australia and UK, while those that had the lowest IDV scores were Guatemala, Ecuador and Panama.

- *Masculinity versus femininity* is concerned with the distribution of emotional roles and the male/female divide. It is argued that women give more importance to social goals, such as relationships, while men give more importance to ego goals, such as careers and money. Respondents were mostly male, so Hofstede called this the masculinity index (MAS). Japan was at the top of this scale. German-speaking countries such as Austria, Switzerland and Germany also scored high. Countries that had the extremely feminine side included The Netherlands and Nordic countries, such as Sweden and Norway.

- *Long-term versus short-term orientation* concerns the extent to which a culture encourages its members to accept deferred gratification of their material, cultural, social and emotional needs. Hofstede also created a long-term orientation index. East Asian countries, such as China, Hong Kong and Japan, scored highest, while Western countries scored rather low, and some developing countries, such as Zimbabwe, Nigeria and Pakistan, scored lowest.

Trompenars

Fons Trompenars' work has some similarities with Hofstede's work as they are both studies of cross-cultural management, both have developed cultural theories and both propose a set of cultural dimensions and dominant value systems that can be placed and ordered on these dimensions (e.g. see Trompenars and Hampden-Turner, 1998). These value systems impact on factors such as human thinking, feeling and acting. Both writers show the problems that society has to cope with and both have different solutions. They are also both very significant writers in their field. As Holden says:

> As a subject of management teaching, cross-cultural management has been based on a small number of textbooks ... Hofstede (1980) and Trompenars (1993) of course feature to a greater or lesser extent in all these offerings. (Holden, 2002: 306)

Concerning relations between people, for example, both Hofstede and Trompenars consider the importance of examining cultural groups, but use different terminology to express this. Hofstede refers to individualism and collectivism, whereas Trompenars refers to universalism versus particularism and individualism versus communitarianism. Similarly, while Hofstede and Trompenars both recognise the importance of time, Hofstede focuses on long-term versus short-term orientation, while Trompenars focuses on sequential versus synchronic and inner versus outer time. Trompenars also distinguishes between achieved versus ascribed status, where achievement is based on what a person has actually achieved, and ascription focuses on status.

Bird and Metcalf and applying Hofstede

Bird and Metcalf (year unknown) applied Hofstede's cultural value dimensions to negotiating behaviour in six countries by using a 12-dimension framework. This model could also be applied to KM, I suggest. This section provides an overview of their findings, and how these can be applied to KM, and indeed, how Hofstede's cultural theory can be applied to KM in general.

Bird and Metcalf examined Japan and five of its main trading partners – namely USA, Germany, China, Mexico and Brazil. They classified each country's negotiating behaviour on 12 negotiation dimensions according to a high, medium and low scheme. They ranked each of the six countries according to their index values on Hofstede's five dimensions of cultural variability – i.e. power distance, individualism, masculinity, uncertainty avoidance and long-term orientation. This framework can aid with providing more effective negotiation. It was found that negotiating behaviours were largely formed around one or more of Hofstede's dimensions.

The first type of negotiation that was examined was distributive versus integrative. Integrative negotiators take more of a problem-solving approach than distributive negotiators. This can be related to Hofstede's masculinity/femininity value dimension, for example. Members of the masculine culture, according to Hofstede are more likely to resolve conflicts through competition, and there is more emphasis on the survival of the fittest and the need to be aggressive and competitive. Members of feminine cultures, on the other hand, are more likely to resolve conflicts through problem solving, cooperation, and intuition rather than decisiveness. With regard to KM, research suggests that the feminine qualities of diversity, listening and cooperation are all important skills to possess for the implementation of successful KM programmes, and so integrative negotiators are likely to be better suited for effective KM programmes.

Second, there is task versus relationship-based negotiation. Negotiators from countries where relationship issues are more important spend a lot of their time building trust and friendship between different members of the team. Hofstede says that in collectivist cultures the personal relationship is more important than the task, whereas in individualistic cultures the task is more important than personal relationships. KM programmes are likely to be more successful in relationship-based, collectivist cultures, I would suggest, given that sharing knowledge, information and ideas etc. can only really be achieved by a relationship-based, collectivist approach.

Third, there is the selection of negotiators, and the focus here is on the difference between abilities and status. Managers from achievement-based cultures consider job-specific skills, knowledge and/or expertise, and focus on areas such as education and skills. Managers from status-based cultures, however, give preference to candidates that they know or with whom they are connected. Hofstede argues that power distance affects the importance of the status of negotiators. Low power distance cultures, for example, attach little importance to inherited privilege and status. Instead, respect is earned on the basis of how effectively they perform. Achievement-based cultures are probably better environments for engendering successful KM programmes. Status-based cultures could even inhibit knowledge flows. People could be too frightened to say what they think to those who have a higher status, while those with higher status might not want to share information with those lower down the hierarchy. An achievement-based culture is likely to reward those that are more forthcoming in both articulating and sharing their knowledge, I would suggest.

Fourth, there is collectivism versus individualism. Individualistic negotiators are emotionally independent of the organisation, whereas collectivist negotiators have a strong sense of identity with the organisation. Collectivism is likely to be conducive to effective knowledge flows. Individualistic people are likely to feel less tied to the organisation, so might leave the group/organisation and take their knowledge with them. However, individualistic people might be more likely to formulate new ideas, which is also very necessary today. Indeed, both types are probably needed, which reflects one of the many contradictions in capitalism.

Fifth, there is independent versus consensus decision making. According to Hofstede, cultures with high uncertainty avoidance scores prefer consultative decision-making processes, whereas cultures with low uncertainty avoidance prefer independent decision-making processes. Consensus decision making is likely to be highly beneficial for the implementation of effective KM systems, although independent thought is also important for the generation of new ideas.

Sixth, there is monochromic versus polychromic time dimension. Negotiators from monochromic cultures think that time is money, whereas negotiators from polychronic cultures tend to think that time is never wasted. This can be related to uncertainty avoidance. Cultures that are high in uncertainty avoidance prefer to operate in an environment where there is clarity and structure, but low uncertainty avoidance cultures can work in an environment where there is more ambiguity. Polychromic cultures are likely to be more conducive to effective KM programmes, I would have thought, given that the generation of knowledge and ideas cannot be easily encapsulated into a simplistic time-dimension, such as the 9–5 day.

Seventh, there is the risk-taking dimension, with risk averse versus risk tolerant, which focuses on negotiators' willingness to take risks. Hofstede suggests that there is a relationship between risk aversion and uncertainty avoidance. Cultures with tendencies toward lower uncertainty avoidance accept both familiar and unfamiliar risks, but cultures with high uncertainty avoidance scores prefer to limit risks to known risks. Risk-taking is likely to be more conducive to effective KM programmes, because people who are willing to take risks are more likely to feel bolder about putting forward new and different ideas, and to being generally proactive and breaking new ground.

Eighth, there is the basis of trust dimension. Two different types of trust are identified – external trust and internal trust. With external forms of trust, trust exists because a formal contract has been drawn up. But with internal forms of trust, the trust exists because of the relationship that has been built up. People from high uncertainty cultures tend to prefer to deal with people that they know, thereby limiting risks. Internal forms of trust are likely to work better for the implementation of effective KM systems. Trust is an important factor for successful KM programmes, as people are only likely to be willing to share and distribute knowledge if they think that they can trust the people in their group and/or organisation.

Ninth, there is formal versus informal protocol. Negotiators from countries where there is much enthusiasm for protocol will tend to conform to strict rules. Hofstede and Usunier (1996) suggest that negotiators from high uncertainty-avoiding cultures prefer highly-structured procedures during negotiations, whereas those in low uncertainty-avoiding cultures can cope more easily with ambiguities in the procedures. Informal protocols with low uncertainty-avoiding cultures are likely, on the whole, to result in better KM systems, as flexibility is an important factor for the implementation of effective KM programmes and knowledge flows.

Tenth, there is style of communication, which can be high-context or low-context. This reflects the extent to which people rely on non-verbal communication. Negotiators from high-context cultures focus more on non-verbal communication. Gudykunst and Ting-Toomey (1988) say that high-context communication is used mainly in collectivist cultures, whereas low-context communication is used in individual cultures. Hofstede is also of this opinion and notes that what is self-evident in collectivist cultures often has to be communicated in a clearer and more explicit way in individualistic cultures. Both high-context and low-context communication is likely to be valuable for effective KM programmes. This is because collectivist cultures (with the emphasis on non-verbal communication – i.e. high-context) are likely to induce an environment of knowledge sharing, while verbal communication (i.e. low-context) is also a very important part of sharing and imparting knowledge, especially for the recording of tacit knowledge which might not previously have been recorded.

Eleventh, there is the nature of persuasion, which is involved with factual-inductive versus affective. Factual-inductive negotiators base their arguments on empirical facts and use linear logic. Affective negotiators, on the other hand, base their arguments on abstract theory and ideals. Hofstede says that cultures with low uncertainty avoidance scores tend to prefer inductive reasoning, but those with high uncertainty avoidance scores prefer deductive reasoning. Both factual-inductive and affective methods are likely to be needed for effective KM programmes.

Finally, there are different forms of agreement, these being explicit contract versus implicit agreement. This refers to the preferred form of agreement between parties, whether this is a written formal contract or an informal agreement. Hofstede says that high uncertainty-avoiding cultures want to avoid ambiguous situations and so they prefer written agreements. Once again, cultures that are low on uncertainty avoidance and are less concerned about formal agreements are likely to produce better KM systems, given that flexibility is an important factor for effective KM programmes, I would suggest.

In conclusion, Bird and Metcalf's findings show the usefulness of Hofstede's cultural dimensions in identifying a given culture's position on different negotiation dimensions. They say that:

> Because the framework is straightforward and can be aligned with cultural values, managers should be able to draw upon the extensive body of research replicating Hofstede's work to inform their understanding of negotiations. (Bird and Metcalf, year unknown: 811)

They argue that rather than just looking at negotiation in one country as though it is something unique, researchers can use the framework to allow comparisons to be made across different countries. In this way, their model could also be applied to KM.

Summary

Bird and Metcalf had a 12-dimension framework for negotiation and related this to Hofstede's five dimensions. This framework can also be applied to KM and I have given some examples of this, although much more work needs to be done on this area, and there was not the space to include references from the KM literature in this section. Some of the main points are summarised below, under the 12 headings for negotiation.

1. Distributive versus integrative negotiators:

   – Integrative negotiators – take more of a problem-solving approach. This can be related to Hofstede's masculinity/femininity dimension. Males tend to resolve conflicts through competition and being decisive, whereas females tend to prefer to resolve conflicts through problem solving and cooperating.

   – *Implications for KM*: Feminine qualities, integrative negotiators probably more valuable.

2. Task versus relationship, collectivist versus individualistic:

   – Relationship-based, collectivist cultures spend a lot of time building up trust; personal relationship is more important than the task.

   – *Implications for KM*: KM programmes likely to be more successful in relationship-based, collectivist cultures because knowledge can only really be shared effectively in such an environment.

3. Selection of negotiators – abilities versus status:

   – Power distance can affect importance of status of negotiators. Low power distance gives little credit to status.

   – *Implications for KM*: Achievement more important for KM programmes. Relationship/collectivist better for KM.

4. Collectivism versus individualism:

   – Collectivism more dominant in developing countries; individualism more dominant in developed countries.

   – *Implications for KM*: Collectivism probably better for KM.

5. Independent versus consensus decision-making:

   – High uncertainty avoidance cultures prefer consultative decision-making.

   – *Implications for KM*: Both useful for KM.

6. Monochromic versus polychromic time-dimension:

   – Monochromic – time is money; polychromic – time is never wasted.

   – Hofstede says cultures high in uncertainty avoidance seek clarity and structure.

   – *Implications for KM*: Polychromic – better for KM.

7. Risk-taking – risk averse versus risk tolerant:

   - Lower uncertainty avoidance cultures accept risks.

   - *Implications for KM*: Risk-taking – important for effective KM programmes.

8. Basis of trust dimension – internal and external trust:

   - Formal/informal contracts.

   - *Implications for KM*: Internal forms of trust better for KM.

9. Formal versus informal:

   - Hofstede and Usunier say negotiators from uncertainty-avoiding cultures prefer structured procedures.

   - *Implications for KM*: Informal protocols with low uncertainty-avoiding cultures are likely to result in better KM systems.

10. Style of communication – high-context versus low-context:

    - High-context cultures rely more on non-verbal cues. High-context is collectivist.

    - *Implications for KM*: Both high-context and low-context are likely to be valuable for effective KM programmes.

11. Nature of persuasion – factual-inductive versus affective:

    - Factual-inductive – arguments based on empirical facts and linear logic; affective negotiators – arguments based on abstract theory and ideals.

    - Low uncertainty avoidance cultures prefer factual-inductive reasoning.

    - *Implications for KM*: Both needed for KM.

12. Different forms of agreement – explicit contract versus implicit agreement:

    - Uncertainty avoiding cultures avoid ambiguous situations, prefer formal written agreements and contracts.

    - *Implications for KM*: Low uncertainty avoidance less concerned about formal agreements – better for KM.

Summary

This chapter focused briefly on definitions of KM and related concepts and definitions of culture. It then briefly examined KM in the developed and the developing world. From here, it considered cultural theories, focusing on Hofstede's work, and Hofstede's five dimensions of cultural variability. It then examined Bird and Metcalf's work on negotiating behaviour, and how they applied Hofstede's five dimensions to their own work. Following on from this, it considered how this could be applied to KM. Other such models could be applied to KM. More work needs to be undertaken on this.

Thus, in this chapter I have aimed to highlight some of the most important work being undertaken on cultural theories, and how this work can be applied to KM. However, although benefits can be gained from this work, in terms of improving KM practices both within and across different cultures, thereby assisting with the sharing and effective dissemination of knowledge, at a deeper level these theories are quite limited. How can an indexing system, such as Hofstede's actually result in objective measuring, for example? I would suggest that any such measuring and weighting system is ultimately impossible, but that instead, we need to move out of this mode of thinking altogether, and apply an Open Marxist theoretical framework to the whole topic, and to use Marx's concepts and tools in order to enhance our understanding and analysis. I also consider the weighting and balancing problem in *Globalisation, Information and Libraries,* in relation to the balance in copyright. As I say:

> ...how does one go about measuring the weighting? ... It is impossible to achieve this balance in any idealised sense while we live under global capitalism, as far as I am concerned. More specifically, we are asking the wrong set of questions altogether. Rather than focusing so closely on the notion of balance and other ethical issues, we need to address and work with Marx's concepts, as these concepts expose the intrinsic workings of the capitalist system. (R. Rikowksi, 2005a: 226)

In addition, while the Bird and Metcalf/Hofstede framework could be applied to KM, I am certain its many limitations would become apparent once examined in more depth. Furthermore, none of this would lessen the inequalities in the world, whereby in practice knowledge transfer and knowledge flows are always likely to benefit the developed world more than the developing world, while we live in global capitalism. The Open Marxist theoretical framework that I am developing on this topic is considered further in Chapter 11 of this book.

The following chapter considers KM and cross-culture issues more widely and KM in the developing world.

Knowledge sharing and organisational learning in the developed and developing world

Ruth Rikowski

Introduction

Much has been written and talked about knowledge management (KM) from varying perspectives and positions and there is also a wealth of literature on culture and cultural theories; however, less has been written about KM within and across cultures specifically. In the previous chapter, I demonstrated some of the connections and emphasised how more work needs to be undertaken on this. In this chapter, I will consider some of the work that has already been undertaken.

Knowledge management and cross-culture

Introduction

As Michailova and Husted emphasise, 'the relationships between culture and knowledge management ... are not explored in depth in a coherent manner in mainstream texts' (Michailova and Husted, 2002: 3).

Despite this, it is interesting to note that some people believe that cultural issues are one of the most important aspects of KM. Torrey and Datta, for example, argue that 'the greatest hurdles to successful knowledge management are not the technical or process issues, but the cultural issues' (Torrey and Datta, 1998: 1).

Thus, culture could perhaps make or break an effective KM system. Torrey and Datta are also of the opinion that:

> ...from the lack of knowledge about unfamiliarity with different social milieu and cultural situations, organisations fail to see the richness of support for knowledge management inherent in the various cultural frameworks of their global enterprises. (Torrey and Datta, 1998: 5)

Thus, they clearly think that different cultures can enrich KM, but that it is not sufficiently recognised. They go on to say that:

> Much has been written about the cultural implications for knowledge management and knowledge sharing in modern enterprises. It is generally accepted by practitioners that the greatest hurdles to successful knowledge management are not the technical or process issues, but the cultural issues. (Torrey and Datta, 1998: 1)

If the open sharing of knowledge is to take place effectively, the hurdle of knowledge hoarding must be overcome.

Issues surrounding KM and culture in the developed world obviously differ from those in the developing world. Consideration will be given to this throughout this chapter, but the focus will be more on the developing world than the developed world.

Knowledge management in the developed world

Knowledge management and the effective utilisation of effective KM practices in the developed world today are crucial. This is because capitalism always needs to be reinventing itself. It needs to be forever finding new ways in which to create and extract value from labour, thereby ensuring its continued success. In order to achieve this successively, capitalism must go through various phases. First there was the agricultural revolution, then the industrial revolution and now we are moving into the knowledge revolution. Stephen Byers, who at the time was the UK Trade and Industry Secretary speaking at the Confederation of British Industry conference, in 1998, said that:

> We must ... prepare the UK to take advantage of the new knowledge driven economy. Success in this fast moving world depends critically on how well we exploit our most valuable and distinctive assets: our knowledge ... The first industrial revolution was based on investment in capital and machinery. The revolution we are going through now requires investment in human capital – skills, learning and education. (Byers, 1999)

Furthermore, as I say:

> Today, we are moving into the knowledge revolution, which is the latest phase of capitalism. This knowledge revolution is dependent on knowledge, information, skills, human capital, intellectual capital, ideas, services, intangibles, brainpower, education and brand names. (R. Rikowski, 2005a: 1)

Meanwhile, Potter makes clear that:

> My thesis has been that we are in the relatively early phases of a major economic revolution. This revolution is based around the concept of a post-industrial era where making things is increasingly automated and routine; creating things is difficult and value therefore derives from creation and from the intellectual capital or knowledge base of the firm or nation. (Potter, 1999: 7)

I consider these different phases further in Chapter 11 of this book.

So, capitalism as a system is continually changing, moving and evolving, going through various phases as it adapts, changes and progresses in its quest to seeks new ways of creating value, new commodities and new markets. As Schumpeter (1951: 66) says, the fundamental impulse for the development of capitalism is 'new combinations'. Furthermore, 'capitalism ... is by nature a form or method of economic change and not only never is but never can be stationary' (Schumpeter, 1952: 82).

So, today, the emphasis in the developed world is on the exertion of intellectual labour and the creation and extraction of value from intellectual labour.

Knowledge management practices can assist with the creation and extraction of this value from intellectual labour. Various writers in the business and information literature have highlighted the fact that we need to be creating value from knowledge and intangibles in the knowledge revolution in the developed world today. As Meyer says, 'value is in the intangibles like knowledge, information, services, software and entertainment (Meyer, 2000: 193).

There is also the need to differentiate value from profit. As Welch makes clear:

> The organisation has to recognise that its prime objective (perhaps its only objective) is to add value NOT to cut costs. Making more profit, increasing the share price, increasing the value of intellectual assets (including brands) is what makes a company fit to survive. (Welch, 2000: 10)

Meanwhile, Broadbent emphasises the importance of knowledge management in this regard, saying that, 'Knowledge management is about enhancing the use of organizational knowledge through sound practices of information management and organizational learning. The purpose is to deliver value to the business' (Broadbent, 1998: 24).

In the empirical data that I gathered for my dissertation on KM, many of the participants recognised the importance of creating value from knowledge. One participant (P7) said, for example:

> ...I believe that the *value* comes out of *managing knowledge*, whether people recognise it as that or not ... In reality, you are always *managing knowledge* to create an application and create *value* out of ... a situation ... you might not actually recognise it as knowledge management but you're still doing it. (R. Rikowski, 2003c, my emphasis)

Meanwhile, another participant (P8) said:

> I think the whole point ... of *managing knowledge*, information and people ... is to produce *value* for the organisation and beyond the organisation ... but that *value* isn't always produced in monetary terms, or measurable in monetary terms. (R. Rikowski, 2003c, my emphasis)

I have written several articles around the broad topic of KM in the developed world and why it is so crucial, so I will not explore this in great depth in this chapter. Instead, I point the reader to these other articles – see references at the end of this book. Furthermore, in Chapter 11 of this book, I explore the topic at a deeper, theoretical level. However, there is a short section on KM, culture and organisations in the developed world in the section below.

Literature overview

This section will briefly consider some of the literature on KM, culture and organisations, focusing largely on the literature in the developed world. Sue Newell et al.'s book *Managing Knowledge Work* is a useful resource in this regard. Newell et al. argue that structural conditions that encourage flexibility and self-managed teamworking are important preconditions facilitating knowledge work tasks, but that:

> ...the cultural conditions within the firm will be at least as important in ultimately facilitating knowledge work processes that are largely conducted autonomously. It is the cultural conditions within a knowledge-intensive firm that primarily promote responsible autonomy ... and a workforce that can be trusted to work in the interests of the firm, that is, working autonomously but working very hard and to the best of their abilities. (Newell et al., 2002: 32)

They argue that it is appropriate cultural conditions that promote autonomy, and a trustworthy workforce that can then help to ensure that knowledge flows freely throughout an organisation.

Meanwhile, writers such as Grant (1996) and Lowendahl (1997) emphasise the fact that there is a need for diversity across the workforce for innovation. The argument here is that there is often now a need for knowledge from different fields and, therefore, leaders and managers of creative knowledge-intensive firms need a highly diverse workforce, with people from different ages, ethnic origins, social class etc., and with a variety of different skills and expertise. Thus, the cultural differences that employees have in an organisation can become valuable resources.

However, Newell et al. also say that workers need to be able to identify with the organisation and that 'by identifying with the organization workers then internalize the dominant organizational ideology – values, beliefs and norms – and behave in the interests of the firm' (Newell et al., 2002: 33).

To what extent, though, can and should knowledge workers identify with the organisation and its dominant culture, one could ask? Is it in their long-term interest? Leaders and managers of creative knowledge organisations need to think further about such matters.

Two distinct perspectives on organisational culture can be identified – an integration perspective and a fragmentation perspective. The 'integration perspective' views culture as an organisational variable that can be shaped and adapted to the needs of the firm. The emphasis here is on homogeneity and consensus within the knowledge-intensive firm. However, predictable behaviour could stifle innovation and creativity. This is another problem and demonstrates one of the many contradictions in capitalism.

Schein (1992) focuses on the integration perspective and considers how leaders of firms themselves can create and shape organisational culture. Schein says that leaders of firms are responsible for implementing primary and secondary embedding mechanisms, which coincide with the dominant, core values held by the leaders. Examples of primary mechanisms include the criteria for selection and recruitment, performance management and reward, while examples of secondary mechanisms include organisational design and structure. So, the aim here is for leaders/managers to recruit employees that are likely to fit in well with the dominant culture of the firm and to also create an organisational structure that is conducive to effective KM for the benefit of the firm. Schein says that knowledge sharing in an organisation can be encouraged when knowledge workers start to realise that knowledge sharing is a core value in the firm.

However, Schein's work and many others writing in the business literature also assume that it is possible for leaders to bring about this integration. But as Newell et al. say, 'it should not simply be assumed ... that knowledge workers in knowledge-intensive firms will necessarily be willing to subsume their identity and own personal value systems to those of the firm' (Newell et al., 2002: 34).

Indeed, one could ask, why should knowledge workers subsume and camouflage their identity in this way and perhaps not have their original contribution recognised? (Although knowledge workers in some cultures and countries are likely to be more willing to subsume themselves in this way than others.) However, knowledge workers surely need to have confidence that they will benefit personally in some way or other. As Newell et al. also say, 'leaders of knowledge-intensive firms may ... have to acknowledge that knowledge workers will naturally hold a variety of beliefs, which cannot necessarily be altered or subsumed within a competing organizational value system' (Newell et al., 2002: 34).

Thus, knowledge workers will not necessarily conform to the organisation's value system and goals, and this needs to be taken into consideration when considering KM processes. Furthermore, it might not always be in the organisation's interest anyway – because new ideas and knowledge can emerge out of conflict situations.

The alternative perspective is for management to adopt a looser, fragmented approach. Martin's (1992) work, for example, refers to this 'fragmentation perspective on culture'. The suggestion here is that culture should be viewed as a metaphor rather than as a variable – i.e. something that an organisation *is* rather than something that it *has*. From this perspective, culture is only loosely structured and partially shared. There is recognition that individuals in organisations might hold a variety of meanings and beliefs. Perhaps managers need to recognise that they can only manage organisational culture in a very fluid way and that it is important that they seem to be supporting values with which knowledge workers want to identify. They therefore need to give adequate consideration to the value systems of knowledge workers.

Thus, these two approaches (integration and fragmentation) view management involvement in KM quite differently. The integration perspective is of the view that management can control the worker's value system and related KM processes, while the latter thinks it is more useful to adopt a looser, more flexible management approach, which facilitates rather than dominates knowledge flows.

Newell et al. also note that a number of different factors can help an organisation to develop an organisational culture that is supportive of knowledge sharing (rather than knowledge hoarding) – i.e. creating a knowledge-sharing culture. These include appropriate incentives and motivation; adequate resources; a range and depth of skills and expertise and a committed project champion/leader.

Thus, this section has briefly considered some of the literature on KM, culture and organisations and has highlighted some of the more important themes.

(The above section has all been referenced from Newell et al., 2002.)

Knowledge transfer across cultures

Overview

This section will briefly consider the transferring of knowledge across cultures specifically. This is clearly important if knowledge is going to be shared in an effective way and on a global basis. However, not everyone is going to be willing to share knowledge in this way, and there are also many practical problems, such as language barriers. Furthermore, cultures have different ways in which they communicate and transfer knowledge. In some cultures, for example, workers only really want to accept knowledge from top management (i.e. knowledge flows are top-down), but other cultures adopt a looser approach and are happy and willing to receive knowledge from people on varying positions in the hierarchy (i.e. knowledge flows can be top-down, bottom-up, or middle up and down).

However, there are also contradictions embedded within capitalism itself, particularly concerning the contradiction between wanting and needing to engender an environment that facilitates knowledge sharing with one that wants and needs to protect knowledge. I consider this in my book *Globalisation, Information and Libraries* (R. Rikowski, 2005a), particularly in regard to the World Trade Organization's agreement on Trade-Related Aspects of Intellectual Property Rights (TRIPS). In essence, TRIPS is about transforming intellectual property rights, such as patents, into international tradable commodities. Thus, organisations take knowledge, patent it, commodify it and then sell it in the marketplace, thereby making a profit out if it. At one level, this is clearly protectionist – protecting knowledge for the benefit of individual organisations, especially for large corporations, and this goes against the free flow of information. At another level, in order for this to work effectively, an environment that encourages a free flow of knowledge and information needs to be encouraged. As I say:

> ...various elements of the free flow of information are necessary to enable global capitalism to thrive. Companies need to be able to obtain some information easily ... and creators need some easy access to information and, indeed, this also extends to the public at large. It is impossible to predict where the next pocket of success for capitalism might lie – it seeks new markets, new ideas and new means for obtaining value from everywhere. It must be looked at within this context. Thus only the free access to information that is beneficial to global capitalism is celebrated. But obviously, it can be difficult to decipher where this actually resides. So, we have many anomalies in capitalism, and many contradictions arise within its never-ending quest for new markets, new commodities and new forms for establishing and perpetuating trade. (R. Rikowski, 2005a: 228)

Thus, this is a problem reflecting one of the many contradictions embedded within capitalism.

However, another fundamental point concerns who is likely to gain most benefit from this knowledge transfer process. Clearly, the developed countries are generally likely to benefit at the expense of the developing countries. The developed world might, and probably will, pay lip-service to the developing world, and seem to 'care' and to provide them with useful knowledge, but in reality, any such actions must always be subservient to the wider capitalist agenda, and therefore, the knowledge wants and needs of those in the developed world are always likely to dominate. We need to keep this firmly in mind when examining knowledge transfer.

Transferring knowledge: developing and developed countries

Transferring and sharing knowledge between developing and developed countries can provide various benefits, although it is always likely to benefit the developed world more than the developing world. There are, however, various general problems as well.

First, value systems in the developed world are likely to be different from value systems in the developing world. This could obviously cause problems for the effective transfer and sharing of knowledge and it might also lessen the relevance of any knowledge that is transferred. Furthermore, any form of effective knowledge transfer can surely only take place if people respect one another's cultures. Given the wide variety of differences between different cultures though, this can be very difficult. From the African cultural perspective, for example, the transfer or knowledge transfer should be mutually beneficial to all parties involved in the exchange, but this is likely to be very difficult to achieve in practice. There are also various other problems, such as language barriers and literacy problems themselves, particularly in the developing world.

Furthermore, some local communities in the developing world do not think that knowledge can be owned by either individuals or organisations – that instead, all knowledge belongs to God and/or Nature (also considered in R. Rikowski, 2005a). This could cause both problems and benefits for transferring knowledge. On one level, the indigenous population might be more willing to share their knowledge, as it is not owned by them personally; but on the other hand, they are unlikely to be very enthusiastic about recording the knowledge, particularly given that many of the local population cannot read or write anyway. If the knowledge is not recorded, then it will be more difficult to share it from one perspective – it will be more difficult to house it in a library and information resource centre, for example. On the other hand, it will probably be easier for companies to just appropriate this knowledge, patent it and make money out of it. This can be seen to be 'knowledge transfer' or knowledge sharing on one level – but in a strictly limited way – i.e. knowledge transfer for the benefit of large corporations, to enable them to make more profits, which might then go to transfer knowledge in the developed world, but only to those that can afford to pay. But it is not knowledge transfer for the benefit of the local, indigenous population, that is for sure.

Furthermore, it might have taken hundreds of years for the indigenous population in the developing world to have built up traditional knowledge, but this traditional knowledge can then be appropriated by large corporations, without giving due recompense to the local community. By this means, the local indigenous population can become very exploited, while once again, knowledge transfer only takes place between the well-off and those that can afford to pay.

Various studies have been conducted regarding knowledge transfer across cultures.

The tt30 project on knowledge transfer systems (intercontinental, intercultural and intracultural knowledge transfer), for example, started in September 2003 (see Edozien et al., year unknown). It aimed to view methods and mechanisms by which knowledge is transferred, both between and within cultures, and how this influences development trends in three regions: West Europe/North America, South-East Asia and Sub-Saharan West Africa. It had a number of objectives, including identifying key indicators of indigenous knowledge transfer in various cultures, compiling a comparative analysis of knowledge potential for the three regions and suggesting measures to influence existing patterns in knowledge transfer.

The study emphasised that tacit knowledge is not transferable without communication between individuals and that trust and understanding are important ingredients for the sharing of knowledge between individuals. They highlighted the fact that knowledge transfer can be improved by having employee involvement and a trained workforce, effective leadership and a culture based on trust and understanding. As Edozien et al. say, 'the key to understanding how to create a successful transfer of information between cultures is to see it from a perspective that promotes development among parties' (Edozien et al., year unknown).

Thus, many factors need to be considered regarding knowledge transfer and sharing, some of which have been highlighted here.

Interfaces between culture and knowledge

Michailova and Husted (2002) outlined a research agenda for the dynamic interfaces between culture and knowledge and this is considered in this section.

Michailova and Husted say that knowledge production is heterogeneous and international, and is not limited by the boundaries of an organisation – thus, they appreciate the global cultural context in which KM now often operates. They emphasise the importance of virtual organisations within the context of KM and culture, as well as the different mechanisms for networking. Michailova and Husted say that:

> The specific knowledge production and application relevant to the value creation in the individual organisation is no longer limited by the boundaries of the organization. Instead it takes place under the labels of virtual organization in dynamic organizational forms such as loosely coupled networks. Moreover, the ability of knowledge-based companies to develop and exploit new knowledge efficiently and innovatively is highly related to their networking capabilities. (Michailova and Husted, 2002: 3)

Thus, effective networking mechanisms and virtual networking assist with the development, exploitation and transfer of knowledge.

Furthermore, they say that knowledge creation, sharing and utilisation take place within different cultural contexts, but that 'the relationships between culture and knowledge management ... are not explored in depth in a coherent manner in mainstream texts' (Michailova and Husted, 2002: 3).

Michailova and Husted say that while some writings consider the importance of culture for knowledge creation, many do not explore the topic at a sufficiently deep level. Their proposal aims to fill the gap in the literature and it focuses on the creation and sharing of new knowledge and knowledge practices with a cultural perspective.

Four levels of culture were identified in the project. These were professional subcultures (both functional differences within one company and across different industries); organisational cultures; cultures in inter-organisational networks; and national cultures.

All subcultures tend to develop their own identities and specific languages and shared beliefs, and apply their own criteria in defining knowledge. Michailova and Husted say that 'organizational cultures are central to knowledge creation, sharing and utilization and they are increasingly recognized as a major barrier to leveraging intellectual assets' (Michailova and Husted, 2002: 7).

Thus, the aim of the study was to focus on establishing and developing knowledge networks – both intentional (formal) networks and unintentional (informal) networks. The central theme of the project was the nature of the relationship between KM and culture, focusing on content. The project also questioned the usefulness of more traditional conceptions of knowledge work and networking.

In sum, Michailova and Husted identified a number of key factors regarding the dynamic interfaces between culture and knowledge. These included the importance of virtual organisations as networking facilitators, the significance of professional subcultures, and the importance of establishing and developing both formal and informal knowledge networks.

Knowledge management in a cross-cultural setting: a case study

Introduction

This section will consider KM and knowledge sharing across different cultures with the focus on Ford and Chan's (2002) article 'Knowledge sharing in a cross-cultural setting: a case study', which described an exploratory case study that they undertook on this topic. This study looked at the relationships between cross-cultural differences and knowledge transfer within an international subsidiary. The study examined a Japanese manufacturing subsidiary in west USA.

Organisational culture is seen to be a key factor in the success of KM practices. The study looked at KM and cross-cultural issues and organisational culture and how these areas interact. It also explored the extent to which knowledge transfer (or knowledge sharing) is dependent on national culture.

Thus, the main purpose of the study was to examine whether cross-cultural differences within an international subsidiary influenced knowledge flows within the company. As Ford and Chan say:

> In an increasingly globalized business context, companies need to understand if and how cross-cultural differences influence knowledge management. The purpose of this study was to investigate whether or not cross-cultural differences within an

international subsidiary influence knowledge flows within the company, and if so, how. (Ford and Chan, 2002)

The results showed that language differences can create knowledge blocks and that cross-cultural differences can explain the direction of knowledge flows within an international subsidiary.

Ford and Chan say that four processes characterise KM – namely, knowledge generation, knowledge codification, knowledge transfer (or knowledge sharing) and knowledge application. The study focused, in particular, on knowledge transfer – i.e. the dissemination and sharing of knowledge from one individual or group to another within the organisation, although people do not necessarily want to share their knowledge. Ford and Chan emphasised the importance of knowledge sharing for effective knowledge transfer, saying that:

> The challenge facing companies wishing to gain a competitive advantage through knowledge management is to create a culture and environment in which knowledge sharing will thrive. Without an appropriate culture, knowledge transfer is at best very difficult and most likely will not occur. (Ford and Chan, 2002: 5)

Organisational culture, national culture and knowledge transfer

Various other studies have looked at the effectiveness of knowledge transfer and knowledge sharing and have found that cultural differences impact on information flows, KM processes and knowledge transfer (e.g. Simonin, 1999). This also needs to be linked to organisational culture. Simonin, for example, concludes that cultural distance between firms increases the difficulty of performing these different knowledge and information processes well. How then can companies, where employees have many cross-cultural differences, encourage knowledge sharing in their work environments? Various factors influence the effective transfer/sharing of knowledge, such as trust, language and beliefs.

Hofstede also recognised the importance of the relationship between organisational culture and national culture. He says that an organisation's culture is embedded within a national culture, and that organisational theory is not independent of national culture. Thus, national culture influences human resource practices, organisational behaviour and many other factors. Research such as Davenport and

Prusak's (1998), has found that the type of organisational culture is important for the success of KM practices. The importance of trust, common cultures and frames of reference were emphasised.

Hofstede's five dimensions can also be applied here. The different dimensions can influence knowledge processes and knowledge transfer both within and across organisations. Cultures that measure high on individualism, for example, might have more difficulty in knowledge sharing and knowledge transfer than those high on collectivism, while countries that have high power distance might have more hierarchical structures. With hierarchical structures, knowledge is more likely to flow from the top down and knowledge flows will probably be more limited than knowledge flows in cultures that have less power distance. Meanwhile, members in long-term orientation cultures might be more willing to work for long-term goals, which might be better for promoting effective KM over a long period. While cultures high in masculinity may have less knowledge transfer between organisation members if there is a very competitive, individual-based environment.

Yoo, Ginzber and Ahn (1999) have focused on the likely impact of national culture on organisational KM processes. They formulated a research proposal to examine whether national culture influenced organisational KM processes. Little research had been undertaken on this area prior to this. The plan was to conduct case studies at multiple sites within a consulting firm, covering both USA and Korean sites. They had a number of research questions in this regard. First, to investigate the effectiveness of KM practices across cultures; second, to examine which dimensions are culture-specific; and third to consider whether there is an underlying theory that can explain any differences.

Finally, an examination of different national cultures, such as the difference between Japanese and US culture and the knowledge transfer processes is interesting, as they can differ so greatly, regarding various factors such as history, language and religion. Japan has a largely homogeneous culture, for example, whereas that of the USA is more heterogeneous. Such differences will clearly have a major impact on knowledge flows in organisations in these different countries.

Ford and Chan's research: methodology and findings

Ford and Chan asked the following research questions:

- *Research question 1*: How does national culture relate to knowledge transfer and flow within an international subsidiary?

- *Research question 2*: How does knowledge transfer across cultural groups differ from knowledge transfer within cultural groups (if it does differ) within the subsidiary?

Ford and Chan say that organisational culture, national culture and knowledge processes are best measured in a natural setting. Thus, they choose to look at a Japanese manufacturing subsidiary in west USA. The president of the subsidiary was Japanese; top management of the subsidiary were American and Canadian, while middle management was a mix of Americans, Japanese, Canadians and other cultural groups (e.g. Chinese, Indian). The employees were Americans who consisted of other minority groups and different cultures living in the USA.

The case study research strategy was used, and a variety of research methods was adopted, including questionnaires, interviews, site observations and documentation. Interviews were conducted with 21 employees.

One of the first indicators of different cultures is the different languages. This has been highlighted by a number of different writers and researchers, such as Triandis (1989) and Hofstede (2001). Three languages were being spoken in the company that was being researched: English, Japanese and Spanish. Language as a knowledge block is considered further below.

During the interviews, some individuals spoke about other cultural differences – for example, perceived work ethic differences between Japanese and Americans. One respondent said:

> It's sort of cliché, but if you were to put a Japanese and American worker next to each other, the American worker will look lazy, and the Japanese worker will look stupid. A Japanese will spend ten hours of cleaning a machine with a toothbrush, the American will grab a hose, rinse it down and walk away.

Formal knowledge teams were being formulated in different departments and there were various top-down knowledge flows and knowledge sharing during meetings. There were also informal KM practices. The research discovered that there were also various knowledge blocks.

Knowledge flows: qualitative data analysis and some key results. Ford and Chan said that knowledge can flow through a company in different ways:

- knowledge can flow through knowledge sharing between two individuals;

165

- knowledge can flow from one individual to a group via meetings, e-mail, or other versions of documentation (e.g. intranet web pages);
- knowledge can flow in different directions – from top to bottom, across co-workers or bottom-up.

Questions about knowledge flows in the organisation were asked during the interviews. It was found that sharing problem-solving knowledge took place, but that it was not supported by management, and so was not formally rewarded. All the respondents were willing to ask for advice, but they asked different people. Americans were more willing to discuss problems with co-workers and people below them in the hierarchy. In general, people sought out others that had the relevant knowledge and expertise to help them to solve their problems.

Knowledge sharing was determined by the willingness of employees to share their knowledge. Only four of 20 interviewees said that knowledge was shared readily. However, everyone had 'buddies' – i.e. people that they enjoyed socialising with. Concerning casual networks, Ford and Chan say:

> These casual networks would often discuss work in more philosophical terms, or enjoy other casual, more personal conversations. It is possible, therefore, to consider these as informal flows of knowledge throughout the organization. In this case, the flow is more lateral than the more formal knowledge flows, and these knowledge flows tend to fall more along nationality and language lines. (Ford and Chan, 2002: 16)

There was an 'information sharing' questionnaire in the study. This consisted of five questions on a seven-point Likert scale, which assessed people's perceptions of employee's willingness to share information within the company. The average score was 4.437, which indicates that a moderate level of sharing was taking place.

Knowledge blocks: qualitative data analysis and some key results. Various 'knowledge blocks' can stop knowledge from flowing freely in an organisation. These include factors such as different languages, different frames of reference, distrust, lack of management support and knowledge hoarding. The study examined these knowledge blocks.

Languages were particularly significant. Nine out of 21 respondents, for example, said that people speaking different languages did create difficulties and only four said it did not create any difficulties. One of the main problems was individuals' ability and willingness to learn different languages. Two said that key information was not passed along when there were full conversations in languages other than English. Thus, although, some overall understanding might have been conveyed, some vital pieces of information were sometimes lost. The language barrier was the largest block to knowledge sharing in the organisation. There were also differences between the language being spoken and the types of knowledge being blocked.

In the front office, there were two paths of knowledge – the Japanese path and the English path, with different language-dependent knowledge blocks. One significant block was that between Japanese and English speaking managers and employees. In the marketing department, for example, the top manager was fully bilingual, and was willing to translate during meetings, but this was only enough for conversation purposes.

In the back office, there were some knowledge blocks due to language. This was commented on largely with regard to front-line employees and managers. Managers mainly spoke English but many front-line employees only spoke Spanish. Some supervisors were bilingual, speaking Spanish and English, but it was not their job to translate. This created knowledge blocks, for getting knowledge to and from the front line.

With regard to management support, from the quantitative data gathered from a seven-point Likert scale, management did not discourage knowledge sharing but it did not actively support it either. Some interviewees commented on the fact that there was a lack of formal management support for knowledge sharing and that this could cause problems. People who hold on to knowledge might not realise that it could be of interest to others, for example. This happened to some extent in the customer service, distribution and production areas.

Knowledge hoarding and distrust also created knowledge blocks on an individual level.

Summary of main findings. A number of salient points emerged from the study – first, for cross-culture in general, and second, for KM in particular. These are listed below.

Cross-cultural findings:

■ It was found that nationality predicted cross-cultural differences, but there were not as many differences as were expected. The largest expected differences (Japanese versus American) were in reality the smallest differences, and the smallest expected differences were found to be the largest differences (Canadian versus American) among the four main groups.

- Participants did not refer explicitly to cultural groups, although they were visible in the organisation, such as with seating arrangements during meetings and casual conversations in the office. There were many reasons for group formation, including language, personal friendships and perceived commonalities.

Knowledge management findings:

- There were no formal KM practices in the company, but there were some informal KM practices.

- There were several different types of knowledge flows in the company, but the main flow was bottom-up, with a little flowing middle-down.

- The connection between knowledge flows with advice seeking differed for North American employees and Japanese employees. North American employees sought advice from co-workers, subordinates and superiors – thus, there were bottom-up, lateral and top-down knowledge flows. While the Japanese sought knowledge from a small body of individuals, which resulted mainly in top-down knowledge flows.

- There were different knowledge blocks – these included language barriers, a lack of formal management support, different frames of reference, distrust and knowledge hoarding. The most significant, though, were language barriers. A lack of formal management support blocked knowledge flows, but the blocks existed across the whole organisation and were not between specific cultural groups. Knowledge hoarding and distrust created knowledge blocks on an individual level, but many thought that those individuals that behaved like this would not remain in the company for very long.

Research questions readdressed:

- *RQ1: How do cross-cultural differences relate to knowledge transfer and flow within an international subsidiary?* Cross-cultural differences affected the flow of knowledge/knowledge transfer within the organisation – these differences included different languages, heterogeneity versus homogeneity of national cultures and culturally acceptable advice-seeking behaviour.

  Language was a particularly significant knowledge block between Japanese and English employees. Some knowledge was transferred between the two groups (e.g. through a bilingual individual) but a lot of knowledge was lost in translation. Various other writers (e.g. Davenport and Prusak, 1998) have cited language as a knowledge block for the transfer and sharing of knowledge.

With regard to informal networks, Japanese employees created a separate network that was homogeneous, with shared frames of reference, experience, culture and vocabulary. Such an environment helped to engender an environment for knowledge sharing between the Japanese employees.

With regard to knowledge flow through advice seeking, Japanese and North Americans differed about who they asked for advice to solve problems, with Japanese people largely preferring to take advice from top-down. There are various possible explanations for this, one of which is the power distance dimension that differs between the two cultures. Traditional Japanese culture has higher power distance than traditional US culture and a country that is high in power distance is more likely to have top-down instruction and knowledge flows.

- *RQ2: How does knowledge transfer across cultural groups differ from knowledge transfer within cultural groups (if it does differ)?* There were some differences between knowledge flows within and between cross-cultural groups. Knowledge flows between cross-cultural groups tended to be on formal lines and work-related. Cultural differences were more noticeable in informal groups. Thus, the majority of knowledge flowing across cultural groups was formal, and knowledge flow within cultural groups was informal. Knowledge flows for Japanese people tended to be more top-down, while knowledge flows for North American employees/management were more diverse, and included top-down, lateral and bottom-up.

Conclusions and recommendations of the case study

This section has examined a case study about knowledge sharing in a cross-cultural setting (Ford and Chan, 2002). The study examined a Japanese manufacturing subsidiary in west USA, focusing on cross-cultural differences and knowledge transfer within an international subsidiary. The findings were also related to Hofstede's five dimensions.

There were a number of important findings. These included, first, the fact that there were a number of knowledge blocks in existence, the most prevalent of which being the language barrier. Second, informal networking and KM practices were taking place. Third, sharing problem-solving knowledge was evident, but management did not formally support the sharing of such problems. Fourth, nationality predicted cross-cultural differences, but there were not as many differences as were expected. Fifth, there were several different types of knowledge flows in the company, but the main flows were bottom-up, with a little flowing middle-down.

There were a number of recommendations leading on from the study, for optimising knowledge flows throughout an international subsidiary. One was that management should lay out guidelines for knowledge sharing practices along formal structures within an organisation. Second, that barriers to knowledge flows should be broken down. Buckley and Carter (1999) recommend the creation of a team of employees responsible for coordinating knowledge that is created locally, as a method for encouraging knowledge flows. This might also help to break down the language barrier to some extent, which was a significant knowledge block. Third, the value of informal knowledge flows should be considered further, such as through communities of practice (McDermott, 2000; Wenger and Snyder, 2000). This might not fit in with a company's objectives; however, if management is willing and able to work with these communities, then informal knowledge flows can perhaps be integrated with some formal knowledge flows. That said, some KM writers and consultants (e.g. McDermott, 2000; Everest, 2001) say that informal flows should not be managed and formalised. This might alter the knowledge in some way, and might also discourage people from sharing knowledge informally in the future. Thus, careful consideration needs to be given to the possible integration of formal and informal knowledge flows.

Concluding comments in regard to Ford and Chan's study

Ford and Chan's study has provided a valuable contribution to the literature on KM and culture, focusing on the issues that surround people from different nationalities and cultures working together in an organisation, and how these differences can affect knowledge transfer and sharing. Not surprisingly, language was a significant knowledge block. The hierarchical structure in the organisation was also an important factor. Some cultures prefer to receive knowledge only from the top-down, whereas others prefer a more fluid approach. The structure of informal knowledge networks also differed between cultures.

Thus, if there are different cultures and nationalities working within a particular organisation, management needs to consider these differences carefully, if it wants to engender an environment for effective knowledge sharing. With regard to language, for example, more bilingualists could perhaps be employed and employees could be encouraged to learn other languages. However, this is not a knowledge block that can be solved easily, and management should try to avoid putting unfair expectations on their workers. With regard to knowledge flows throughout the hierarchical structure, although the learning curve here is not so steep, changing culture beliefs that have been established over a long period, could prove difficult to overcome. For example, it will be difficult for cultures that are only used to receiving knowledge from top-down to adjust suddenly to a more fluid approach. In addition, one could question the extent to which one culture should impose its value/belief system on another culture. Thus, if knowledge is to flow freely in such organisations, subtle management techniques will be required to facilitate such an environment.

Concluding comments

This section has considered knowledge transfer and sharing across cultures. It has focused on a number of issues in this regard, including knowledge flows throughout the hierarchical structure of an organisation and how this varies between different cultures; the contradiction between the free flow of information and the protection of intellectual property; different cultures value/belief systems in regard to who owns knowledge; virtual organisations; formal and informal knowledge networks; language barriers and knowledge hoarding.

However, 'knowledge transfer' also seems to imply some notion of a 'happy global family' framework, within which the 'there is no alternative' (TINA) philosophy dominates. The TINA philosophy views globalisation/global capitalism as the best social, economic and political system that we can have, even though it recognises that it is not an ideal system. Thus, the assumption seems to be that knowledge transfer will work to the benefit of all cultures across the world in one way or another; it simply remains for us to work out how to achieve that. However, while we live in global capitalism, it will be impossible to distribute knowledge in a fair and equitable way, I would suggest. Instead, knowledge transfer is bound to benefit one group of people at the expense of another – the rich will benefit at the expense of the poor, and the developed world will benefit at the expense of the developing world. Thus, knowledge transfer will not help to bring about any type of 'happy global family', or any real sense of fairness in the distribution of knowledge resources.

Knowledge management and organisational learning in the developing world

In an objective sense, in order for capitalism to thrive, the emphasis must be on how KM can help an economy to prosper and not on how it can help the poor. Interestingly though, much of the literature on KM in the developing world tends to focus on the fact that KM is often not being used to the advantage of the poor, and it then considers how this situation can be rectified. Drawing on the work of Inge Hovland, I will now examine some of this literature in relation to KM and organisational learning.

Review of the literature

Ing Hovland has provided a valuable contribution to the topic of KM and organisational learning in the developing world. She wrote a paper entitled 'Knowledge management and organisational learning: an international development perspective', which was published by the Overseas Development Institute (ODI) in 2003. The paper is essentially an annotated bibliography, which reviews the current literature on KM and organisational learning, particularly in the international development field, and as such, it is a very useful resource. The paper is part of a Research and Policy in Development (RAPID) programme at the ODI, aiming to promote 'pro-poor' policies, so the emphasis was on how KM can work to the benefit of the indigenous populations in the developing world.

The ODI programme had a number of general aims. These included improving knowledge about research-policy links among development practitioners, a consideration of policy-makers and researchers in the area and improving KM and learning systems in both southern and northern agencies. In addition, it set out to help both southern and northern KM researchers and practitioners to communicate their KM research findings more effectively and to influence policy. Finally, it aimed to emphasise the importance of this research, to raise awareness about it and to highlight how the research can be accessed. Hovland's annotated bibliography focuses mainly on improving KM and learning systems in both southern and northern agencies.

As Hovland emphasises, most of the work on KM and organisational learning has been carried out in northern or international development non-governmental organisations (NGOs). Furthermore, this reinforces the point that I have already made that the successful implementation of KM in the developed world is more important than developing effective KM practices in the developing world. There is also more literature on KM and learning in the development field in the corporate sector than within NGOs in general.

Furthermore, King (2001) notes that most issues around KM and learning in the development sector have focused on the internal knowledge needs and processes of northern agencies. Less attention has been given to the knowledge gaps in southern organisations. King suggests that northern KM projects should consider how they can best support southern knowledge bases and systems, rather than just seeking to further their own agendas. Once again, then, the needs of those in the north are paramount.

However, NGOs have, and are, also making a valuable contribution. Some NGOs, such as Oxfam, for example, have provided guidelines for KM and learning systems (see Powell, 2003). There have also been various surveys of NGO learning (see, for example, BOND, 2003) and various academics have endeavoured to develop theories of learning processes within NGOs (see, for example, Davies, 1998).

As Hovland also notes, different groups (whether they are different through political reasons, economic resources, culture, social background or religion etc.) are likely to have a different understanding of various concepts used in KM, such as 'leadership', 'information' and 'monitoring'. This will clearly influence any KM programme in the developing world. The anthropologist Bailey (1971), for example, examined the concept of 'leadership' in a peasant community in India. It was found that traditional leaders got respect by giving orders, and not seeking cooperation. This can clearly have implications when endeavouring to implement KM programmes in India, particularly if and when trying to obtain knowledge and information from those lower down the hierarchy becomes important. An authoritarian approach is unlikely to engender an environment that will encourage the necessary cooperation for the giving and sharing of significant knowledge (as much of the research and writing on KM indicates).

In general, there has not been much research and literature in the south on KM and learning environments (compared with the north), although there have been a few studies. Rondinelli (1993), for example, examined public sector development programmes that were undertaken by various southern governments. It was found that the programmes were very control-oriented and top-down and so it was difficult to engender a learning environment. This can partly be explained by the fact that the programmes were often dictated by external donors and aid agencies, who want coherent national development plans.

Others focus on the size of the organisation and regard this as a very important, determining factor. A study undertaken by Carlsson (1998) on African organisations and management, for example, argued that the size of the organisation was important. Small organisations can adapt more quickly to change and, indeed, it is often necessary that they should do so. Managing change effectively in large organisations and public sector institutions, however, can often be more difficult, slower and more cumbersome. Furthermore, Carlsson argues that public sector institutional processes in Africa often change through changes in the environment in which they operate, rather than through their own strategic aims. There are implications of change management for KM. The need to be able to manage change well is clearly important for effective KM systems – for flexible work patterns, effective knowledge sharing etc.

Meanwhile, Hailey and James (2002) built on case studies of nine 'successful' South Asian NGOs in considering how NGOs learn. They concluded that the single most important factor affecting organisational learning is a 'learning leader'. Furthermore, that the most important characteristic of learning leaders in South Asia was their ability to understand and work in a changing and complex environment. It is interesting to contrast this view of 'leadership' with the view of 'leadership' that dominates in some cultures in the developing world, such as the one outlined by Bailey (1971), which emphasised the importance of giving orders. In contrast, Uphoff's study (1992) from Sri Lanka emphasised flexibility. This study looked at the success of a large-scale irrigation system. It was largely successful because farmers engaged in flexible systems of cooperation. However, many NGOs in the south rely on donors, and this can make it more difficult to be flexible.

Heeks (2002) points out that many information and communication technology projects fail in organisations in the south. This is because IT systems that are designed in the north are often not compatible/do not fit in with the IT needs of those in the south. Furthermore, southern institutions do not usually have the same level of technological infrastructure and local skills base as those in the north. Meanwhile, Volkow (1998) makes the point that there is little to be gained from having an IT system if the management structures within an organisation prevent the system from functioning well. In addition, Moussa and Schware (1992) say that ICT innovation and application in the north are largely aimed at the private sector, whereas in the south it is mainly in the public sector. Good and effective IT systems are clearly important for any successful KM programme and the differences between IT systems in the north and the south and the implications of this for KM need to be considered further.

There is not much literature on KM and learning issues in relation to research institutes and think-tanks. March (1991) highlights two different strategies concerning KM: exploitation and exploration. Exploitation involves the reprocessing of past or existing knowledge, whereas exploration involves developing new knowledge. In order to remain innovative, Hovland suggests that a research institution needs to focus on exploration strategies. Effective KM is closely related to innovation, so I would suggest that more attention should be given to this area.

Clearly, then, organisations function in different ways in different cultural, political and economic contexts. As Hovland says, 'to put it crudely, the best KM, learning and evaluation strategies in the UK are not necessarily the best KM, learning and evaluation strategies in Uganda' (Hovland, 2003).

Thus, cultural differences impact on KM and learning.

Gaps in the literature

Hovland identified some of the main gaps in the literature on KM and organisational learning in the developing world and examined this under four headings. This is considered further below.

Learning and responsiveness

Effective civil society organisations (CSOs) can provide a voice so that the poor can be heard. Hovland asks whether improved KM and learning systems can enable CSOs to do this better. King (2001) points out that KM and learning processes do not necessarily make NGOs more responsive to southern needs. Instead, he says that northern NGOs often implement KM in order to ease their own information blockages, and that this is based on the profit motive, rather than using KM to address issues in the south. Further work needs to be undertaken on this area.

Learning and impact on policy

Northern development NGOs often have to carry out advocacy work on evidence that is obtained from the south. Hovland asks whether improved KM and learning systems in development agencies can enable them to influence policy processes in a way that will benefit them. But one problem is that the clients of agencies in the development sector are often separate from their funders (Edwards, 1994), so there can be a conflict of interest. Senge (1990) examined the corporate sector and refers to 'the learning organisation' as if everyone in the organisation was working together in harmony. But as Hovland says, 'this conclusion must be modified in line with the particular tensions experienced by development organisations' (Hovland, 2003: 13).

Again, further work needs to be undertaken to examine a number of areas, such as whether KM/learning can increase southern and northern development organisations' impact on policy.

Learning and impact of policy on practice

How much of a policy is taken up in practice and how quickly does it happen? Hovland asks whether improved KM and learning systems can enable development agencies to translate policy into practice more effectively. A few case studies have been undertaken here about what happens regarding development policies.

Mosse (2002), for example, presented a case study on rural development for the Department for International Development, UK (DFID) project in India. It was found that participatory development legitimated action rather than guided it. This also helped to secure funding from donors. Once again, further work needs to be undertaken in this area, to consider issues such as whether KM/learning can increase the ability of institutions to translate policy into institutional practice.

Learning and southern engagement

As Hovland says, northern NGOs should try to build a better relationship with southern NGOs, in order to try to utilise knowledge in an endeavour to lessen poverty. As the DFID's research policy paper says, 'the evidence suggests that the capacity of developing countries to generate, acquire, assimilate and utilise knowledge will form a crucial part of their strategies to reduce poverty' (Surr et al., 2002: v).

Hovland asks whether KM and learning systems in development agencies can enable them to bridge the gap between northern and southern development institutions or whether it will widen the gap.

Hovland suggests that one way to ensure that KM works for southern agencies and not just northern ones is to focus on knowledge needs and challenges of those in the south. Northern and southern staff could work together on this. Again, further work needs to be undertaken to examine whether KM/learning can help to connect southern institutions and northern institutions and processes.

Summary

Hovland highlights a number of gaps that need to be addressed. First, the need for further research on the work of NGOs working with KM and learning systems in the south. Second, the need for further research on advocacy work that NGOs carry out and the effect that KM and learning systems can have on this process. Can KM/learning increase southern and northern development organisations' impact on policy? Third, whether KM/learning can help institutions to transform policy into practice. Fourth, whether KM/learning can help to connect southern and northern institutions and processes.

Conclusion

This section has considered KM in the developing world, focusing on Hovland's work on KM and organisational learning in the developing world and some of the gaps in the literature, as identified by Hovland. It has considered, in particular, how KM can be implemented more effectively to benefit those in the developing world more, through organisations (particularly NGOs) and their learning strategies. For various reasons, however, NGOs often engage more with the knowledge needs of those in the developed world, and further consideration needs to be given in regard to how to overcome this.

In conclusion, while some work on KM in the developing world has been undertaken, considerably more work needs to be done, particularly with regard to further assessing how KM can benefit the poor. However, in reality, this can never be the main thrust of the research – instead, it must always be subservient to the overall capitalist agenda, as far as I am concerned. There are two types of labour in capitalism – manual labour and intellectual labour and value is extracted from both of them, but today, there is an emphasis on extracting value from intellectual labour in the developed world, while the focus in the developing world is more on manual labour. For these reasons, the development and implementation of effective KM practices in the developed world will continue to be more important than the development of such programmes in the developing world.

Furthermore, while KM projects with the aim of helping the poor in the developing world are worthwhile, they can only ever be a form of paying lip-service to the developing world. But if the north does not seem to 'care' about the south at all, then this is likely to have serious implications. Thus, it has to appear to care. But, ultimately, while we live in capitalism, labour will continue to be exploited, alienated and objectified.

(All information for this section was obtained from Hovland, 2003)

Summary

This chapter has examined a number of important areas around the broad topic of KM within and across cultures, with the focus being more on the developing world than the developed world. First of all, it provided a brief literature overview on KM, culture and organisations. Second, it considered knowledge transfer or knowledge sharing across cultures, particularly between developing and developed countries. Third, it focused on interfaces between culture and knowledge, and fourth it examined a case study of KM and cross-culture in a Japanese international subsidiary in West USA, which was undertaken by Ford and Chan. This study focused, in particular, on knowledge transfer and language as a knowledge block. Finally, it examined KM and organisational learning in the developing world, drawing on Hovland's valuable work in this area.

Knowledge management: internal, external and social cultures
Ruth Rikowski

Internal cultures

Introduction

As well as examining the concept of culture as a whole, it is important to differentiate between knowledge management (KM) and both internal and external cultures. The first section of this chapter focuses on internal cultures – i.e. the different cultures internal to an organisation, while the subsequent section considers external cultures.

Various writers and researchers, such as Ford and Chan (2002) have focused on different cultures within the organisation. Some subcultures engender a higher degree of trust than others, for example, and as Baker and Baker say, KM 'thrives in a high-trust culture' (Baker and Baker, 2001: 5).

Various sociological studies have undertaken research and writing on subcultures, such as deviant subcultures. With regard to deviant subcultures, Haralambos and Holborn say that subcultures 'explain deviance in terms of the subculture of a social group'. They argue that certain groups develop norms and values which are to some extent different from those held by other members of society (Haralambos and Holborn, 2004: 335).

These subculture theories state that deviance occurs when individuals conform to the value and norms of the particular social group that they belong to and that this is different from the dominant culture. A deviant subculture is clearly a negative reaction to the mainstream culture, which for various reasons the members of the deviant subculture do not like, or cannot/do not want to fit into.

Many other sectors of society have their own subcultures – these can be based on many different factors such as religion, race and age. All these different subcultures will have their own internal cultures. One example is the culture of 'laddism', where males (often teenagers) join a subculture where the focus is around areas such as sport, music and alcohol. The research of Paul Willis (1977) is very relevant here. His study of a school on a working class housing estate in the Midlands, England, used the observation research technique. A clear 'lad culture' emerged. The school's boys were keen to leave school and get a job, one that involved 'real work' rather than 'pen pushing', as they saw it. Thus, this lad subculture was largely anti-school and learning.

Some interesting research could be undertaken considering in further detail the impact that KM practices could and do have on these various subcultures, how different subcultures respond to KM and how these subcultures fit in (or not) with the dominant culture. For example, given that KM is a relatively new subject, a group of elderly people will probably not respond as well to KM practices as a group of young people. Nevertheless, within this, some elderly groups will respond better than others. With regard to the lad culture in the Willis study, the boys opposed to school, education and learning are clearly not likely to be so well-disposed towards KM either. Upon leaving school, their aim was to undertake manual, not intellectual, work. Thus, different school experiences for various groups of young people are likely to result in different reactions if and when KM practices are introduced into the world of work that they subsequently enter.

'Communities of practice' (CoPs) are a particularly important internal culture for KM practices. Successful CoPs can help to ensure that better KM takes place within an organisation, and they can endeavour to utilise the good parts of various cultures, to help ensure effective knowledge flows. Members of a CoP are often likely to be more willing to share their knowledge, information and ideas; the high level of trust that can be built up is one reason for this. Resources have been put into CoPs over the last few years and many consider it an important new area. 'People to people' connections and communities of practice are now generally recognised to be more important than just having efficient IT systems for KM. Knowledge cannot simply be captured and recorded in an IT system in a simplistic way. A significant shift in thinking has taken place in this regard and increasing importance is being attached to tacit knowledge (both conscious and unconscious tacit knowledge), and CoPs can help to extract this tacit knowledge. However, various questions also need to be asked concerning CoPs. For example, if a CoP works for one organisation, will this necessarily mean that it will work for another? Can KM practices be transferred in this way? Are certain people likely to try to dominate the CoP, and if so, how could this problem be overcome?

Other areas for the creation and engendering of internal KM environments include e-learning, web conferencing, groupware, blogging, intranets and after action reviews. Thus, there are many ways in which small internal cultures can be created for the effective dissemination of knowledge and information.

There is a lack of space to consider different internal cultures further, therefore the focus for the rest of this section will be on communities of practice, as these internal cultures are particularly significant for KM today and are changing the way in which KM practices are currently operating.

Communities of practice

Wenger and Lave (1991) first coined the term 'communities of practice' and the term became entrenched in KM culture after Wenger's *Communities of Practice* (1999). CoPs are also sometimes known as 'knowledge networks'. Wenger describes a CoP as a network of people who share a common interest in a certain area of knowledge and are willing to work together and share knowledge over a period of time. Wenger believes that learning is a social activity and that people tend to learn best in groups. CoPs can vary in their characteristics. They can exist for a long time or just for a specific purpose, while some may be localised, and others are 'virtual communities'. Ives says that 'communities of practice are about connecting individuals with common interests into groups so experience and knowledge can be shared' (Ives, 2003: 3).

CoPs differ from other groups in a number of ways. Membership of CoPs is voluntary, and although the CoPs might have a stated goal, they are not obliged to have one. Neither do they necessarily have to deliver tangible results. CoPs can last as long as their members want.

Benefits of communities of practice

CoPs have many benefits. They can be vehicles for nurturing, developing, sharing and managing specialist knowledge, information and ideas. They can help to avoid workers from 'reinventing the wheel' and they can cut across boundaries in organisations and formal reporting and management lines. CoPs can create an environment that is conducive to the generation of new knowledge and ideas. They can also create a knowledge sharing culture and an environment for cultural change. They are also mainly self-organising.

Benefiting individual members

CoPs can also benefit individual community members in a number of ways. Members can gain knowledge on particular areas from other experts, for example, and can discuss issues in a more open and democratic way within the group. They can help members to feel more confident about their own personal knowledge and assist them with extracting important personal knowledge that can be shared within the group and organisation. New ideas can also be explored in a non-threatening environment. It can also help people to get to know each other better in the organisation, and help to enable people to trust each other more. If they are successful, they could also be potentially beneficial career-wise. However, there are also possible disadvantages for members, such as members' concern that sharing knowledge that will result in benefiting others within the organisation and the organisation itself, but not benefiting themselves. Trust within the CoP therefore becomes crucial.

Setting up a community of practice

How then can a CoP get started? They are often 'organic and self-organising' and come into existence in response to a specific need or problem. They are not usually created from a top-down managerial position. As the National Electronic Library for Health says concerning the formulation of CoPs:

> Communities of practice are organic and self-organising. Ideally they should emerge naturally. Organisations that have tried to create communities 'from the top down' have often failed. Communities can, however, be 'seeded'. Any area or function of your organisation where knowledge is not evenly distributed is a potential target for a community of practice. However, the impetus for a new community usually comes from the recognition of a specific need or problem. (National Electronic Library for Health, 2001: 2–3)

What, then, are some of the pre-conditions for establishing a CoP? A White Paper from SiteScape (2002), gives a list of characteristics for effective CoPs. These are:

1. members have a common interest or affinity;
2. members are often self-grouping;
3. members seek to share information;
4. members seek to further their understanding of practice of areas of interest;
5. members are loosely controlled;
6. membership must be quite large, if it is to be self-sustaining;
7. large communities are often moderated;
8. members are encouraged to read and write content;
9. most members value reading.

Characteristics 1–4 are usually in place in informal communities in every organisation. Sometimes a moderator is needed for a CoP.

Nurturing a community of practice

Once the CoP has been formulated, a number of areas need to be considered and explored. These include, for example, defining the scope – what is the domain of knowledge and who should the membership consist of? Who are the subject experts and will the membership be open or by invitation only? What are the common needs and interests of the group? In addition, what are the terms, purpose and references of the community, and what particular problems need to be addressed? What resources does the group have?

Communities also need to be nurtured, if they are to survive. Members' interest and involvement needs to be maintained, encouraged and nurtured. If the community is to be vibrant and to grow and develop then it can be helpful to recruit new members. Developing a body of knowledge and expertise is also very useful. That said, sometimes the community will fade away, if it is no longer needed.

Supporting and developing a community of practice

CoPs need to be supported and developed in a number of ways. Successful CoPs need support but not too much structure. Particular roles within the CoP can be developed, such as the roles of leader, facilitator and librarian/resource allocator. Consideration needs to be given to the resources that the community needs in order for it to be sustained, such as financial and human resources. CoPs can also be worthwhile sources for housing documents in themselves. As the National Electronic Library for Health says:

> Many communities are becoming the focal point within their organisations for documenting best practice, identifying valuable external resources, writing case studies, and developing frameworks, techniques and tools for their particular knowledge domain. (National Electronic Library for Health, 2001: 5)

Following discussions with a knowledge manager from UK company Shal, Ives (2003) reports that their experience was that CoPs do not need much resourcing and that facilitators only spend about half a day per fortnight in activities or research connected with the community. As such, CoPS did not take up much time, but good returns were gained from shared learning. Thus, CoPs should not be too consuming with respect to resources.

Concluding comment on communities of practice

CoPs are powerful internal cultures in many organisations today. They can provide good returns in facilitating effective KM flows, and for the sharing and distribution of knowledge and information throughout an organisation. However, as Ives says, 'because humans are involved, knowledge management is a mixture of art and science where "formulas for success" must be treated with caution, and outcomes can still surprise us' (Ives, 2002: 12).

Thus, CoPs can be exciting, but rather an unknown quantity. But for those willing to take the risks there are many likely benefits.

(Information for this section has been obtained from a number of sources, including Ives, 2003; National Electronic Library, 2001; SiteScape, 2002 and Wenger, 2002).

Conclusion

This section has considered internal cultures and KM, emphasising that there are many different subcultures within society, all with their own internal cultures. Many sociological studies have been undertaken on subcultures. The section then focused on communities of practice (CoPs) in some detail, as these internal cultures are a very important and valuable part of KM today, and are helping to make KM practices more successful in general.

External cultures

Introduction

External culture is the culture that exists across different organisations and across different countries. This section will largely focus on globalisation as an external KM culture and how it affects KM.

Globalisation

Definition of globalisation

Globalisation is not a new term. One hundred and fifty years ago, Marx and Engels predicted that globalisation was coming, saying that:

> All that is solid melts into air … the need of a constantly expanding market for its products chases the bourgeoisie over the whole surface of the globe. It must nestle everywhere, settle everywhere, establish connections everywhere. (Marx and Engels, 1848: 83)

Many different people have considered the meaning of globalisation, focusing on areas such as the 'death of distance', the exacerbation of international trade, a global approach to norms and values and the increased interconnectedness of the world. The House of Lords Select Committee on Economic Affairs considered some of these different definitions in their 2002 report on globalisation. The report refers to a cross-governmental departmental memorandum, for example, which highlights the fact that globalisation has both an economic and a political dimension. In an economic sense, it is concerned with accelerating international trade and capital and information flows, whereas the political dimension includes the diffusion of global norms and values, the spread of democracy and the proliferation of various treaties (House of Lords Select Committee on Economic Affairs, 2002: 12, Ev 1, para1). The House of Lords Select Committee concludes the section noting that it does not offer a simple definition of globalisation, but that:

> ...it is our view that the period of globalisation represents a new departure in world affairs. Partly this is to do with what has been called 'the death of distance', assisted by the absolute and relative decline in transport costs ... we have one world in an economic and cultural sense, which has not existed before. (House of Lords Select Committee on Economic Affairs, 2002: 18)

Meanwhile, Clare Short, then UK Secretary of State for International Development, has described globalisation as the 'growing interdependence and interconnectedness of the modern world' (Short, 2001: 17).

This includes the increasing ease of movement of goods, services, capital, people and information across different national borders. Such ease of movement is leading towards the creation of a single global economy, she argues. All this is taking place within the age of information technology. She also associates globalisation with the 'spread of democracy', the diffusion of global norms and values and the proliferation of global agreements and treaties.

Glenn Rikowski (2001), however, argues that we need to analyse globalisation at a deeper and more theoretical level. He says that there are four dimensions to globalisation; namely, cultural, the eroding of the power of nation states, commodification and labour taking on the 'value form'. With regard to the cultural dimension, Glenn Rikowski draws attention to the fact that there are two approaches to the cultural issue, but that these are contradictory. One is the recognition and appreciation of cultural differences, while the other is the homogenisation and the bringing together of different cultures into one overall global culture. He states that 'globalisation has been associated simultaneously with the cross-fertilisation and increasing hybridity of cultural forms and identities on the one hand and the homogenisation of culture on the other' (G. Rikowski, 2001: 8).

This contradiction reflects one of the many contradictions that are inbuilt into global capitalism itself and this has various implications for KM. On the one hand, for example, there is the need to recognise and be able to tap into the vast array of different knowledge that exists within different cultures. On the other hand, however, there is also a need to be able to examine areas where significant knowledge is being developed which transcends cultural differences, thereby reflecting and sharing knowledge that has been acquired through global cultural norms and values. To some extent, this can be achieved by the utilisation of effective KM practices, but it is always going to be very challenging, and various problems and contradictions will emerge. In terms of globalisation itself, however, it is impossible to have both the total homogenisation of culture and the diversity of culture at the same time.

Meanwhile, Tomlinson relates globalisation and culture saying that 'globalization lies at the heart of modern culture; cultural practices lie at the heart of globalization' (Tomlinson, 1999: 1).

Tomlinson says that globalisation is multidimensional and that culture can be seen to be one of its dimensions. Furthermore, he suggests that it is dialectic, as globalisation relies on input from the local level, as well as the fact that the local culture operates within a global setting and is influenced by a global culture. Thus, it is not a 'one-way process' that is 'cast in stone'. As Tomlinson says:

> Thinking about globalization in its cultural dimension also discloses its essentially dialectical character ... The fact that individual actions are intimately connected with large structural-institutional features of the social world via reflexivity means globalization is not a 'one-way' process of the determination of events by massive global structures, but involves at least the possibility for local intervention in global processes. (Tomlinson, 1999: 26)

Tomlinson argues that globalisation can disturb the way in which we usually think about culture, because culture tends to be associated with a fixed locality. Eade considers this fact within a sociological context, saying that 'an emphasis on boundedness and coherence traditionally dominated the sociological treatment of the idea of culture' (Eade, 1997: 25).

A sense of 'boundedness' and 'coherence' has been very powerful in sociology, particularly in functionalist approaches. Thus, in order to appreciate the connection between globalisation and culture, this 'fixed' notion needs to be overcome. Once again, an Open Marxist theoretical perspective is highly relevant here, as it recognises the dynamics and interrelationships of Marxist concepts, thereby challenging fixed notions, while at the same time enabling us to analyse global capitalism more effectively.

Meanwhile, Derber relates the 'culture of globalisation' to the market, shopping and buying products, saying that:

> The culture of globalization is based on the vision of billions of people newly liberated to make their own choices in a market offering dignity and endless delights [even though] you recognise that it is a fantasy for most of the world's people ... Engrossed shoppers rush around frantically, buying and buying as if making

up for centuries of deprivation and serfdom. It makes you a believer and makes clear that globalization will not disappear until a new, even brighter vision takes root. (Derber, 2003: 58)

However, globalisation should more accurately be called 'global capitalism', as I argue elsewhere (R. Rikowski, 2005a). Capitalism is now the dominant social, economic and political system in the world and it is pervading every angle of the global – i.e. it is becoming truly global. As I say:

There are many facets and aspects to globalisation or global capitalism and various definitions. Since the supposed death of communism, global capitalism now appears to stalk the earth. We are led to believe that it is the accepted order and, indeed, that we should celebrate it. This is why it is termed 'global capitalism', rather than simply 'capitalism', because of its seemingly all-pervading nature, although the preferred terminology is 'globalisation' as this camouflages the true reality to some extent and sounds more pleasant. (R. Rikowski, 2005a: 14)

The 'TINA' philosophy dominates today – 'there is no alternative' to global capitalism. I also challenge this notion in my globalisation book. Our understanding and analysis of KM and culture will be enhanced once we fully appreciate the fact that we live in a global capitalist world. This is in contrast to being fooled into the notion that we live in a nice, cosy globalisation world, where we are all one 'big, happy, global family'. So, we should really be referring to 'global capitalism' rather than 'globalisation'.

Thus, there are many different definitions of globalisation, some of which have been considered in this section, and briefly considered within the context of culture and KM.

Deterritorialisation and homogenisation

Tomlinson argues that the key to cultural impact of globalisation lies in the transformation of localities themselves, which is referred to as 'deterritorialisation' (Tomlinson, 1999: 29). However, Ulf Hannerz says that:

There is now a world culture, but we had better make sure we understand what this means ... No total homogenization of systems of meaning and expression has occurred, nor does it appear likely that there will be one for some time soon. But the world has become one network of social relationships, and between its different regions there is a flow of meanings as well as a flow of people and goods. (Hannerz, 1990: 237)

Thus, there is no actual homogenisation of systems, but there are networks of social relationships, Hannerz argues. There is a globalisation of culture in terms of complex connectivity, but no total interconnectedness – indeed, this would surely be quite impossible, given the wide range of different cultures that exist in the world today. So, instead we have deterritorialisation.

Hybridisation

'Hybridisation' is another term that is referred to in the literature. This concerns the mingling of different cultures from different territorial locations. Hybridisation can be a useful way of describing deterritorialisation. Deterritorialisation is not a one-way process either. As Tomlinson says, 'where there is deterritorialization there is also reterritorialization' (Tomlinson, 1999: 148) and that:

> ...we are all ... embodied and physically located. In this fundamental material sense the ties of culture location can never be completely severed and the locality continues to exercise its claims upon us as the physical situation of our lifeworld. So deterritorialization cannot ultimately mean the end of locality, but its transformation into a more complex cultural space. (Tomlinson, 1999: 149)

So, the power of the local community and its culture remains, but it is taking on a different form today, and the result is 'more complex cultural space'. Tomlinson also emphasises that:

> The possibility of cosmopolitanism is not ... ruled out by any iron logic of localism, but becomes focused on the cultural project of extending the field of relevance of mutuality to embrace a sense of distant others as symbolically; 'significant others'. (Tomlinson, 1999; 207)

This reflects, once again, the changing nature of the situation. Tomlinson also thinks that it is important not to forget the power of 'moral commitment, mutuality and solidarity' as it exists in modern societies at the local level. Furthermore, he argues that we cannot guarantee the building of any form of 'cosmopolitan solidarity', given the changing nature of the global world today. Thus, deterritorialisation does seem quite a useful term to explain some of the global changes taking place.

Global capitalist culture

Rather than a 'global culture', we should really be referring to a 'global capitalist culture'; similarly, I suggest we should really be referring to 'global capitalism' rather than 'globalisation'. Herbert Schiller (1979, 1985) says that the capitalist world is incorporating all societies into its orbit. Thus, the emphasis here is on global *capitalist* culture rather than global culture. He argues that capitalism determines the global culture itself, with its emphasis on the marketing and distribution of commodities, and on a consumerist mentality and value system.

Some, though, are sceptical about any notion of a 'global culture'. Anthony Smith (1991), a sociologist, argues that this potential global culture is 'fundamentally artificial', 'shallow', 'fluid and shapeless'. He says that it is constructed and that a global culture lacks a sense of temporal continuity and shared memories. This seems to me, however, to be a grossly over-simplistic analysis.

Meanwhile, Tomlinson says that culture does not transfer in a unilinear way and that there is not one clear 'uniform capitalist monoculture'. He says that 'movement between cultural/geographical areas always involves interpretation, translation, mutation, adaptation, and 'indigenisation' as the receiving culture brings its own cultural resources to bear' (Tomlinson, 1999: 84).

Tomlinson refers to Marx's vision of globalisation under communism (Tomlinson, 1999: 76–7) but argues that Marx underestimated the power of ethnic and religious attachments. Given the recent backlash to religion, perhaps religion is an even more powerful force than Marx and many others (including myself) have realised. However, this does not change the basic argument, as far as I am concerned – it just means that it will take longer to overcome religion and religious notions, and for humankind to free itself from the domination of capital in general.

Tomlinson also says that:

> ...arguments that extrapolate from the global ubiquity of capitalist consumer goods and media texts towards the vision of a uniform

capitalist monoculture are to be doubted precisely because they trade on a flawed concept of culture. (Tomlinson, 1999: 85)

Thus, Tomlinson argues that we cannot view the notion of global culture as a global capitalist culture, because this does not recognise the changing nature of culture and the fact that it goes through various mutation processes. Tomlinson implies that the notion of a global capitalist culture assumes that all other cultures can be, and indeed will be, subsumed under it. However, to present this argument in this simplistic and essentially flawed way is reductionist and it is not a helpful analysis. Glenn Rikowski refers to reductionism, saying that reductionism:

> In its general form ... is the notion that one type of category or social phenomena in reality represents another type of category. The reduction is made when we view the former principally or totally in terms of the latter. (G. Rikowski, 2005: 4)

An Open Marxist theoretical analysis is very much against any simplistic notion of reductionism, but instead, demonstrates the dynamic and ever-changing nature of global capitalism – and so it fully appreciates the dynamics embedded within global capitalism as well as the different cultures that exist within it.

Tomlinson argues that the key is the commodification of culture itself, rather than the influence of any one particular set of cultural goods. This is more important than focusing on 'world brands', he says. The commodification process is at the heart of Marxism, and as Marx made clear, any analysis of capitalism must begin with the commodity. So, Tomlinson is perhaps not quite as much 'at odds' with Marxism as he might think. Tomlinson also does say that the global capitalist monoculture needs to be taken seriously and that:

> ...commodification is now deeply structured into modern cultural life in the developed world, and this undeniably represents a distinct narrowing and convergence of cultural experience: a marshalling of 'what we do' into one particular form of doing it. (Tomlinson, 1999: 87–8)

'Commodification' is further considered in Chapter 11 of this book.

Managing knowledge across borders and building strategic alliances

When considering KM and external cultures it can also be useful to consider how knowledge is managed across borders and the building of strategic alliances in this regard. According to Steve Barth, 'There is nothing new about the idea of managing knowledge across borders ... What is the age-old tradition of telling stories around caravan campfires if not a form of international knowledge management?' (Barth, 2000: 1).

So, in one sense, there is nothing new in managing knowledge and information across borders – it is just that, today, it takes on a different form. Barth emphasises the importance of knowledge, saying that, 'beneath the borderless world's free-flow of capital, technology, production capacity and materials is the robust flow of knowledge' (Barth, 2000: 1).

Furthermore, globalisation has widened the field of competition and KM is one response to this. Barth says that, 'practiced in the multinational enterprise, KM can guarantee coordination, synchronize production, develop agility and simultaneously promote a cohesive corporate culture and present a consistent customer experience, regardless of location' (Barth, 2000: 2).

Managing knowledge in a dispersed organisation is difficult. However, managing knowledge across international borders is more complex than across corporate culture, so it is more important to understand ethnic cultures. Indeed, there is a need to consider why an enterprise needs a worldwide KM system.

KM can also assist with and play a part in the building of strategic alliances. Parise and Sasson consider this, saying that 'managers who can leverage information and knowledge across each stage of the alliance process will find that a knowledge-based approach is critical to the success of any partnership' (Parise and Sasson, 2002: 1).

According to Parise and Sasson, KM approaches to alliance management must be based on several important factors. First, they say that well-managed alliances can increase a company's financial returns, through their effective acquiring and utilisation of knowledge, arguing that:

> Firms can no longer develop all the resources, technologies and products to compete in today's dynamic marketplace, and so many of those firms use alliances to acquire the critical skills, knowledge and capabilities that they lack. (Parise and Sasson, 2002: 1)

Second, they say that companies form research and development alliances partly in order to be able to learn and internalise the know-how of their partners and that 'with companies that look on alliances as a way of learning from their partners, practices that enable knowledge sharing, creation, dissemination and internalisation become critical' (Parise and Sasson, 2002: 1).

Third, they add that an alliance KM capability is an important part of alliance success and that it is a differentiating factor. There have been high failure rates resulting from unsuccessful knowledge-based partnerships, so endeavouring to implement all this successfully becomes very important.

In conclusion, further consideration should perhaps be given to the topic of managing knowledge across borders, and building strategic alliances and the external culture in which they operate. Are there a number of different external cultures in existence, for example, or can just one or two external cultures be identified? Just how important is this external culture regarding KM practices? Does it enhance our understanding of global capitalism?

Conclusion

This section has considered external cultures and KM. Within this, it has focused on globalisation and the managing of knowledge across borders and strategic alliances. Regarding globalisation, it examined the meaning of globalisation itself and then considered some of the other terminology used in the associated literature. This included deterritorialisation, homogenisation, hybridisation and global capitalist culture. However, the most important concepts to analyse, as far as I am concerned, are 'global capitalism' and the 'global capitalist culture'.

Social culture

Introduction

In the past, the focus on culture and KM was largely on corporate or organisational culture, rather than 'social culture'. However, some people, such as Torrey and Datta (1998) have now started looking at social culture. The social element to knowledge is even now being talked about on weblogs. For example, Grey in his weblog 'Knowledge-at-work' says:

...knowledge is social rather than personal, needs verification and is difficult to capture. At a personal level, practices may be many times more important than tools, e.g. reciprocity, sharing, listening, supporting and coaching others, being well-linked and connected, being in dialog and the flow, inviting critique, engaging in creative abrasion – not things you can do alone on a desert island or in your individual cube! (Grey, 2004)

Why is social culture important then? It can be related to the importance of CoPs and tacit knowledge for the implementation of effective KM practices, over other factors such as simply using good IT systems. Furthermore, the successful extraction of value from intellectual labour requires more sophisticated and subtle processes, and an analysis of social culture becomes important for the furtherance of this – i.e. on how to get the knowledge worker/intellectual labourer to generate new ideas and impart their knowledge, thus enabling value to be extracted from intellectual labour, thereby ensuring the continued success of global capitalism.

Types of social cultures and their impact on knowledge and KM

How can we define social culture? Torrey and Datta say that social culture can be seen to be the culture of the society in which the organisation(s) exists. This can obviously be related to KM. An enterprise might have a culture that encourages subordinates to engage informally with superiors, for example, to encourage creativity, better communication, and better knowledge and information flows etc. This will clearly help to improve KM practices. However, such a culture might work well in an Israeli culture, even in a US one, for example, but might not work so well in Asian and Japanese environments. This is because the Japanese and Asian cultures tend to encourage subordinates to obey orders from their superiors. If this is reversed, then it is possible that Japanese and Asians will feel confused, and it might even lead to people being less creative and less willing to share their knowledge. Others might see it as an opportunity, but we need to be aware of the fact that simply changing practices and work procedures will not necessarily improve knowledge flows. Social culture can sometimes transcend work practices.

Torrey and Datta refer to a group of US managers that had to set up cross-functional high-performance teams across different corporations in Japan. This exercise illustrates some of the differences between US and

Japanese social cultures, and the impact that these differences can have on KM. The aim of the study was to create an open and free-flowing sharing of knowledge. Managers had to pass concepts along and transfer knowledge to their Japanese counterparts. All members of the teams participated in decision making and leadership was rotated so that a flatter structure was created. However, this did not work, as this was not the way in which the Japanese culture has traditionally operated. Instead, in their culture knowledge came from above and those in subordinate positions were not used to being involved in the free flow of information in this way, within a flatter structure.

In India and other parts of Southeast Asia the supposed 'right' to certain knowledge might depend on age and gender. Only men of a certain age and with a high economic and social status may have the right to 'know' information, or possess knowledge. As Torrey and Datta say, this 'may also cause severe problems in conducting international business across gender, age and status line. Business deals may not mature, conversations may not be frank' (Torrey and Datta, 1998: 2).

A culture of not wanting to advertise one's expertise might also inhibit knowledge sharing. A US executive that transferred to Australia, for example, found that a culture of 'mateship' discouraged individuals from drawing attention to their abilities (Davenport and Prusak, 1998).

Torrey and Datta also refer to a KM system that was developed in Korea. It was found that various culture barriers to knowledge sharing needed to be overcome. There was concern, for example, about expressing oneself openly, regardless of the topic or expertise in front of one's superiors. As Torrey and Datta say:

> Perhaps the most clearly articulated concern, was that 'experts' would see their prestige and position threatened by sharing their knowledge through the system – the 'knowledge hoarding' problem that has shown up all over the world. (Torrey and Datta, 1998: 2)

Thus, experts were concerned that sharing their knowledge could threaten their position. This could obviously lead to knowledge hoarding.

There is also the concept of the 'knowledge community'. A knowledge community can nurture a sense of community and trust. However, it is impossible to really have a seamless knowledge community and as Torrey and Datta say, 'since the practices of knowledge management, knowledge sharing and knowledge creation differ from culture to culture, a seamless knowledge community would be a practical impossibility' (Torrey and Datta, 1998: 3).

It is impossible to separate out an organisation from the social culture in which it operates. However, Torrey and Datta say that each corporation creates its own culture.

> ...many of the largest and most successful multi-national or global concerns go to great lengths to establish a strong organisational culture that is homogeneous across all part of the enterprise and transcends national or social culture. (Torrey and Datta, 1998: 2)

Clearly then, social culture, organisational culture and national culture are all very interrelated and affect one another.

Knowledge sharing

Some form of knowledge sharing is necessary for any effective KM practices. Hustings and Michailova refer to knowledge sharing saying that 'knowledge sharing can be defined as referring more to a learning process whereby there is an assimilation of ideas' (Hustings and Michailova, 2004: 2).

How, then, does social culture affect the sharing of knowledge? Knowledge sharing is more entrenched in the social culture of many traditional Eastern cultures than it is in cultures in the developed world, because of their collectivist approach. Torrey and Datta cited a Korean example that aimed to counteract knowledge hoarding by focusing on strong group loyalty bonds and building strong teams. They said that 'team loyalty and competitive spirit would encourage both the experts to yield up their personal stock of knowledge and others to contribute more openly' (Torrey and Datta, 1998: 5).

However, the developed world could also benefit from more knowledge sharing, to help to counteract the individualistic approach, which can often dominate. There is also the problem, though, that people in the developing world can be further exploited because of their collectivist/sharing culture.

Torrey and Datta emphasise the importance of taking social culture into account when trying to develop 'knowledge sharing environments' in an organisation, saying that:

> If global enterprises desire to take advantage of their organisational intellectual wealth, they should seek to understand the benefits of the social and cultural situations in which they exist and attempt to create an articulate form for acting on these concepts. The mistake

many business organisations make is to jump too readily to conclusions about what is needed to create a knowledge sharing environment without taking into account the underlying social culture. (Torrey and Datta, 1998: 6)

Thus, organisations, in general, should give more attention to the social culture in which they operate.

Conclusion

This section has focused on social culture and how it can influence KM practices. Torrey and Datta think that organisations suffer through a lack of knowledge and understanding about the social and cultural situations that are embedded within them. They say:

> We believe that, from the lack of knowledge about unfamiliarity with different social milieu and cultural situations, organisations fail to see the richness of support for knowledge management inherent in the various cultural frameworks of their global enterprises. (Torrey and Datta, 1998: 5)

Torrey and Datta also suggest that if we do not take social culture into account, it will be very difficult to implement KM successfully. Furthermore, they suggest that with the globalisation of modern business enterprises it becomes more important to take into account different national and social cultures. They think that it is particularly important that we focus more on non-western cultures in this regard. Torrey and Datta conclude by saying that 'there is a wealth of knowledge available in the world's cultures that can vastly enrich the knowledge management culture of today's global business enterprise. It is there waiting to be explored' (Torrey and Datta, 1998: 6).

Thus, further consideration needs to be given to social culture when implementing KM practices.

Summary

This chapter has focused on a number of important areas concerning KM and culture: namely, internal cultures and KM, focusing mainly on communities of practice, external cultures and KM, with the emphasis on globalisation, and social culture. All this helps to illustrate the complexity of the subject of KM and culture overall and the fact that many different factors need to be taken into consideration.

Note

The original idea for exploring the topic of KM and culture was first suggested to me by George Bell, MBA Course Director at London South Bank University, in the Faculty of Business, Computing and Information Management. The thinking behind this was that this topic could form part of the Masters in Business Administration programme. Hopefully, in the future, this will prove to be a realistic possibility.

An Open Marxist theoretical analysis of knowledge management within and across cultures

Ruth Rikowski

This section has covered a large number of areas in regard to knowledge management (KM) within and across cultures. In this chapter, I will place KM and culture within an Open Marxist theoretical perspective.

The concept of *value* is essential for an understanding of KM and culture, I would suggest. I explore a Marxist analysis of KM in some detail, in Chapter 11 of this book (focusing in particular on value and the commodity), as well as Open Marxism specifically, so this chapter will be quite short. It will extrapolate relevant parts from Chapter 11, to help us to understand and analyse the topic of KM within and across cultures. In this regard, I am only touching the surface. Furthermore, the focus will be largely restricted to the cultural differences between the developing world and the developed world.

The key point I want to make is that the utilisation of effective KM practices is more important for cultures in the developed world than for those in the developed world. Furthermore, cultures in the developed world need to be seen to working in cooperation with KM and KM trends, to ensure that KM practices are implemented successfully. To understand why this is the case, we need to return to Marx's concepts of 'labour', 'value', 'the commodity' and 'capital'. Value is the substance of the social universe of capital. As Neary and Rikowski say, 'We live in the social universe of capital. This is the social universe that was the focus of Marx's three volumes of *Capital*. The substance of this social universe is value' (Neary and Rikowski, 2002: 60).

Furthermore, in Postone's critique of capitalism he refers to the 'essential relational structures' of this 'social universe' (Postone, 1996: 143).

Workers undertake two types of labour – manual and intellectual – from which value is created. Logically, it is only possible for labourers to undertake these two types of labour. They always undertake *both* types of labour, but one type of labour will tend to exhaust the labourer more than the other. Furthermore, one type of labour will tend to result in the creation and extraction of more value than the other. Thus, capitalism goes through various phases. In the industrial revolution, it was largely manual labour that exhausted the labourer, and it was the creation and extraction of value from this manual labour that ensured the continued success of the industrial revolution while the focus was on the production of manufactured goods. In the knowledge revolution, however, intellectual labour exhausts the worker, and it is the creation and extraction of value from intellectual labour that ensures the continued success of the knowledge revolution. A simple example can be given here. A computer programmer undertakes both manual and intellectual labour. The programmer types into a keyboard (manual labour) and designs and creates programming code and computer programs (intellectual labour). However, it is the creating and designing of computer programs that exhausts the worker (and the thinking that is involved with this), and value is largely extracted from this intellectual labour. Thereby, software packages, for example, are created, commodified and sold in the marketplace for profit, and this profit can only ever be derived from value. All this ensures the success of the company and the continuation and perpetuation of the knowledge revolution and thus, of capitalism itself. Thus, in the knowledge revolution the focus is on intangible goods and intellectual labour.

Capitalism is always seeking to create new commodities – this is its *raison d'etre*. It needs then to be forever finding new ways to create and extract value from labour, so that this value can then be embedded in these commodities. All this is explored further in Chapter 11. The important point to emphasise here though is that because of all this, capitalism today needs to be creating and extracting more value from intellectual labour.

Hence, in the developed world – which is at the forefront in terms of pushing forward the global capitalist agenda, the knowledge revolution is gathering pace at an ever-accelerating rate. Within this, effective KM practices become necessary, in order to effectively extract value from intellectual labour. The question then becomes one of how to extract ideas, knowledge, information etc. effectively out of the intellectual labourer. This can even include knowledge that the labourer did not know that they had – unconscious tacit knowledge. For this reason, creating effective KM practices in the developed world becomes more important than creating effective KM practices in the developing world. Subtle processes need to be introduced, in order to be able to obtain ideas and knowledge out of labourers effectively. Considerable thought, through the utilisation of effective KM practices, needs to be given to this.

In the developed world, the focus is more on manual labour, and the creation of manufacturing goods, which are obviously still necessary. For this reason, KM practices in the developed world are bound to be more primitive than those in the developed world. In addition, while they must adapt to the cultures of those in the developing world, this will always have to be secondary to the culture of the developed world, as will be reflected in their KM practices. Furthermore, to the extent to which the developing world seems to 'care' about the developing world in regard to preserving its culture and helping it in regard to topics such as KM and organisational learning (as outlined by Hovland, 2003, for example), depends only as long as this fits in with the overall global capitalist agenda. It is not being undertaken for humanitarian reasons per se.

In what other ways then can an Open Marxist analysis be applied to KM within and across cultures? Can Marxism be applied to Hofstede's work, for example? As far as I am concerned, Marxism provides a better theoretical analysis and understanding of global capitalism than other social scientific theories do, so a Marxist analysis can be applied to any social, economic and political situation in the modern world. This is not to say that we should deify Marx – far from it. If some of Marx's concepts, tools and ideas no longer apply for any particular aspect of the global capitalist world today, then they should be abandoned, but this does not change the fact that Marx's work, in general, provides a far better understanding, analysis and explanation of capitalism than other theories. Sometimes we simply need to develop, change and apply it.

Thus, while Hofsteded's five dimensions can help us to understand different cultures and how they operate, this does not lessen the significance of Marxism at all. Marxism focuses on the big picture – what makes capitalism tick. Within that bigger picture, variations and cultural differences will emerge. With regard to Hofstede's uncertainty avoidance dimension, for example, some cultures can handle uncertainty better than others, as Hofstede makes clear. But as far as capitalism is concerned, it needs some people, organisations and cultures that can handle uncertainty, but it also needs some that cannot handle it so well. An uncertainty culture can create an environment where people are more likely to come up with original ideas, for example, which can benefit the organisation, increase profits, and thereby help to perpetuate capitalism itself. However, too much uncertainty could mean that some of the basic work would not be done. So, cultures that are high on uncertainty avoidance are also needed in capitalism. It then becomes a matter of fitting this all together in the jigsaw, and this reflects one of the many contradictions in capitalism. There is not the space to explore this further in this book, but I hope that the task that needs to be done has become somewhat clearer.

In conclusion, I have laid the groundwork for a Marxist theoretical analysis of KM within and across cultures. In particular, I have highlighted the fact that it is more important for cultures in the developed world to be able to work successfully with KM, because of the increasing importance of intellectual labour and intangible assets for the furtherance of global capitalism. This does not mean, however, that cultures in the developed world will necessarily be more conducive to effective KM practices. Cultures in the developed world often focus on an individualistic approach, for example, rather than a collectivist approach, yet in order for knowledge to flow freely, a collectivist approach is important. In this regard, many cultures in the developing world might well be able to implement KM practices more effectively. However, elements of individualism are also necessary, in order to engender an environment that is conducive to the creation of new ideas, which is needed for the extraction of value and for the advancement of KM. Thus, once again, the situation is complex. But objectively, there is a need for better KM practices in the developed world than in the developing world.

Furthermore, knowledge is always needed, whether one lives in a culture that is dominated by the production of tangible goods, or whether one lives in a culture that is increasingly preoccupied with the production of intangible goods. Knowledge is needed to be able to design a car or a washing machine, for example – i.e. to be able to design and then produce manufactured goods. In the knowledge revolution, however, knowledge is being marketed in its own right, such as through patents, and the creation and extraction of value from intellectual labour becomes of ever-increasing importance.

There is a need for further Open Marxist analysis on other areas of KM and culture. However, we must also try to avoid the danger of letting these other issues detract us from the core analysis – which revolves around how to most effectively understand and analyse global capitalism itself. To that extent, my Marxist analysis of KM in the developed and the developing world and the importance of intellectual labour in this regard, remains key.

Part 4
Theoretical perspectives

There are two chapters in this theoretical section – the first by Dr Leburn Rose, Head of the Department of Mathematics, Statistics and Foundation Studies at London South Bank University and the second by myself. Once again, there are many different theoretical perspectives on knowledge management (KM) that could be examined, although those that are directly related to KM are often very inadequate, and indeed, many could hardly be called theories at all. Instead, they are just models and tools to help KM practitioners and experts to implement KM more effectively. I explore some of these tools, charts and diagrams in two articles of mine (R. Rikowski, 2000a, 2000b) and demonstrate some of the inadequacies of such approaches. I also consider why we need to re-examine philosophical perspectives on knowledge. From these early articles, I then moved on to examine KM from a much deeper theoretical perspective and some of this work will be examined in this section.

Thus, both Dr Leburn Rose and I seek to get beyond this surface approach. I will be examining KM from a Marxist social scientific theoretical perspective, while Leburn Rose examines KM from a scientific theoretical perspective, drawing on the laws of thermodynamics. Interesting parallels can be drawn between these two theoretical perspectives – it does not have to be an either/or situation. This in particular, is in relation to energy and value. I suggest that science and social science need to be brought together more in this way, both in KM and in other areas of life, and I hope more progress can be made in this regard, in the future. Various great thinkers and theoreticians throughout history have recognised the need for this. We must remember, for example that Einstein, while being a scientist, had very clear views about the type of social universe that he wanted to live in – i.e. he wanted to live in a socialist world. But he also realised that great advances needed to be made in economics as a social scientific theory, before a better social world could ever begin to be imagined, let alone realised.

Dr Leburn Rose aims to understand knowledge management concepts through the three laws of thermodynamics and the concepts of energy. His chapter focuses on thermodynamic and energy principles, which are then related to knowledge. In particular, Rose builds on Nonaka and Takeuchi's knowledge work, arguing that while their work has provided a sound foundation for an analysis of KM within organisations, it is also inadequate in some ways, because it does not fully appreciate the dynamics of the knowledge process. The dynamics of life need to be appreciated more in general. Rose moves beyond Nonaka and Takeuchi's (1995) model and he designs an alternative schema for knowledge creation in an organisation.

Rose argues that the relevance of thermodynamics lies in the fact that organisations can be described as systems into which various resources, such as intellectual capital and energy (which, as previously stated, can be related to value), undergo transformations and then 'leave the system in the form of products and/or services' (i.e. as commodities – thereby, once again, returning to the relevance of Marxism).

Rose begins his chapter by referring to the three laws of thermodynamics, which are all idealised. The first law establishes the principle that in a totally closed system, it is not possible to lose energy, but only to change its form. The second law suggests that even if a system is totally isolated from its surroundings, the energy flows that take place will result in degrading the high-grade energy of the system to low-grade energy, thus causing an 'irreversible decline of the system's total energy'. Meanwhile, the third law 'establishes an idealised physical limit at zero entropy (and zero energy) in an isolated system, which irrespective of the number of energy flow processes that occur, can only be approached, but never actually reached'.

This means that successive energy flows will 'progressively degrade the system' and various strategies are needed to try to maintain the system's operation as far as possible from the equilibrium state.

While the science of thermodynamics 'dictates that flow processes should result in a change in state, shape or location of the object that absorbs the quantity of energy', this can also be related to organisational structure, Rose argues. He says that:

> ...where organisations manage to achieve a good degree of alignment between their communication (human and technological) and structural architectures, predictions on the basis

of thermodynamics are likely to yield results that are close to the true valuations of their flow processes.

In this way, thermodynamics can provide a useful tool for modelling knowledge flow processes. But 'many problems arising from weaker causality between flow processes stem from poor alignment of the architectures that make up the organisation'.

Instead, the continuity of flow processes, including knowledge flows, can be interrupted in an organisation for various reasons, such as through political and cultural conflict. Organisations devise various schemes and methods, in an endeavour to overcome this problem.

Rose then relates this energy to knowledge in a very innovative way. He considers Nonaka and Takeuchi's tacit and explicit knowledge model, arguing that while their model is useful it might be rather too simplistic and idealised. Instead:

> A richer interpretation of the tacit-explicit and structure-process relationships may be to conceive them as idealistic states on a spectrum, which describes knowledge states that are part tacit, part explicit, part structure and part process.

In this way, knowledge can be seen to be dynamic and changing rather than static, and interesting parallels can also be drawn with an open Marxist dynamic approach.

From here, Rose formulates an alternative schema for knowledge creation in an organisation, which proposes four processes through which knowledge is transferred: conduction, convection, radiation and combustion. He says that each process is enveloped by a unique combination of 'knowledge form' and 'organisational architecture'. These processes can be seen to be on a continuum from tacit-organic through to explicit-rigid. Furthermore, the firm can be represented in two dimensions – architecture and knowledge forms. The architecture can be seen to be on a continuum of organic to rigid, and knowledge forms on a continuum of tacit to explicit, and firms can be positioned along this continuum. He concludes by making the point that 'the science of thermodynamics offers an intriguing and fresh perspective for understanding the nature and scope of knowledge management in organisations'.

In Chapter 11, I outline an Open Marxist theoretical analysis of KM. This approach appreciates the ever-changing nature of social systems. I first consider the evolutionary nature of social systems and the evolutionary nature of subsystems within each phase. I suggest that this evolutionary process needs to be established as a fact/theory, in the same way that Darwin's evolution of the species is accepted as a fact/theory and is taught in schools. Thus, the evolutionary nature of social systems should also be taught in schools. Only once we accept this fact, and have a firm grasp of it, can we then really seek to change the tide – i.e. be proactive and try to change our social system, rather than merely waiting for evolutionary processes to take their course. From here, I focus on the commodity and the extension of the commodification process, highlighting that, following on from Marx, we need to begin our analysis of capitalism with the commodity. Commodities have a physical natural form and a value form. The physical form of a commodity consists of the different materials and substances that make up the physical components of a commodity, such as plastic, wood and iron. However, the value form can only be created through human labour. There are two different types of value in the commodity – use-value and exchange-value, and I examine both types in this chapter. Value must also be distinguished from use-value and exchange-value, and as Glenn Rikowski (2002) says, value is social energy.

This is followed by a section on value, and the fact that capitalism needs to be forever creating value from labour. This section also considers surplus value and added value, the valorisation of value and the law of value. For example, with regard to these, I say that:

> Value is continually expanded and perpetuated and it becomes a dynamic force, multiplying itself time and time again in capitalism. This is accomplished through the creation of and then the continual expansion of surplus value. Surplus value becomes a 'dynamic totality', which Postone refers to as the 'valorisation of value', the 'valorisation process' or 'self-valorising value.'

From here, I move on to emphasise how value is created and extracted from labour, and that only labour can create value. Workers undertake two types of labour: manual labour and intellectual labour. But in the knowledge revolution, there is a greater exertion of intellectual labour than manual labour in the developed world. Value is increasingly being extracted from this intellectual labour. I then consider the fact that it is impossible to determine the length of the working day for intellectual labour within this scenario. Thus, effective KM practices become crucial, in order to be able to extract the ideas, knowledge and information out of the knowledge worker, or more accurately, out of intellectual labour, thereby creating and extracting value from intellectual labour.

From here, I focus on the objectification of labour, the value of Open Marxism as opposed to traditional Marxism and social scientific theory in general and Marxism. An Open Marxist approach appreciates the dynamic, ever-changing nature of capitalism, while Marxism uncovers the fact that there is a need for more rigorous social scientific theory in general. I conclude by emphasising that we need to overthrow capitalism and abolish value as its means of sustenance within the commodity. Furthermore, I argue that we need to find ways in which our knowledge and understanding can be used to liberate us rather than dominate us.

Thermodynamics and knowledge: principles and implications
Leburn Rose

Introduction

The gradual emergence of knowledge management in recent years has accompanied much deliberation on the concepts, themes, frameworks and practices that should define the discipline. There is a wide body of literature aimed at addressing knowledge management both conceptually and in practice (Polanyi, 1966; Nonaka, 1991; Nonaka and Takeuchi, 1995; Zack, 1999a, 1999b; Gao and Li, 2003). One major review by Kakabadse et al. (2003) presented knowledge management as a multi-disciplinary 'field of thinking and praxis' consisting of multiple approaches and modelling perspectives. These differing knowledge management perspectives range from the philosophical, cognitive, networking, community of practice, through to the quantum theoretical.

One important implication of seeing the knowledge management discipline in different but complementary ways is that organisations themselves could well consist of different approaches to, and ways of perceiving knowledge. As such, the idea of seeing the organisation as a landscape consisting of spaces in which knowledge is conceived of, and used in different ways, holds intriguing possibilities for developing knowledge management strategies.

The science of thermodynamics lies behind much of what we experience and take for granted in the physical world around us, and the organisations in which we work. The laws of thermodynamics encompass a wide range of phenomena from interactions at the molecular level to the unlocking of much of the secrets that lie in our universe. At the same time, these laws also provide important insights into the complex interactions between the processes and structures within our organisations.

This chapter uses thermodynamic and energy principles as a conceptual basis for deriving definitions of data, information and knowledge. From the synthesis of these definitions, a clearer understanding of the difference between information management and knowledge management is then articulated. A framework for managing knowledge in organisations that accounts for the different ways in which knowledge is conceived and used is then presented and described. This framework proposes that organisations consist of four distinct knowledge spaces, in which the knowledge created and/or converted emerges from the nature and purpose of the physical space.

The science of thermodynamics

Thermodynamics is defined as:

> that branch of physics which is concerned with the storage, transformation and dissipation of energy, including the flow of heat from which the term is derived. (Heylighen, 2005)

It is enshrined within three fundamental laws of nature that govern energy, biological and ecological processes. The relevance of thermodynamics rests on the notion that organisations may in general be described as systems into which resources such as intellectual capital, raw materials and energy flow, undergo transformation, and leave the system in the form of products and/or services. Of particular interest to thermodynamics are the nature and characterisation of the process interactions that organisations undergo during the transformation of inputs into outputs, and the relative efficiencies of these process interactions. The principles of thermodynamics also offer a powerful analogy for conceptualising data, information and knowledge, and for understanding the systemic processes that lead to organisational learning.

The first law of thermodynamics establishes the principle that in a totally closed system, it is not possible to lose energy, but merely to 'transform' it to another form. This law establishes the principle of the 'conservation of energy' within a system's flow processes, and in these circumstances it is neither possible to increase the total quantity of energy originating from the system, nor to 'get something for nothing'.[1]

By contrast, the second law of thermodynamics is a subtle, but highly significant corollary of the first law. For it suggests that even if the system remains totally isolated from its surroundings, the energy flows that take place will, to a lesser or greater degree, be associated with losses from the totality of the system's energy. This is the law of entropy[2] associated with closed systems, and is of fundamental importance in understanding that successive energy flows will result in irreversible decline of the system's total energy. Thus, in closed systems involving energy transformation processes, 'it is not even possible to break-even'.[3]

The third law of thermodynamics establishes an idealised physical limit at zero entropy (and zero energy) in an isolated system, which irrespective of the number of energy flow processes that occur, can only be approached, but never actually reached. It is not possible for the elements of this system to transfer energy from the idealised zero energy state. So as successive energy flow processes occur from higher to lower energy states, and fractions of the system's total energy are ceded to other elements in accordance with the second law, it becomes clear why the idealised state of absolute zero can never be obtained. This means that once initiated within the system, successive energy flow processes will, ad infinitum, progressively degrade the system. In turn, this creates a condition in which all entities within the system approach equilibrium one with another. In this sense, the third law initiates a game from which we cannot extricate ourselves.[4] So to slow down the inevitable decline of the system, strategies are needed for maintaining operation of the isolated system as far as possible from the its equilibrium state. In this way for an isolated system to survive, it is bound to operate at energy levels occurring far-from-equilibrium.[5]

Matter, fuel and energy versus data, information and knowledge

When a gaseous fluid is heated, the energy transferred reveals itself in the excitation of the molecules that constitute the fluid. The more heat is applied, the greater will be the state of excitation of molecules.[6] The heat applied to the fluid is converted into molecular kinetic energy, and confers a capability for the fluid to circulate its surroundings. While this chain of events describes how heat (a motive force) energises a fluid and causes it to circulate, does it present a plausible explanation of the circulation of knowledge in an organisation? In their most basic form, the molecules of a fluid exist purely as matter. However, to be constituted as a gas such as methane, these elements of matter would need to assume a structural form. Methane is thus a specific structural form consisting of a single molecule of carbon and four molecules of hydrogen. Energy would thus be defined as the result of the chemical combustion of methane in a manner that produces the potential to do useful work.

There is a remarkable analogy between the physical relations of matter, fuel and energy, and the organisational relations of data, information and knowledge. If data are analogous to molecules in their basic form, then like fuel, information is bits of data that exist also in structural form. Therefore, it follows that as energy results from the chemical combustion of fuel, likewise, knowledge[7] could also be the psychosocial processing of information in a form that achieves added value. As with the conversion of matter to fuel, the first and second laws of thermodynamics suggest important consequences for converting data to information.

Geological and chemical processes contrive to convert matter to fuel over geological time-spans. But set against the enormity of these time-spans, the period of a century and a half over which the world's hydrocarbons (such as methane) have been exploited is by comparison infinitesimally small. Hence the continued exploitation of fuel sources at rates that exceed those of their replenishment will result in exhaustion of fuel supplies. This principle of the finiteness of energy resources is directly analogous to the principle of the finiteness of information resources. In converting data to information, the most accessible (or valuable) forms are likely to be exploited initially. When the scarcity value of these accessible forms diminishes they are then abandoned, and richer sources of data and denser forms of information are sought. Thus the consequence of the continued mining of data will be a progressive reduction of the utility (or added value potential) of information. This describes information's scarcity or economic quality. In defining the scope of information management, it thus concerns decisions within the organisation about where to strike the balance between the form of information needed and the quality and cost of data with which it is to be produced.

A further consequence of the second law of thermodynamics arises from the notion that knowledge results from the psycho-social processing of information. Like energy, once knowledge is created there will be a natural tendency for it to diffuse. This process of diffusion occurs through various carriers and/or repositories, which may be within or external to the organisation, and each responsible for a fractional loss of knowledge's overall potential. Thus, once knowledge is diffused (disaggregated), it cannot be re-constituted. Losses of knowledge are, therefore, inevitable and avoidable, and can only be slowed down. In effect, this is knowledge's entropy or (irreversible) quality. In contrast to information management, knowledge management thus concerns a different set of decisions within the organisation; namely, how to balance the natural losses of knowledge the organisation must undergo with the need to sustain and develop its mission-critical knowledge capital.

Conduction, convection, radiation and combustion

The three modes of energy transfer provide important insights regarding the transfer of knowledge through the objects, physical spaces and processes in organisations. The first of these, conduction, describes the process of energy diffusion through direct physical contact between objects. The logical connection between objects is in this case determined by the flow of energy from objects at a higher temperature (or potential) to those at lower temperature. The conductive efficiency would also depend largely on the relative ease with which energy is transferred between connected objects. The second mode, referred to as convective energy transfer, is where diffusion takes place by means of a buoyancy effect, resulting in the cyclical replacement of warmer, rarer fluid currents in a physical space with denser, cooler air. The source of and motive force for convective energy transfer would probably be a radiant heat source. In addition, the convective flux would depend on factors such as the density of the convective medium, the intensity of the radiant source, and the pressure differential between the warmer and cooler air currents. The final of these modes, radiation, is where energy is diffused from one object to another, but with no physical contact between objects. Here the intensity of radiation will depend on factors such as the temperature of the source object, the proximity between objects, and properties of the medium across which the radiant energy is transferred. The process of combustion differs from conduction, radiation and convection, in that while the former process creates energy, the latter three processes facilitate energy transfer. Combustion is a chemical process in which substances react together to produce a significant rise in temperature and the emission of light. With a gaseous fluid, combustion would arise from the synthesis of matter in two structural forms (e.g. methane and oxygen) in the presence of a source of ignition or catalyst. Combustion is also a highly inefficient process that demands the obliteration of significantly higher proportions of potential energy to produce useful energy. Wasted energy, or, increased thermodynamic entropy as dictated by the second law of thermodynamics, is thus a logical consequence of the production of useful work. Combustion is also not a 'clean' process of synthesis and transformation, as it is always associated with the production of by-products. Some of these by-products may be benign, others may be inert substances that help to moderate the consequent rise in combustion temperature, and others may be harmful. Finally, efficient combustion demands an environment in which the proportions of the substances and the temperature of ignition are optimally controlled and maintained.

Thermodynamics and organisation

The use of thermodynamic principles as a means of understanding organisational transformation raises a number of interesting questions about the correspondence between thermodynamic and organisational concepts. Can thermodynamic energy also be conceptualised as 'organisational energy' in its various forms? How far can the concept of energy be ascribed to the inputs and outputs of real organisations? Does the thermodynamic notion break down when the problems of quantification and use of energy are confronted within the organisation?

Classical physics defines energy as the capacity of a physical agent to do work. The movement of an entity over a particular distance, as are the awesome and destructive forces liberated by earthquakes and hurricanes, are all examples of mechanical work. Similarly, the flow of heat from an entity of higher temperature to one of lower temperature provides an example of a thermodynamic flow process. Energy is also endowed with an ability to be transformed into different forms and to be stored in different ways. The storage of energy in a flywheel, in chemical formulations, and behind large dams provides examples of the capacity for storing energy.

Among the transformed and transforming inputs to the organisation, only fuel can strictly be described as energy in the thermodynamic sense. While all other inputs, including capital, human resources and technology are expended in the organisation's business processes, they do not, at least in the short term, undergo a change of physical state. However, one way in which the thermodynamic concept of energy may correspond with the notion of 'organisational energy' is to conceive of such inputs as possessing 'potential energy', much akin to that stored at a height in a water reservoir, which is brought into use when needed. In this way, these particular inputs could also be regarded as potentially degradable over the medium or longer term of the organisation, and as such be subject to the second law of thermodynamics. A practical example would be the application of depreciation to a fixed asset to reflect the incremental loss of value associated with its use over a fixed time period during the life of the organisation. An adjustment of this kind would prevent an 'over-estimation' of the organisation's net book value, and thereby help to slow down the rate of growth of entropy.

In a strict sense, the science of thermodynamics dictates that flow processes should result in a change in state, shape, or location of the object that absorbs the quantity of energy. There is a direct relationship – a causality or connectivity – between flow processes. Further constraints imposed by the first and second laws of thermodynamics on these flow processes also dictate the conditions, direction and relative efficiencies by which transfers of energy should take place.

In organisations, causality or connectivity among individuals, groups and departments is more often indirect, than direct; especially where the organisation has a traditional architecture that prevents the natural flow of ideas across departments or functions. In this respect, because causality is more likely to arise from indirect or secondary effects, there is significant potential in real organisations for the dissipation of thermodynamic energy. In addition, factors such as structural inflexibility, and political and cultural conflict, which are a daily feature of organisational life, can undermine the continuity of flow processes, and result in further diffusion of an organisation's finite energies. The strong causal relationship between flow processes, which the science of thermodynamics expects, but which real organisations cannot deliver, is probably more accurately depicted by a causality that is weaker, fuzzier and chaotic. In this important context, the science of thermodynamics may fail to provide an appropriate basis for determining the complex web of causality that is a feature of all organisations. This is not to say that thermodynamics is not valid for all organisational architectures. The point is that where organisations manage to achieve a good degree of alignment between their communication (human and technological) and structural architectures, predictions on the basis of thermodynamics are likely to yield results that are closer to the true valuations of their flow processes. It follows, therefore, that many problems arising from weaker causality between flow processes stem from poor alignment of the architectures that make up the organisation.

The contribution of direct labour[8] (mechanical work) to the business processes of organisations is self-evident, and within the scope of these processes, thermodynamic principles can help to quantify energy flows. However, the increasing significance of knowledge work in the last 25 years or so raises an important issue of the valuation of work in ways that recognise the central role of knowledge in the performance of the modern organisation. Concomitant with this rise of knowledge work has been the progressive deconstruction of the traditional organisational structure into flatter and more flexible architectures capable of responding to crises and change imposed by the business environment. As a consequence of the challenges of globalisation, newer organisational architectures with fuzzy boundaries have also emerged. One case in point is Nike's 'hub to spoke' organisational architecture designed to maintain its core competences and capabilities in marketing, design and innovation at the hub of the organisation while off-shoring its manufacturing function to overseas suppliers. Among the vast array of organisations, those that still possess strong elements of the traditional architecture, are likely to lend themselves more readily to the valuation of mechanical and intellectual work on the basis of thermodynamic principles. For in these organisations, accounting methods and conventions have long recognised at least the pecuniary contributions of mechanical and intellectual (managerial) work. However, for newer organisations whose prime capabilities and competences lie significantly in knowledge work and whose workers are mobile, the thermodynamic valuation of their work becomes problematic in terms of its quantification and auditing. Therefore, while all organisations to some degree lend themselves to valuation on thermodynamic grounds, the efficiency with which their mechanical and intellectual work can be valued will depend on the organisation's architecture, and the extent to which it engages in work that is predominantly mechanical or knowledge-based.

Knowledge creation as dynamic, but not necessarily spirals

In the same way that energy can be stored in various physical media, there are also a number of repositories in which knowledge is stored within the organisational boundary. Some of these include written reports, databases, design specifications, rituals and stories, and experience. Although Nonaka and Takeuchi (1995) categorise this knowledge in terms of the two broad forms of tacit and explicit, this bipolar conception may be misleading. To categorise knowledge in this way serves merely to reinforce the structure-process[9] paradox and to underplay the possibility that structure and process may well be two sides of the same coin. A richer interpretation of the tacit-explicit and structure-process relationships may be to conceive them as idealistic states on a spectrum, which describe knowledge states that are part tacit, part explicit, part structure, and part process. In this way, what emerges is a more enlightened notion of knowledge as an entity that is dynamic and changing, rather than a set of bipolar stationary states. This proposition thus invites us to consider knowledge transfer media in more creative ways.

For example, a written report, according to the Nonaka and Takeuchi conception would be categorised as a repository of explicit knowledge. It is clear, however, that for knowledge conversion or creation to occur, a more dynamic perspective of this written report as a catalyst for change would need to be taken. The project team would aim initially to internalise the content, conclusions and recommendations of the written report into the tacit form needed for mental processing. Implementation of the report's recommendations would then occur through different combinations and permutations of new, existing, and explicit and tacit forms of knowledge. From this state of flux, manifestations of the report's recommendations into more explicit forms of knowledge, emerge gradually.[10]

This example suggests that the bipolar perspective of knowledge as either tacit or explicit fails to properly convey the dynamic quality of knowledge: that it exists in a persistent state of *becoming* and is neither sterile nor static. This further suggests that the 'positioning' of forms of knowledge on the tacit–explicit continuum is not fixed, but fluid; and probably subject to changes in both directions of the tacit–explicit knowledge continuum. Knowledge creation possesses potentialities for effecting changes both in an organisation's structure and in its forms of knowledge. Conversely, organisational structure and knowledge form impacts on a firm's ability to convert and create knowledge.

Nonaka categorises knowledge creating organisations as those exhibiting four distinct modes of behaviour in 'dynamic interaction, a kind of spiral of knowledge' (Nonaka, 1991: 98). These behaviours stem from the four permutations that result from the synthesis of tacit and explicit forms of knowledge within the organisational envelope. Nonaka describes these behaviours as socialisation, articulation, internalisation and combination, and he views knowledge creation as a dynamic process. However, his notion that knowledge is transmitted throughout the organisation in unimpeded upwards and downwards spirals is instructive, but idealised. As we have argued, the traditional organisation is not a continuous, interconnected whole. It possesses physical, political, cultural, and socio-technical barriers that are delineated broadly along functional lines, and these contrive to prevent the unimpeded rippling of knowledge throughout the organisation. In these circumstances, Nonaka's four modes of behaviour are much more likely to be enacted within the functional department, rather than in the organisation as a whole. In these conditions of confinement, knowledge is neither created nor transferred, but recycled. Eventually, if isolation persists, there is a danger that knowledge may degrade irreversibly.

An alternative to Nonaka's thesis is to conceive of knowledge creation as a process that is not only behaviouristic and unimpeded, but also one that is systemic and arises from the need to reconcile the form of knowledge with the design of the organisation's architecture. Figure 10.1 presents this alternative schema in terms of a two-dimensional matrix.

Figure 10.1 A schema for knowledge creation in organisations

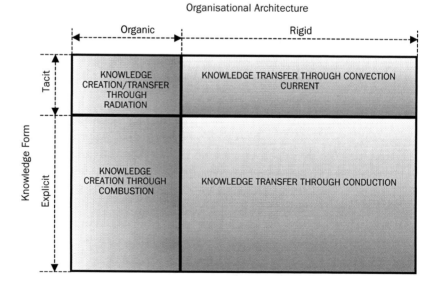

The schema could be thought of as representing the unique configuration of 'knowledge form' and 'organisational architecture' in a given firm. For example, this particular configuration might be typical of that found in a manufacturing or processing firm, where the predominant portion of the architecture exists to support the volume manufacture of goods. In this case, as the horizontal portion of the schema depicts, the architecture will be predominantly rigid in construction, so that modifications to the design could only be countenanced in the long term. The remaining smaller horizontal portion depicts the organic part of the firm that can respond more flexibly to the needs from change and innovation. This flexibility arises from the under-utilisation of physical and intellectual resources resulting from the firm's unexploited economies-of-scale. The vertical axis of the schema depicts the relative proportions of explicit and tacit knowledge contained in the firm. Again, as the substantive purpose of the firm is to support the manufacturing of goods, then explicit rather than tacit knowledge might be expected to predominate. So the unique configuration of this manufacturing firm is one whose 'knowledge form' is explicit-dominant, and architecture, rigid-dominant.

This schema presents a perspective on knowledge creation and conversion that sees the organisation as a disaggregated whole, consisting of distinct knowledge zones. The structure, content and form of knowledge created and converted arises from the nature and purpose of the knowledge space.

The schema further proposes four processes through which knowledge is transferred: through conduction, convection, radiation, and combustion. Each process is enveloped by a unique combination of 'knowledge form' and 'organisational architecture'.

Organisational knowledge as conductive energy

Numerous objects, physical spaces, and processes facilitate the conductive transfer of knowledge in an organisation. Written reports, e-mail messages, software, symbols,[11] hardware, products, manuals, policies and databases are all examples of physical objects that lend themselves to knowledge transfer. Manufacturing processing plant and organisation-wide information systems and architectures also provide examples of the infrastructure through which conductive knowledge transfer is made possible. Similarly, the functions of marketing, research and development, human resources, manufacturing, and finance, could also be construed as physical elements of the traditional organisation. In these circumstances, the parallel for conductivity relates to the direct physical contact and the logical connectivity between these physical objects. For example, an e-mail message can via an attachment transfer a written report, which can in turn be converted into a printed document. Similarly, by the click of a mouse, a sequence of instructions can result in the delivery of a product. These examples reveal both the conductive property of knowledge, and its capability for storage in a number of different forms. They also lend credence to the 'cognitive' perspective of knowledge management suggested by Kakabadse et al. (2003).

In the schema described in Figure 10.1, knowledge transfer by conduction is seen to fall within the tacit-rigid envelope of the firm and concerns the explicit articulation and enactment of rules, guidelines, policies and processes. This form of explicit knowledge is rigidly adhered to, and demands the precise interpretation and application of predetermined rules. The conductive metaphor arises from the direct physical connectivity between parts of the firm, and knowledge transfer is assumed to occur mechanistically and without loss of efficiency. The tacit-rigid envelope thus depicts that part of the firm concerned with the normal day-to-day operation and the provision of goods and services for existing customers and markets. For example, the International Organization for Standardization (ISO) 9000 series Quality Assurance and Control Standards and the US Food and Drug Agency Guidelines for Good Manufacturing Practice, are two examples of explicit knowledge that demand a conductive transfer process.

Organisational knowledge as convective energy

Convective energy processes are enacted within the tacit-rigid envelope of the organisation. The circulation of convective currents within and around the physical spaces of the organisation provides an important parallel for knowledge transfer. Convective knowledge transfer, as was noted earlier, arises in part from the intensity (potency) of the radiant knowledge source, and in part from the conditions of density and pressure difference in the medium through which the knowledge transfers take place. So the two key notions of the potency of knowledge sources, which are exclusively those associated with human capital, and the contextual environment of the organisation, are fundamental to the effective diffusion of convective knowledge within the organisation. Knowledge potency connotes the political, charismatic and expert influences (the tacit knowledge) that individuals and groups often wield in the organisational arena. To liberate these individual and group potentialities from the structural rigidities of the organisation, those who lead are responsible for creating an environment which is open and tolerant, perceives conflict as a necessary condition for learning and development, and above all, respects the principle of individual and group autonomy. Contextual conditions allude to the qualitative aspects of the working environment, such as the design and accessibility of physical spaces, and the extent to which informal and chance mechanisms for enabling convective knowledge circulation are supported and encouraged. For example, mechanisms such as coffee shops, accessible meeting rooms, open, attractive and well-lit spaces, and space-time,[12] are likely to enhance convective knowledge circulation significantly. It is in this organisational milieu that myths, stories, rumour, rituals and symbolism are rehearsed and enacted through what Geertz (1973) describes in Hatch (1997) as 'webs of significance [man] himself has spun'. Nonaka and Takeuchi's process of 'socialisation' in which sense-making among individuals and groups is enacted through the integration of tacit forms of knowledge is also an allusion to Geertz's so-called 'webs of significance'. The 'community of practice' perspective of knowledge management noted by Kakabadse et al. (2003) and the notion of culture as a socially constructed phenomenon (Hatch, 1997), also lend strong support to this convective metaphor of organisational knowledge.

Organisational knowledge as radiant energy

Radiant modes of knowledge transfer and creation are made possible by the presence of and interaction between people, processes and physical spaces within the organisational arena. Nonaka and Takeuchi's process of 'socialisation', which they argue stems from the integration of the tacit knowledge sources of the organisation, is not dissimilar to this notion of radiant knowledge transfer and creation. The metaphor also lends support to the 'philosophical perspective' of knowledge management proposed by Kakabadse et al. (2003). Thus training and coaching, formal and informal meetings and briefings, brainstorming and teamwork are exemplars by which the radiant transfer and creation of knowledge is made possible.

The process of radiant energy transfer and creation demonstrated in Figure 10.1 lies within the tacit-organic envelope of the firm. The 'knowledge form' is contained within the minds of individuals and concerns ideas about how to improve the operations and/or strategy of the firm in its industry. According to Zack (1999b) the source of these ideas stems from 'direct experience and action, usually shared through highly interactive conversation, story-telling and shared experience' (Zack, 1999: 46). As the fundamental medium for radiant knowledge transfer is through oral communication and auditory perception, structure can be a significant impediment to effective knowledge flow in organisations. Attenuation of knowledge can also result from individual physical limits and nuances associated with oral and auditory perception, from cultural, political and language differences, and from common prejudices. The myriad of possible routes through which radiant knowledge can be dissipated makes it the most wasteful (or entropic) of the remaining two modes of knowledge transfer. Yet if deployed thoughtfully and appropriately it is the most potent form of knowledge for creating change and transformation in the organisational. So in the deployment of the radiant mode of knowledge transfer, there is a tension of purpose between the need to accept that, along with a degree of wastefulness, comes also the potential for creative transformation of the organisation. The creative use of structure as a means of directing and containing radiant knowledge is a key strategy for managing this tension. For example, whereas seating at a conference would be arranged so that an expert speaker occupies a central position in relation to the audience, such an arrangement would clearly be inappropriate for, say, a team of designers. In the former case, the knowledge transfer process would be predominantly radiant, with only minimal two-way communication between the expert and audience to address points of clarification. In the case of the latter, however, radiant knowledge transferred by one designer would, in effect, be the spark that ignites a random sequence of radiant knowledge transfers from designer to designer, much like the random flickering of individual light bulbs in a cluster of light bulbs. These random, controlled events could lead to a new synthesis of ideas and thus potentially transform the organisation.

Knowledge creation by combustion

The process of combustion uses energy in the form of heat to initiate a chemical reaction that results in the fusing together of different forms of matter. During this chemical reaction, significant quantities of heat and light are generated in association with the release of different forms of matter, which are often less stable and of lower energy potential. The production of heat and light are a logical consequence, therefore, of the aggressive deconstruction and transformation of matter. The catalyst, which in this case is usually an intense transient heat source such as a spark or match, is vital in initiating and establishing the combustion reaction. Such is the intensity of heat generated by the combustion reaction that a coolant or moderator is often required to control the process within the specified process parameters.

Combustion is thus a powerful metaphor for seeing how information (matter in structural form) is synthesised through psycho-social processes to create knowledge in the organisation. The metaphor reveals that a necessary condition for the creation of useful knowledge will be the deconstruction or fusion of existing explicit forms of knowledge. Again, this would appear to be consistent with the 'network' perspective of knowledge management noted by Kakabadse et al. (2003). The metaphor also suggests that the knowledge creation process is concomitant with the procreation of by-products (or spin-offs). Some of these may yield useful avenues for further knowledge creation, while others could be potentially wasteful of the organisation's finite energies. The metaphor also alludes to the importance of creating an appropriate organisational context for knowledge creation.

The process of combustion resides within the explicit-organic envelope of the firm and consists of an adaptive process or organisational learning. It integrates explicit knowledge into novel permutations, the source of which may be within either the firm or the industry. A process of combustion, for example, might use 'value engineering' to integrate a number of separate manufactured components into a single part. The result would be a dramatic reduction in material and manufacturing costs and remarkable increases in technical efficiencies and product reliability. There may be natural limits in the degree to which the process of combustion can significantly transform the fortunes of the firm. Eventually, as higher value sources of explicit knowledge are increasingly integrated within the firm, diminishing returns may set in and prevent further attempts at adaptation.

In summary, an interpretation of the schema illustrated in Figure 10.1 and articulated above, suggests that the firm can be represented in two dimensions: on one side by its architecture, and on the other, its knowledge forms.[13] A unique signature of a firm is thus the extent to which the architecture is predominantly organic or rigid, and the knowledge forms predominantly tacit or explicit. The result is the formation of envelopes or organisational spaces in which particular modes of knowledge creation reside. Conduction, the first of these four knowledge creation processes, reproduces explicit knowledge, while convection, the second of these processes, fine-tunes and refines the firm's tacit knowledge resources. The third process, radiation, is created and transferred by the expert tacit knowledge and ideas of individuals, and offers substantial potential for transforming the organisation. The final process, combustion, enables the creative adaptation of the organisation's scarce repositories of explicit knowledge. However, knowledge creation through this process may eventually decline due to the onset of diminishing returns.

Conclusions

The science of thermodynamics offers an intriguing and fresh perspective for understanding the nature and scope of knowledge management in organisations. The discussion of the three laws of thermodynamics in relation to matter, fuel and energy, alerts us to the remarkable correspondence between matter, fuel and energy, on the one hand, and data, information and knowledge on the other. By pondering these differences, we are thus able to see that, whereas decisions about the use of information in organisations surround the issue of information scarcity, those relating to the use of knowledge are concerned with knowledge entropy. Information management answers questions about the economic utility of one form of knowledge against that of another. Knowledge management is concerned with wider strategic questions about how to conserve mission-critical knowledge forms, in ways that maximise the organisation's competitive advantage.

The science of thermodynamics also provides us with powerful metaphors for characterising the nature of knowledge and the mechanisms by which it is created and transformed. Conduction is a metaphor for direct knowledge transfer, and the conversion and re-constitution of knowledge repositories within the tacit-rigid organisation envelope. Convective knowledge transfers are enacted within the tacit-rigid envelope of the organisation and involve the incidental circulation of losses from the organisation's radiant and conductive knowledge repositories. These incidental knowledge transfers may be circulated predominantly through the medium of organisational culture. Radiant knowledge transfer is essentially a creative, individualistic process, which is augmented by the Nonaka and Takeuchi socialisation process, and so resides in the tacit-organic envelope of the organisation. The metaphor of combustion suggests a crucible-like process in which information is synthesised through psycho-social processes within the explicit-organic envelope of the organisation. A necessary condition for knowledge combustion will be the diffusion of existing explicit forms of knowledge.

The thermodynamic perspective on knowledge creation and transfer has considerable relevance for the way organisations should approach the formulation of knowledge management strategy. This perspective offers a two-dimensional, rather than a one-dimensional view of knowledge strategy; one that is a function of organisational architecture as well as knowledge forms. It suggests that the organisation is represented as a series of four knowledge zones: tacit-organic; tacit-rigid; explicit-organic; and explicit-rigid. These zones appear to be differentiated because of the nature of the human capital, and the physical structures and processes which these zones contain. The plausibility that such zones of knowledge could exist in an organisation is supported by the four taxonomies of knowledge management proposed by Kakabadse et al. (2003). Thus an organisation's capability for work conducted in one knowledge zone as against that conducted in another depends on the extent to which the zone is loosely or rigidly structured. If these knowledge zones do exist, then they could offer fascinating possibilities for managing knowledge capital in organisations.

One important implication of this zoned perspective is that it offers a means of characterising organisations in terms of the relative predominance of, or emphases placed on one knowledge zone, over another. So whereas one organisation might be characterised as tacit-organic dominant, another would, perhaps, be classified as explicit-rigid dominant. In this way, perhaps, approaches to establishing balanced knowledge portfolios in organisations, much in the same way as that established by the Boston Consulting Group on product portfolio analysis, could be fruitfully explored. This possibility also suggests the need to investigate the extent to which the operating environment contributes to shaping the organisation's knowledge portfolio. It would also be interesting to consider whether there may be factors in the organisation's operating environment that could contribute to a dynamic interchange between a growth and/or decline of particular knowledge zones in accordance with the lifecycle concept.

Finally, the analysis, synthesis and discussion of the content of this chapter, presents an overall perspective on knowledge management that is located in classical scientific thinking. However, an emerging theme from the knowledge management literature, which holds fascinating prospects for the near future, will doubtless be the contribution of quantum and chaos thinking to the continued development, articulation, and embedding of this important discipline.

Acknowledgement

I would like to acknowledge Gareth Morgan's seminal work, *Images of Organization*, published by Sage in 1986. This perennial text, with its evocative and powerful imagery, has had a continuing and profound influence on my own thinking on organisational life.

Notes

1. This clever encapsulation of the first law of thermodynamics is borrowed from the British scientist C. P Snow. For more information, see *http://en.wikipedia.org/wiki/Thermodynamical_system* (accessed 19 July 2006).
2. This systems concept is explored more fully later on in the chapter. It describes a natural tendency for systems, when left to themselves, to approach a state of disorder.
3. Ibid., C. P. Snow.
4. These words are the author's, and the idea that of C. P. Snow.
5. Far-from-equilibrium is a concept first used by the late Nobel Laureate Illya Progogine who observed a propensity for systems to self-generate and develop structure in chaotic contexts existing far from thermodynamic equilibrium.
6. This phenomenon, known as Brownian motion was first discovered by the scientist Robert Brown in 1827, when under the microscope he noticed the random movement of particles of pollen on the surface of water. This discovery later on gave rise to the molecular theory of matter.
7. This close correspondence between energy and knowledge suggests that, as energy depends on the movement of a physical entity (a unit of mass over some predetermined distance), knowledge can only be so defined if it comes about through some form of 'movement' or 'processing' of information. In this sense, the word 'processing' is what confers knowledge its dynamic character. Thus, a certain dynamic is in fact implied when the word 'knowledge' is used.

8. Direct labour is taken here to mean physical and not intellectual work that is conducted at the point of manufacturing a product or performing a service. In the limited sense, energy or work is not expended unless it results in the movement of a force over a distance.

9. In this context, the structure-process paradox describes the age-old dilemma with which organisations have always grappled, which is how to structure the work of the organisation in ways that deliver its operational goals as well as its need for innovation and change. The structure-process paradox is also taken to be synonymous with the hybrid term rigid-organic.

10. These new explicit manifestations of knowledge will also be associated with new tacit forms. For example, commissioning is a process of transforming the tacit knowledge gained in the design and manufacture of a new technology (an explicit knowledge form) from the manufacturer to the purchaser. In this sense, explicit knowledge is concomitant with both new and existing forms of tacit knowledge.

11. To the extent that a symbol is a material representation of an abstract idea, it can also be taken to be a physical object.

12. The term space-time alludes here to the need for these convective knowledge transfer mechanisms to be designed in the organisational space, in a manner that maximises the possibility of staff encounters and the opportunities for the cross-fertilisation of ideas.

13. Knowledge form could be taken here to connote a notion of time and its contribution to the relative fluidity of knowledge, though in the long term, all forms of knowledge could be construed as changeable. For example, a recently commissioned printing press could be regarded as having an explicit/rigid knowledge form as its technology is fixed and codified. However, the process skills of a designer would be tacit/organic knowledge form as it is clearly transferable.

Knowledge management: an Open Marxist theoretical perspective and analysis

Ruth Rikowski

Introduction

Leburn Rose in the previous chapter situated knowledge management (KM) and knowledge within the science of thermodynamics and energy. He asks 'Can thermodynamic energy be … conceptualised as organisational energy in its various forms? How can the concept of energy be ascribed to the inputs and outputs of real organisations?' He says that energy could be defined as:

> …the result of the chemical combustion of methane in a manner that produces the potential to do useful work. There is a remarkable analogy between the physical relations of matter, fuel and energy, and the organisational relations of data, information and knowledge.

Furthermore, that:

> …it follows that as energy results from the chemical combustion of fuel, likewise, knowledge could also be the psychosocial processing of information in a form that achieves *added value*. As with the conversion of matter to fuel, the first and second laws of thermodynamics suggest important consequences for converting data to information. (my emphasis)

Thus, he seeks to bring science and social science together, focusing in particular on the relationship between thermodynamics, energy, the organisation, knowledge and KM and how the laws of thermodynamics can be applied to knowledge and KM.

Energy is thus an important concept. Glenn Rikowski refers to *social energy*, saying that:

> ...value, within the social universe of capital, constitutes a social force field analogous to gravity as a force within the known physical universe ... value is a social energy whose effects as a social force are mediated by the movements of capital (in its various forms) and the social relations between labour and capital. (G. Rikowski, 2002: 183)

Thus, value (including the value that is created from knowledge) is actually social energy. Mike Neary and Glenn Rikowski also say that:

> Value can be viewed as being social energy that undergoes transformations ... Value is a multi-dimensional field of social energy – a social substance with a directional dynamic but not social identity. It is the matter and anti-matter of Marx's social universe. (Neary and Rikowski, 2002: 60)

Energy then needs to be related to value theory – and this brings us back to Marx and his theory of value. We can now start to visualise the way in which concepts and, indeed, life are interconnected. Einstein's focus, for example, was clearly on scientific development, but he appreciated the fact that science and social science needed to be brought further together more, and indeed, he had a clear political position – he was a socialist. Einstein wrote an article about his socialist views in the first issue of *Monthly Review*, in 1949. In this article, he emphasised that economic science is still in a relatively primitive state and that it needs to be developed further.

In this chapter, I will present the argument that an Open Marxist theoretical perspective on KM, more than any other social scientific theory, provides a better explanation and analysis of KM and its importance in the modern global capitalist world. This includes social scientific theories such as functionalism, post-modernism, Weberianism and critical realism. Having said this, I will not be presenting the explanations and analyses of global capitalism from other social scientific theories. There is not the space, and in any case, I do not readily see the need – it can just waste time. As I say elsewhere:

> ...I would not readily see the need to investigate other social scientific theoretical perspectives anyway. It is not my task to investigate whether or not other social scientific theories can provide an adequate explanation and understanding of capitalism ... That task can be left to those theoreticians themselves. My background reading on different social scientific theories over many years has led me to conclude that Marxism provides a far more adequate understanding and explanation of capitalism than any other social scientific theory. So then my task becomes one of developing Marxism, particularly given the limitations of time and the fact that the horrors in capitalism are so severe, are intensifying and urgently need to be exposed and addressed. (R. Rikowski, 2005a: 302)

However, there is a short section on social scientific theory and Marxist theory in this section, highlighting how Marxism calls for a re-examination of social scientific theory itself and demands that it becomes more rigorous.

This chapter builds on my writing and research in this area, which I have been developing over the last few years (see R. Rikowski, 2000a, 2000b, 2003b, 2003c, 2004a, 2004b, 2005a, 2005b). I am building up a whole body of theory and ideas – developing an Open Marxist theoretical analysis on the knowledge revolution, knowledge management, information technology and globalisation. We need to make Marxism applicable to the global capitalist world that we find ourselves in today. Furthermore, Open Marxism challenges the traditional somewhat deterministic, boxlike Marxist approach and recognises the dynamic and ever-changing nature of global capitalism. This will all be considered in this chapter.

With regard to a Marxist analysis of KM, in essence, in the knowledge revolution in the modern developed world, the extraction of value from intellectual labour becomes of ever-increasing importance, and effective KM practices assist with this process. By this means, capitalism is sustained and perpetuated, while labour continues to be exploited, alienated and objectified. This will all be explored further in this chapter.

Evolutionary nature of social systems

Establishing the fact/theory

As I have been arguing throughout this book, we are now in the knowledge revolution in the developed world, because of which, effective knowledge management practices are very important for the continued success of the economy in global capitalism. Why, though, am I so firmly of this opinion? To understand this we need to consider how we have arrived at this capitalist mode of production.

To do this, we need to fully appreciate the fact that social systems evolve. We need to accept the evolutionary nature of social systems. Despite the various discourses on the subject, it has not been accepted as an established fact/theory. It needs to be established as a fact in a similar way to how Darwin's evolutionary theory of the species is accepted as a fact/theory. Obviously, some religious fundamentalists still do not accept Darwinism, but most people today accept Darwin's evolutionary theory of the species. Darwinism is taught in schools as part of the school curriculum. Similarly, the evolutionary nature of social systems also needs to be established as a theory and needs to be taught in schools. This is a new idea that I developed while writing my book on globalisation (R. Rikowski, 2005a, 2005b).

What then do I mean, exactly, by the evolutionary nature of social systems? In the course of history, there have been different economic, social and political systems. As Marx pointed out, there was, for example, ancient slave-based systems and later feudalism. And now we have capitalism. These systems have evolved – this is what needs to be more clearly understood. One system exists for a certain period; then, as society changes and progresses, the system gradually changes and eventually evolves and becomes a different system, one that more accurately represents the needs of the people at that particular time. Thus, just as apes undertook various activities and used their brains more and more, they gradually evolved into human beings, as these bodies were more appropriate for their needs – i.e. they did not need to climb trees so much, but they needed to be able to use their brain more. By the same token, feudalism became no longer an appropriate system, as factories started to be built and people moved from rural areas to urban areas, and so capitalism emerged/evolved out of this feudal system.

The important point to appreciate is that capitalism has evolved from other economic, political and social systems and that it is not a system that we have worked out and chosen by using our intellect. Only once we fully appreciate and understand this can we start to appreciate why capitalism can seem to be such a madhouse, and why there is so much death and misery in it. In essence, capitalism is a crazy system based on irreconcilable contradictions. Even supporters of global capitalism cry 'TINA' (there is no alternative) rather than 'IDEAL'. So, here the argument is that 'there is no alternative', that global capitalism is the best social, economic and political system that we can ever possibly have, so we just have to put up with it. However, no one really argues that it is the best possible, 'IDEAL' system that we could ever hope for. In *Globalisation, Information and Libraries* (R. Rikowski, 2005a), I give various possible explanations for this 'TINA' mentality. There is not the space to consider this further here, but it is important to consider why people want to accept 'TINA'. It is indeed strange why people believe that we simply have to tolerate a less than adequate system – one that causes such poverty, misery, human suffering, destructiveness, injustice and death.

Others have argued that capitalism is essentially a bad system and is ruled by nasty capitalists. This notion also has to be challenged. This is because, once again, social, economic and political systems are evolving processes. Capitalism is not a bad, nasty system, and capitalists are not simply bad and nasty people. This goes back to a simplistic understanding of good and bad, which are linked to religious notions, and which I also explore in my globalisation book. No, capitalism is a better system than those previous. It has provided a far better health and education service than other systems could have provided, for example. There was a need to find a better system, and so capitalism evolved out of previous systems, in order to cope with this need. This can be compared with the way in which humans have evolved from apes. Humans are a more advanced species – the survival of the fittest. Similarly, capitalism is the social, political and economic system that has survived – the fittest system at this particular point in time.

However, just because capitalism is better than previous systems, this is no reason to conclude that it is the best possible economic, social and political system that we could ever possibly have. Indeed, even proponents of 'TINA' are not saying that. Yet we have good intellects, so why are we arguing from this 'TINA' mentality? We can use our intellect to travel in space, to create wonderful IT systems etc. but we cannot seem to find it within ourselves to use our intellect to try to create a better economic, political and social system for ourselves.

Now that we have accepted the evolution of the species, we can be proactive and try to design and change our bodies for ourselves, rather than waiting for evolutionary processes to take their course. Indeed, a very active transhuman movement is working on this area (e.g. see G. Rikowski, 2003). So, today with the ever-increasing use of computers, good eyesight becomes very important, for example. We now have the beginnings of the technical ability to design ourselves better eyes to cope with this computer age, rather than waiting for evolutionary processes to take their course, and for better eyes to evolve gradually, which could take hundreds of years. Furthermore, given the pace of change in the computer world, the need to be able to be proactive in this way is increasingly important. So, we have the ability to take control of our bodies. Choosing the sex of our babies is another example here, as is the patenting of genes and cloning. We might not like all these changes, or want them to come into effect, and there might be various moral objections etc., but the point is that we now have this capability. What I am arguing, however, is that had we not accepted Darwin's evolutionary theory of the species, we would not have been able to realise our capability here. If we had not accepted the theory, then we would still have been stuck in the dark age of a religious mentality. Furthermore, we are only just now starting to take control of our bodies in this way, yet Darwin's theory is over 150 years old. This shows the slow pace at which change takes place. This, in itself, is another area that needs to be given further consideration. Social change can take hundreds of years. We need to exercise some patience in our quest and desire for a better social system and not just cry 'TINA' when things seem to get a little tough.

It is interesting to note that Professor Charles Oppenheim, in his review of my globalisation book in the *Journal of Documentation*, argues that I am developing conspiracy theories. According to him:

> ...conspiracy theories are not appropriate for a book such as this, and her claims certainly don't convince me, who tends to believe in cock ups rather than conspiracies as being the main driver of world events. (Oppenheim, 2005: 684)

However, I do not develop conspiracy theories at all. I say that certain outcomes might be the result of certain decisions, such as the fact that the UK Best Value initiative can help to bring in the General Agreement on Trade in Services (GATS). I also make it clear, though, that these various scenarios might not come to pass. But then I also emphasise that capitalism is basically a madhouse, and that it has evolved from previous systems, and so I quite agree with Oppenheim that it is based on 'cock ups'. It seems that he has not read my book properly! He also says that

I argue that the answer to the problems I raise is not to readjust the treaties, or even to readjust capitalism, 'but a world-wide movement towards Marxist economics' (Oppenheim, 2005: 682).

However, I do not say that Marxist economics is the solution. Instead, I say that Marxist economics provides us with a better and more adequate explanation and analysis of global capitalism than any other theory does. Indeed, Einstein recognises the need for more rigorous economic theory, and in this regard says that:

> Since the real purpose of socialism is precisely to overcome and advance beyond the predatory phase of human development, economic science in its present state can throw little light on the socialist society of the future. (Einstein, 1949: 2)

Thus, he also emphasises that this is necessary in order to move beyond the 'predatory phase of human development' and, indeed, evolutionary processes. So, to understand capitalism, we need to develop economic theory more, which means developing Marxist economic theory, as far as I am concerned. Once we have done this, we can then seek to move beyond the predatory, evolutionary 'phase of human development' and indeed, to move beyond the evolutionary nature of social systems.

Once we have this clear analysis, we can then proceed to try to create a better, kind and fairer world for ourselves – i.e. to work towards a communist system. But all that will take a very long time, and can only be arrived at by using our intellect, and thinking about how to create a better world for ourselves. It cannot be done through a bloody revolution – it is impossible to build a wonderful world out of bloodshed, I would argue.

However, getting beyond religion and religious notions is essential in order to be able to accept the evolutionary process in itself. So, as I say in my globalisation book, although we have got rid of religion on a formal basis in many ways, we have not got rid of religious notions, and we still cling on to notions of 'good' and 'bad'. Marx emphasised the need to criticise religion in *A Contribution to the Critique of Hegel's Philosophy of Right* saying, 'For Germany, the criticism of religion has been essentially completed, and the criticism of religion is the prerequisite of all criticism' (Marx, 1975: 243).

Furthermore:

> Religious suffering is at one and the same time the expression of real suffering and a protest against real suffering. Religion is the sigh of

the oppressed creature, the heart of a heartless world and the soul of soulless conditions. It is the opium of the people. (Marx, 1975: 244)

It is, indeed, 'the opium of the people' and we must get beyond it, as far as I am concerned. As I then go on to say in my globalisation book:

> If we were to accept the evolutionary nature of social systems as an established theory and an established fact, in the same way as we accept Darwin's theory of the origin of species through natural selection, we could then consider how to break free from this evolutionary process. We could then seek to be proactive (rather than just letting evolutionary processes take their course) and work towards creating a better social, economic and political system. (R. Rikowski, 2005a: 291)

So, the fundamental point to realise is that the evolutionary nature of social, economic and political systems needs to be established as a fact and a theory in the same way as Darwin's evolutionary theory of the species is accepted as a fact. This then needs to be taught in schools. This will only ever be achievable once we are beyond religious notions, as well as religion itself. In many ways, we are beyond formal religion itself, although obviously not completely; indeed, there has been some backward movement recently with the emergence of Creationism and the insistence that this be taught in some schools. But in many ways we have moved beyond formal traditional religion, otherwise Darwinism would never have been accepted in the first place. We now need to get beyond religious notions. Once all this is accepted, we can then proactively seek to change our system, rather than waiting for evolutionary processes to take their course. We can do this by using our intellect. This involves developing a Marxist theoretical analysis of capitalism, or more specifically an Open Marxist theoretical analysis, which challenges the somewhat deterministic, box-like approach of traditional Marxism. Once we have a clear understanding of capitalism we can then think about how to create a better world for ourselves, where as Marx says, 'From each according to his ability, to each according to his/her needs!' (Marx, 1858: 17).

Marx and Engels themselves refer to evolutionary processes, and how communism seeks to get beyond these (which once again, shows their great foresight), saying:

> Communism differs from all previous movements in that it overturns the basis of all earlier relations of production and

intercourse, and for the first time consciously treats all naturally evolved premises as the creations of hitherto existing men, strips them of their natural character and subjects them to the power of the united individuals. (Marx and Engels, 1846: 89–90)

Furthermore, Einstein also emphasises that humans are dependent on society and cannot live in isolation from it. However, humans are different from other species because they can think, be proactive and influence and change the society in which they live. Einstein says that:

> ...the dependence of the individual upon society is a fact of nature which cannot be abolished – just as in the case of ants and bees. However, while the life process of ants and bees is fixed down to the smallest detail by rigid, hereditary instincts, the social pattern and interrelationships of human beings are very variable and susceptible to change ... This explains how it happens that, in a certain sense, man can influence his life through his own conduct, and that in this process conscious thinking and wanting can play a part. (Einstein, 1949: 3)

Thus, let us look towards a brighter future and a better world, where we can be proactive and do not just have to wait for evolutionary processes to take their course.

With regard to where knowledge management specifically, fits into this picture, as I have already indicated, the knowledge revolution is an evolutionary phase of capitalism – and it is the phase that we are now in, in the developed world. The success of this knowledge revolution is more dependent on intellectual labour than manual labour, and for the extraction of value from intellectual labour. This means trying to utilise the knowledge, information and ideas that knowledge workers/intellectual labourers have, through effective KM practices. By this means, intellectual labour becomes exploited – and then we have to question whether we want to live in a system that is based on such exploitation.

Sub-phases of evolving social systems

Not only do social systems in themselves evolve, such as the feudal system evolving into the capitalist system, but there are also phases within the social system, so any one social system is an evolving and a changing process. A social system will go through different phases; one phase will evolve into another, as the system adapts to the changing world in which it finds itself. It will do this until the changes become so significant that it actually evolves into another system entirely. This can also be compared with the evolution of the species. A species changes, adapts and evolves until the changes become so significant that they actually constitute a new type of species, such as the ape changing and evolving until it eventually evolved into a human. The same principle applies to the evolutionary processes of economic, social and political systems.

Thus, capitalism as a system is continually changing, moving and evolving, going through various phases as it adapts and progresses, continually seeking new ways of creating new commodities, value and new markets. As Schumpeter (1951: 66) says, the fundamental impulse for the development of capitalism is 'new combinations'. Furthermore, 'capitalism ... is by nature a form or method of economic change and not only never is but never can be stationary' (Schumpeter, 1952: 82).

As Tony Blair, the UK Prime Minister said at a speech he gave to the CBI Conference in Brighton, in the industrial revolution, 'capital was in short supply and labour was comparatively cheap. In the twenty-first century ... intellectual capital will be in short supply' (Blair, 1999).

On another occasion, Blair also refers to a 'new industrial revolution' saying that 'knowledge and the ability to innovate ... are the raw materials of this revolution' (Blair, 1999).

The need for this continual change is absolutely essential for capitalism. This is because in order to continue to survive and flourish it *must* be forever seeking to commodify more and more aspects of social life. Furthermore, the drive to extract value from labour (and value can only ever be extracted from labour), which then becomes embedded in these commodities, is infinite.

Yet, various people have questioned whether the 'knowledge revolution' is really something real, and whether concepts like 'knowledge management' are actually something that is useful. Ironically, on these counts I find myself very much agreeing with various supporters of the neo-liberal agenda, such as Blair, Byers and Leadbeater. Leadbeater, for example, speaks about the knowledge economy saying that 'our institutions, public and private, will all have to change quite fundamentally for us to release the potential of the knowledge-driven economy' (Leadbeater, 1999: 52).

The knowledge revolution is certainly something very real, as I have repeatedly emphasised in my published works.

Interestingly, when Marx and Engels wrote the *Communist Manifesto* in 1848, workers in capitalist enterprises in Europe were very much in the minority, and they only comprised about 5 per cent of the European workforce. But, the industrial revolution developed rapidly in England, and so by 1851 workers in capitalist enterprises formed a majority of workers in England. Thus, parallels can be drawn here with knowledge workers. Knowledge workers are currently very much in the minority, just as industrial workers were much the minority in Europe when Marx and Engels were writing. England, however, was at the forefront of the industrial revolution, pushing capitalism forward, so the numbers of industrial workers in the country rapidly increased. Similarly, there might only be a relatively small number of knowledge workers at the current time, but this does not mean that these workers are insignificant or irrelevant – instead, they indicate future trends, the way in which capitalism is developing and moving forward. In the not-too-distant future, the number of knowledge workers will probably increase quite dramatically in the developed world, particularly in the USA, given that the USA is at the forefront of global capitalism.

Having provided a brief overview of the commodity and value, this will now be considered in more depth, to help understand some of the fundamentals concerning Marx's theory of capitalism, and how it helps to understand and analyse the modern global capitalist world, in general, and the role that KM plays within this, in particular.

(This section has been taken from extracts from R. Rikowski, 2005b)

The commodity and the extension of the commodification process

Introduction

Labour is the core of capitalism – without the continued injection of labour the capitalist mode of production would simply collapse. Marx emphasised how labour is the core of capitalism, saying, 'the whole system of capitalist production is based on the fact that the workman sells his labour-power as a commodity' (Marx, 1867: 406).

Postone in reinterpreting Marx's critical theory clearly emphasises how labour is the 'true source of wealth' in capitalism, saying:

...Marx's critical analysis of capitalism is primarily a critique of exploitation from the standpoint of labor: it demystifies capitalist society, first, by revealing labor to be the true source of wealth, and second, by demonstrating that that society rests upon a system of exploitation. (Postone, 1996: 8)

Furthermore, as Marx says, 'in capitalist society spare time is acquired for one class by converting the whole life-time of the masses into labour-time' (Marx, 1867: 496).

However, Marx begins his analysis of capitalism with the commodity, and this, indeed, is where our analysis must begin. Marx began the first volume of *Capital,* by examining the commodity, saying that:

The wealth of those societies in which the capitalist mode of production prevails, presents itself as an 'immense accumulation of commodities', its unit being a single commodity. Our investigation must therefore begin with the analysis of a commodity. (Marx, 1867: 43)

As Postone also says, Marx 'analyzes the commodity as the most fundamental and general social mediation of capitalist society' (Postone, 1996: 390).

Furthermore, in the *Grundisse,* Marx spoke about the commodity towards the end of the book (and not at the beginning), in a section on value, but he says that 'This section to be brought forward. The first category in which bourgeois wealth presents itself is that of the commodity' (Marx, 1858: 881).

Thus, he realised that his earlier thinking needed to be changed to some extent, as his understanding of capitalism deepened, and he realised that an effective analysis of capitalism *must* begin with the commodity. Endeavouring to understand capitalism is not an easy task. There have been occasions when I have asked myself *why* I am trying to understand and explain this madhouse and that, indeed, perhaps it is not really possible to intellectually analyse this mad system anyway. But then again, my thinking tells me that we have no option. We live and breathe in capitalism on a daily basis, and in order to live and cope with it, we have to try to make some sort of sense of it. So, I am driven by the need to analyse it, and in order to be able to do so effectively we must begin our analysis with the commodity.

Thus, the logic of capitalism is the commodification of all that surrounds us. It is very important that we grasp this basic fact. This is impossible to achieve in reality, but this is because capitalism is essentially a madhouse, and as already indicated, it is a system that has just evolved; it is not a system that we have chosen to live in , nor is it one that we have designed and worked out by using our intellect. We have not sat down and thought about, and tried to work towards creating a better, kinder and fairer economic, political and social system for ourselves. No, instead, capitalism has evolved, and there are many contradictions within it. Thus, in reality, the commodification of all that surrounds us is impossible, but capitalism still strives to achieve this nevertheless. In the same way, it aims to be forever creating value, and extracting this value from labour.

Today, we witness the commodification of many areas of life such as the beaches and water. The World Trade Organization (WTO), for example, is very much about the extension of this commodification process, and this includes the commodification of services (through the General Agreement on Trade in Services) and the commodification of intellectual property rights (through the agreement on Trade-Related Aspects of Intellectual Property Rights). Once it has helped to create more commodities, it then seeks to trade them. I consider this further elsewhere (R. Rikowski, 2005a). We must keep firmly in our mind what the WTO is – the World *Trade* Organization.

Why then, we might ask, did Marx begin his analysis with the commodity? It is essential for humans to have various goods in order to survive (such as bread and water) no matter what type of society they live in. In capitalism, however, these goods become 'commodities' and are traded in the marketplace. As such, the basic wants and needs that humans have in order to live become perverted at a very early stage in capitalism, and come to dominate us. Thus, it becomes necessary to begin a critique of capitalism with an analysis of the commodity. To extend this further, the logic of capitalism implies the commodification of everything that surrounds us (water, the beaches, our bodies etc.), and this is increasingly happening on a global scale. Similarly, although humans need to labour, no matter what form of society they live in, in capitalism labour takes on a particular form, which becomes realised as value, through the commodity. Therefore, it is through the commodity that the 'gem', the value within labour becomes real, so an analysis of capitalism must begin with the commodity, rather than with labour.

Commodities: physical natural form and value form

So, what makes the commodity that exists in capitalism different from a mere 'good'? Marx says that commodities have two forms – their physical natural form and their value form. He says that 'they manifest themselves therefore as commodities ... only in so far as they have two forms, a physical or natural form, and a value-form' (Marx, 1867: 54).

The physical form of a commodity consists of the materials and substances that make up the physical components of a commodity, such as plastic, iron and wood. However, the value form is created specifically and only through human labour and as Marx says, 'the value of a commodity ... is determined by the quantity of labour contained in it' (Marx, 1867: 203).

It is both the value form of the commodity, and the way in which the value is realised that makes the commodity a type of good that is specific to capitalism. 'A given quantity of any commodity contains a definite quantity of human labour. The value-form must therefore not only express value generally, but also value in definite quantity' (Marx, 1867: 59).

Thus, as I say:

> ...Marx introduces the concept of value – the value-form of the commodity can only be created through human labour. Thus, it is human labour that creates value, and in turn, it is value that feeds and perpetuates capitalism – and so, value is the life-blood of capitalism. Without the continued injection of human labour, which creates value, the capitalist mode of production would collapse. (R. Rikowski, 2003b)

Value form: value, use-value and exchange-value

Marx distinguishes between two main different types of values in the commodity – use-values and exchange-values. At the beginning of the first volume of *Capital*, Marx refers to 'use-value' saying:

> The utility of a thing makes it a use-value ... A commodity, such as iron, coal or a diamond, is therefore, so far as it is a material thing, a use-value, something useful ... Use-values become a reality only by use or consumption. (Marx, 1867: 44)

So, commodities are useful, and have a use-value. Exchange-value, on the other hand, involves the exchange of commodities, and as Marx says:

> ...when commodities are exchanged, their exchange-value manifests itself as something totally independent of their use-values...

[furthermore] exchange-value is the only form in which the value of commodities can manifest itself or be expressed. (Marx, 1867: 46)

Thus, the exchange of commodities is a fundamental part of capitalism. Exchange-value, in essence, is the way in which the value in the commodity can be quantified/measured in an objective sense, and in capitalism, this is achieved through money. Commodities can be exchanged equally (they acquire an equivalence), through the money-form. However, money is, in essence, simply another way of expressing the labour that is embedded in the commodity. It is embedded in the commodity in the form of abstract labour.

Returning to the basic concept of the commodity, as Marx says, on initial inspection 'a commodity appears ... a very trivial thing, and easily understood' (Marx, 1867: 76).

However, in fact, the commodity is a mysterious thing, because of the labour that is embedded within it, which becomes objectified.

> A commodity is therefore a mysterious thing, simply because in it the social character of men's labour appears to them as an objective character stamped upon the product of that labour; because the relation of the producers to the sum total of their own labour is presented to them as a social relation, existing not between themselves, but between the products of their labour. (Marx, 1867: 77)

Once again, Marx emphasises that it is the value that is in the commodity that is important.

> Could commodities themselves speak, they would say: Our use-value may be a thing that interests men. It is not part of us as objects. What, however, does belong to us as objects, is our value. Our natural intercourse as commodities proves it. In the eyes of each other we are nothing but exchange-values. (Marx, 1867: 87)

However, it is also very necessary to distinguish 'value' from both 'exchange-value' and 'use-value'. While Marx uses these three terms, and does differentiate value from use-value and exchange-value, as is made clear in the quote above, as Glenn Rikowski points out, Marx does not really define and unravel what 'value' itself is, on its own, in sufficient detail. There is a lack of clarity here. This also demonstrates the fact that we need to build on Marx and not to deify him. So, what actually *is* value?

As previously discussed, Neary and Rikowski (2002) have defined value as *social energy*. Energy in general, and social energy in particular, and how it relates to knowledge and information, is considered further in the paper 'Reframing sustainable sources of energy for the future' (Anon, 2006), although the emphasis in the paper in regard to social energy is on social relationships and people skills, rather than on an objective definition of social energy.

In an objective sense though, embedded within the commodity is value itself, use-value and exchange-value. Humans will labour no matter what form of society they live in and this labour creates social energy. Through labour, social energy becomes 'value' in capitalism, and this value is embedded in the commodity. This is because, as has already been discussed, the continued creation and exchange of commodities in the marketplace is essential for the continued success of capitalism. Furthermore, the social wealth that emanates from these commodities can only be realised through value, and this value is created by labour. So, this is value, pure and simple.

As already stated, however, commodities also have a 'use-value'. For example, bread has a use-value, because we need to eat it in order to live; likewise a chair has a use-value as we can sit on it. On initial inspection, however, one obvious problem is that many commodities are now created that seem, in fact, to be useless. Capitalism is always trying to create new demands and trying to persuade us to buy products that we never thought we needed. How can this situation be reconciled? Very simply – capitalism *must* be forever creating and exchanging commodities – it is essential for its survival. As long as there is a market for the product, that is all that matters. For example, with a mobile phone, people can be contacted in an emergency, wherever they might be; indeed, many people now consider a mobile phone to be essential – thus, it has a use-value. The mobile phone is a relatively new commodity, a new product that was created in capitalism a few years ago. If it had not been successfully sold and exchanged in the marketplace then its use-value would never have been realised. Indeed, the manufacturers might have argued that its various functions demonstrated its use-value, but if people were not convinced and did not buy it, thinking that the mobile phone was useless, then the use-value would not have been realised. However, when the commodity is successfully marketed, then the use-value becomes something real – and so, the mobile phone in capitalism has a real use-value. Another product might not be marketed successfully in this way. An author might write a novel, for example, that does not sell in the marketplace. In such a case, this novel has no use-value under capitalism, or at least, its use-value is not realised.

So, although commodities have a use-value no matter what type of society we live in (to come back to the basic point – we need goods such as bread and water in order to survive), once again, in capitalism use-value takes on a particular form. It includes the use-value in the commodities that we need in order to be able to survive, but in addition, it includes any commodity that in reality is seen to be useful (i.e. any commodity that can be successfully traded in the marketplace).

Meanwhile, as already indicated, exchange-value simply represents the objective way in which commodities can be exchanged, and this is realised through money. As Adam Smith says, 'at the same time and place ... money is the exact measure of the real exchangeable value of all commodities' (Smith, 1776: 140).

To return to the basic point, that the *value* in the commodity is created through labour, it is also important and interesting to note that Adam Smith recognised that the value of any commodity is equal to the quantity of labour. Furthermore, he explored the meaning of exchange-value, arguing that labour is the real measure of exchange-value:

> The value of any commodity ... to the person who possesses it, and who means not to use it or consume it himself, but to exchange it for other commodities, is equal to the quantity of labour which it enables him to purchase or command. Labour, therefore, is the real measure of the exchangeable value of all commodities. (Smith, 1776: 133)

He continues, emphasising how labour is the only accurate measure of value, saying:

> Labour ... is the only universal, as well as the only accurate measure of value, or the only standard by which we can compare the values of different commodities at all times, and in all places. (Smith, 1776: 140)

Smith also emphasises that:

> Labour alone ... never varying in its own value, is alone the ultimate and real standard by which the value of all commodities can at all times and places be estimated and compared. It is their real price; money is their nominal price only. (Smith, 1776: 136)

Thus, labour is the only real standard by which the value of all commodities can be compared and realised.

Similarly, it is because of the value that exists in the commodity through the injection of labour, that a common measure for commodities can be realised – i.e. by the adoption of money. As Marx says:

> It is not money that renders commodities commensurable. Just the contrary. It is because all commodities, as values, are realised human labour, and therefore commensurable, that their values can be measured by one and the same special commodity, and the latter be converted into the common measure of their values – i.e. into money. Money is a measure of value, is the phenomenal form that must of necessity be assumed by that measure of value which is immanent in commodities, labour-time. (Marx, 1867: 97)

This, as already indicated, is exchange-value. Adam Smith also describes how money is used, as it is a more convenient means of expression/ measurement than the quantity of labour, even though labour is the real measure. He argues, 'but though labour be the real measure of the exchangeable value of all commodities, it is not that by which their value is commonly estimated' (Smith, 1776: 134).

Thus, by considering both Marx and Adam Smith we can begin to have a real grasp of 'exchange-value'. This also demonstrates that Smith, like Marx, understood and appreciated the fact that value is created by labour.

Therefore, we have value itself (which is social energy – and in this way, we can also start to bring science and social science together), and this becomes embedded in the commodity in various forms; namely, in the form of use-value and exchange-value. We need to maintain a firm grasp and an understanding of this fact, so that we can clearly analyse the capitalist mode of production. We also need to appreciate that Marx did not actually consider 'value' in sufficient detail on its own, in abstraction from other forms and aspects of value.

Conclusion

An analysis of capitalism must begin with the commodity. Capitalism can only be maintained by the continual creation and exchange of commodities in the marketplace. Value that is created from labour is embedded in the commodity and this takes on different forms – namely, use-value and exchange-value. There are also aspects of value – namely, surplus value and added value, and these will be considered subsequently.

It is the particular way in which these different forms and aspects of value interact and operate together that is peculiar to capitalism. The dynamics of the situation needs to be fully appreciated here.

Capitalism forever needing to create value from labour

Introduction

So far, I have emphasised how labour is essential for the continuation of the capitalist mode of production, but that in order to analyse capitalism, we need to begin our analysis with an examination of the commodity, as Marx did. From here, we were able to establish how value extracted from labour is embedded in the commodity. Postone endeavours to clarify the meaning of value further, saying that:

> …Marx conceives of value as a social form that is not manifest but is determining of a deep structural level of modern social existence, and operates behind the backs of the social actors. Value, according to Marx, is constitutive of consciousness and action and, in turn, is constituted by people, although they are unaware of its existence. (Postone, 1996: 390)

Thus, Marx emphasises that value is constituted by people and encourages us to look at value in a different way.

Postone emphasises how the foundation of capitalism is based on value, saying that:

> …for Marx, the category of value expresses the basic relations of production of capitalism – those social relations that specifically characterize capitalism as a mode of social life – as well as that production in capitalism is based on value. In other words, value, in Marx's analysis, constitutes the 'foundation of bourgeois production'. (Postone, 1996: 24)

However, Marx emphasises that it is 'surplus value', in particular, that is the 'sum and substance of capitalist production', saying:

> …the production of surplus-value, or the extraction of surplus-value, is the specific end and aim, the sum and substance of

capitalist production, quite apart from any changes in the mode of production, which may arise from the subordination of labour to capital. (Marx, 1867: 281–2)

This will be considered further below.

Surplus value and added value

This section will focus specifically on surplus value and added value – these being aspects of value.

Surplus value

Surplus value is crucial in Marx's analysis. Surplus value (as opposed to other concepts of value) takes on a momentum of its own. It becomes self-valorising, it can expand value and it can multiply value – thus, the creation of surplus value is essential for the perpetuation of capitalism. In referring to the capitalist, Marx says that 'his aim is to produce ... not only use-value, but value; not only value, but at the same time surplus-value' (Marx, 1867: 181).

Meanwhile, Postone says that:

> Surplus value is created when the workers labor for more time than is required to create the value of their labor power. That is when the value of labor power is less than the value this labor power valorizes in the production process. (Postone, 1996: 281)

Marx's formula for surplus value is 'M-C-M' (Marx, 1867: 267), and this expresses the circulation of capital: money-commodity-money. With regard to M-C-M, Marx says:

> This increment or excess over the original value I call 'surplus-value'. The value, originally advanced, therefore, not only remains intact while in circulation, but adds to itself a surplus-value or expands itself. It is this movement that converts it into capital. (Marx, 1867: 149)

Thus, in short, surplus value is created by the following process, whereby 'value ... becomes value in process, money in process, and, as such, capital', for:

In simple circulation, C-M-C, the value of commodities attained at the most a form independent of their use-values, i.e. the form of money; but that same value now in the circulation M-C-M, or the circulation of capital, suddenly presents itself as an independent substance, endowed with a motion of its own, passing through a life-process of its own, in which money and commodities are mere forms which it assumes and casts off in turn. Nay, more: instead of simply representing the relations of commodities, it enters now, so to say, into private relations with itself. It differentiates itself as original value from itself as surplus-value; as the father differentiates himself from the son...Value therefore now becomes value in process, money in process, and, as such, capital. (Marx, 1867: 152–3)

Postone emphasises how important the creation of surplus value is for the continued success and expansion of capitalism, saying that:

...although competition among capitals can be used to explain the existence of growth, it is value's temporal determination that, in Marx's analysis, underlies the form of that growth. The particular relation between increases in productivity and the expansion of surplus value shapes the trajectory of growth in capitalism. (Postone, 1996: 313)

Furthermore, Marx says that 'Capitalist production is not merely the production of commodities, it is essentially the production of surplus-value. The labourer produces, not for himself, but for capital' (Marx, 1867: 477).

So, surplus value is the continual expansion, growth and magnification of value. It is a dynamic process, and it is part of the valorisation process. It is a continuing, never-ending, self-perpetuating process, into the infinite. This surplus value is derived from labour. It will go on and on in a never-ending cycles, as long as we have capitalism.

Added value

Marx also refers to 'added value' or 'new value'. This term is commonly used today, especially in the business literature – the importance of 'adding value' is repeatedly highlighted. But, added value is not a new concept. As Welch says, 'the organisation has to recognise that its prime objective (perhaps its only objective) is to *add value*' (Welch, 2000: 10).

Marx says that the labourer, by virtue of his labour being of a specialised kind, creates additional/new value – i.e. added value. He says:

> While the labourer, by virtue of his labour being of a specialised kind that has a special object, preserves and transfers to the product the value of the means of production, he at the same time, by the mere act of working, creates each instant an *additional or new value*. (Marx, 1867: 201 – my emphases)

Marx continues:

> Suppose the process of production to be stopped just when the workman has produced an equivalent for the value of his own labour-power, when, for example, by six hours' labour, he has *added a value* of three shillings. This value is the surplus, of the total value of the product, over the portion of its value that is due to the means of production. It is the only original bit of value formed during this process, the only portion of the value of the product created by this process. Of course, we do not forget that this *new value* only replaces the money advanced by the capitalist in the purchase of the labour-power, and spent by the labourer on the necessities of life. With regard to the money spent, the *new value* is merely a reproduction; but, nevertheless, it is an actual, and not, as in the case of the value of the means of production, only an apparent, reproduction. The substitution of one value for another, is here effected by the creation of *new value*. (Marx, 1867: 201 – my emphases)

Furthermore, Marx refers to the new value created and how it differs from the value that is already in existence, saying:

> He is unable to add new labour, to create *new value*, without at the same time preserving old values; and this, because the labour he adds must be of a specific useful kind; and he cannot do work of a useful kind, without employing products as the means of production of a new product, and thereby transferring their value to the new product. The property therefore which labour-power in action, living labour, possesses of preserving value, at the same time that it adds it, is a gift of Nature which costs the labourer nothing, but which is very advantageous to the capitalist inasmuch as it preserves the existing value of his capital. So long as trade is good, the capitalist is too

much absorbed in money-grubbing to take notice of this gratuitous gift of labour. A violent interruption of the labour-process by a crisis, makes him sensitively aware of it. (Marx, 1867: 200 – my emphasis)

So, the old value is preserved, and yet, new value is also added.

In conclusion, value is social energy and much of this social energy is derived from human labour (it can also be derived from animals, such as workhorses and circus animals, but this will not be explored here). In order to provide further clarity, I have analysed and categorised value according to two main types – aspects of value and forms of value. Each time the labourer labours, they create new/added value (while also preserving the old value) and this added value is then magnified, and is turned into surplus value. Surplus value is constantly magnified, expanded and self-valorised. While we live in capitalism, this cycle will continue into the infinite. It is an all-pervasive, all-powerful force. Value, added value and surplus value are all aspects of value, or social energy. These different aspects of value are embedded in the commodity in capitalism, in different forms; namely in the form of use-value and exchange-value. Thus, both the aspects of value and the forms of value are embedded in the commodity. The commodity and the way in which value is realised in the commodity is the key for the continued success of capitalism. Furthermore, what also ensures its continued success is the way in which value and the different forms and aspects of value interact and operate together – a unique process is undergone which is specific to the capitalist mode of production itself.

The continual expansion of value in capitalism

Value is continually expanded and perpetuated and it becomes a dynamic force, multiplying itself time and time again in capitalism. This is accomplished through the creation of and then the continual expansion of surplus value. Surplus value becomes a 'dynamic totality', which Postone refers to as the 'valorisation of value', the 'valorisation process' or 'self-valorising value'. As Postone says:

> ...Marx analyzes the valorization process – the process of creating surplus value – in terms of the process of creating value; his analysis is concerned not only with the source of the surplus but also with the form of the surplus wealth produced. Value ... is a category of a dynamic totality. This dynamic involves a dialectic of

> transformation and reconstitution that results from the dual nature of the commodity form and from the two structural imperatives of the value form of wealth – the drive toward increasing levels of productivity and the necessary retention of direct human labor in production. We can now extend that analysis further. As we have seen, capital is 'self-valorizing value', according to Marx; it is characterized by the need to expand constantly. When value is the form of wealth, the goal of production necessarily is surplus value. That is, the goal of capitalist production is not simply value but the constant expansion of surplus value. (Postone, 1996: 308)

So, value is the form of wealth, and the goal of capitalist production is not just surplus value, but the constant creation and expansion of surplus value. Emphasising this, Postone indicates that 'industrial production is intrinsically capitalist insomuch as it is a valorization process as well as a labor process. Its ultimate goal is not material wealth but surplus value' (Postone, 1996: 341).

Thus, the valorisation process is the continued expansion and maximisation of surplus value and this continues into the infinite, while we live in capitalism.

Law, theory and the temporal dimension of value

Law/theory of value

We are now in a position to consider the theory of value, which emerges from the analysis of value that has already been explored. Postone examines Marx's theory of value in some depth and he says succinctly that 'far from being a law of equilibrium ... Marx's law of value grasps as a determinate 'law' of history, the dialectical dynamic of transformation and reconstitution characteristic of capitalist society' (Postone, 1996: 300).

Thus, the law of value is dynamic and is fully developed in capitalism, and is not applicable for other societies, and as Postone says:

> The commodity form and, hence, the law of value, are fully developed only in capitalism and are fundamental determinations of that social formation ... For Marx, then, the theory of value grasps the 'truth of the law of appropriation' of the capitalist social formation and does not apply to other societies. (Postone, 1996: 132)

So, the law of value is dynamic, and is wealth-creating, describing a 'pattern of ongoing social transformations' (Postone, 1996); it is specific to capitalism, which is characterised by the domination of value. The law of value cannot be grasped simply in terms of the market and there is a need to explore the theory at a deeper level, to appreciate the 'ongoing transformation of social life'. There is a need to adapt and change and to appreciate the dynamic, all-pervading power of capitalism, as opposed to treating it in a box-like fashion, as many traditional Marxists do. Postone refers to the law, saying:

> I have noted that this 'law' is dynamic and cannot be grasped adequately as a law of the market; at this point I can add that it categorically grasps the drive toward ever-increasing levels of productivity, the ongoing transformation of social life in capitalist society, as well as the ongoing reconstitution of its basic social forms. (Postone, 1996: 300)

So, Marx developed a dynamic and transformative theory of value, the drive of which is towards 'ever-increasing levels of productivity' and is not limited to the law of the market. Furthermore, the basic social forms in capitalism are being continually reconstituted and are not static. Within this, we can now consider the 'temporal dimension' of this value.

Temporal dimension of value

Postone says that the law of value has a temporal dimension – i.e. it only exists within a certain, particular point in time. He then relates this temporal determination of value to the expansion of surplus value, saying that:

> Given this temporal determination of value, the expansion of surplus value – the systematic goal of production in capitalism – can be achieved only if the proportion of surplus labor time to necessary labor time is changed. This ... can be accomplished by extending the duration of the working day (the production of 'absolute surplus value'). Once, however, the length of the work day has been limited (as a result of labor struggles or legislation, for example), surplus labor time can be increased only if necessary labor time is reduced (the production of 'relative surplus value'). This reduction, according to Marx, is effected by increased productivity. (Postone, 1996: 310)

Postone also refers to growth, noting that:

> ...although competition among capitals can be used to explain the existence of growth, it is value's temporal determination that, in Marx's analysis, underlies the form of that growth. The particular relation between increases in productivity and the expansion of surplus value shapes the underlying trajectory of growth in capitalism. (Postone, 1996: 313)

Thus, a grasp of the theory of value and its temporal nature – i.e. the fact that it only exists for a certain, particular time, in this case, within capitalism, is also essential.

Value extracted from labour

So far, I have shown and emphasised how labour is the core of capitalism, and through this how labour produces wealth and ensures the continued perpetuation and success of capitalism. The commodity was then analysed, because this is Marx's starting point in his analysis of capitalism, and I endeavour to explain why I think that Marx started from this point, and indeed, why it is necessary to do so. In the process of unfolding the mystery of the commodity, we discover that it is the value embedded in the commodity that is produced by labour that gives the commodity its unique and powerful ingredient. Thus, the successful perpetuation of capitalism is ensured by the value embedded in the commodity. Value is social energy and takes on various aspects (value, added value and surplus value) and various forms (use-value and exchange-value) in the commodity. It is also the way in which the different concepts interact that is specific to capitalism, and this includes concepts such as labour-power, the commodity, profit and markets, as well as the different aspects and forms of value. However, as I point out (R. Rikowski, 2004a), while the business literature very much realises the importance of value, it largely does not recognise these different aspects and forms of value, and this is a serious omission. We are now in a position to be able to consider how value, and in particular, surplus value, is actually extracted from labour.

Marx says simply that 'labour is the substance, and the immanent measure of value, but has itself no value' (Marx, 1867: 503).

Thus, although labour creates value, it has no value in itself. The value is only realised once the labourer labours and their labour becomes objectified and embodied in the commodity. Expanding upon this further, Marx says that:

...human labour, creates value, but is not itself value. It becomes value only in its congealed state, when embodied in the form of some object. In order to express the value of the linen as a congelation of human labour, that value must be expressed as having objective existence, as being a something materially different from the linen itself, and yet a something to the linen and all other commodities. (Marx, 1867: 57–8)

The way in which value is embedded in the commodity is specific to capitalism. Furthermore,

The general value-form is the reduction of all kinds of actual labour to their common character of being human labour generally, of being the expenditure of human labour-power. (Marx, 1867: 72)

Postone brings us back to the fundamental point, saying that 'Value is a social form that expresses, and is based on, the expenditure of direct labor time. This form, for Marx, is at the very heart of capitalist society' (Postone, 1996: 25).

Labour is the 'substance of value' and as Postone say, 'we have seen that labor, in its historically determinate function as a socially mediating activity, is the "substance of value", the determining essence of the social formation' (Postone, 1996: 166).

All this, then, makes it very clear that it is the value extracted from labour that is necessary for the continued success of capitalism. Yet labour itself does not have value. Instead, the commodity labour-power, the capacity to labour, has value. The labourers sell their labour-power in the marketplace. Once this has been sold, the value is then created when they labour, and this value then becomes embedded in the commodity.

Intellectual labour and value

Introduction

As I have already indicated, labourers undertake two types of labour: manual and intellectual labour. In the industrial revolution, the emphasis was on manual labour, such as on digging up the next lot of coal. In the knowledge revolution in the developed world, however, the emphasis is more on intellectual labour, and it is the exertion of intellectual labour which is increasingly important for the creation and extraction of value from labour, in order to ensure the success of the knowledge revolution and of global capitalism itself. But creating value from intellectual labour is not as easy or straightforward as creating value from manual labour.

The working day, labour and labour-power

The concept of the length of the working day was a very useful concept that Marx formulated in regard to manual labour. Marx emphasised how the length of the working day has been arrived at by a process of negotiation between the capitalist and the labourer, and how the capitalist wants the labourer to work as many hours as possible. However, apart from anything else, it would be physically impossible for the labourer to work for 24 hours a day, as they need to eat and rest – i.e. labour-power, the capacity to labour, needs to be replenished (without this the labourer will die). Marx says that:

> ...the working day contains the full 24 hours, with the deduction of the few hours of repose without which labour-power absolutely refuses its services again. Hence it is self-evident that the labourer is nothing else, his whole life through, than labour-power, that therefore all his disposable time is by nature and law labour-time, to be devoted to the self-expansion of capital. Time for education, for intellectual development, for the fulfilling of social functions and for social intercourse, for the free-play of his bodily and mental activity, even the rest time of Sunday ... – moonshine! But in its blind unrestrainable passion, its were-wolf hunger for surplus-labour, capital, oversteps not only the moral, but even the merely physical maximum bounds of the working day. It usurps the time for growth, development, and healthy maintenance of the body. It steals the time required for the consumption of fresh air and sunlight. It higgles over a meal-time, incorporating it where possible with the process of production itself, so that food is given to the labourer as to a mere means of production itself, as coal is supplied to the boiler, grease and oil to the machinery. It reduces the sound sleep needed for the restoration, reparation, refreshment of the bodily powers to just so many hours of torpor as the revival of an organism, absolutely exhausted, renders essential. (Marx, 1867: 253)

Marx emphasises how 'capital cares nothing for the length of the life of labour-power', instead, its only concern is about how to maximise labour-power. So, it does not care if the life of the labourer is shortened. More precisely, it only cares to the extent that it might be more costly to have to nurture a new lot of labour-power – i.e. nurturing a new labourer, with all that that entails – food, sleep, skills, education, development etc., than it would be to shorten the length of the working day. Shortening the length of the working day enables the labourer to live a healthier and a longer life. Hence, we arrive at the joint desire to limit the length of the working day. But this joint desire to limit the length of the working day is established because it is in the capitalist's interest and not for any moral reasons. We need to appreciate the fact that capitalism has no moral base.

Thus, it is actually in the capitalist's interest to limit the length of the working day and so:

> If then the unnatural extension of the working day, that capital necessarily strives after in its unmeasured passion for self-expression, shortens the length of life of the individual labourer, and therefore, the duration of his labour-power, the forces used up have to be replaced at a more rapid rate and the sum of the expenses for the reproduction of labour-power will be greater; just as in a machine the part of its value to be reproduced every day is greater the more rapidly the machine is worn out. It would seem therefore that the interest of capital itself points in the direction of a normal working day. (Marx, 1867: 253)

Furthermore, 'the creation of a normal working day is … the product of a protracted civil war, more or less dissembled, between the capitalist class and the working-class' (Marx, 1867: 283). Within this formulation of the working day, the capitalist gains because:

> The owner of the money has paid the value of a day's labour-power; his, therefore, is the use of it for a day; a day's labour belongs to him. The circumstance, that on the other hand the daily sustenance of labour-power costs only half a day's labour, while on the other hand the very same labour-power can work during a whole day, that consequently the value which its use during one day creates, is double what he pays for that use, this circumstance is, without doubt, a piece of good luck for the buyer, but no means an injury to the seller. (Marx, 1867: 188)

Therefore, the length of the working day needs to be limited, so that the labourer can rest and labour-power, the capacity to labour, can be replenished. But once this length has been established (e.g. ten hours), the capitalist/manager can then get the labourer to work hard, create value and produce goods. If necessary, the manager can actually observe the labourer at work, and enforce penalties (such as a reduction in pay), if the labourer does not work as hard as the manager thinks he should.

Intellectual labour and the impossibility of determining the length of the working day

With regard to knowledge workers, however, it is impossible to determine the length of the working day in the same sort of way. New ideas can be formulated in minutes, or they could take years. I discuss this further in R. Rikowski (2004b), saying that:

> ...ultimately ... the concept of the working day becomes meaningless in the knowledge revolution ... while we need an appreciation and an understanding of Marx's concept of the working day, having arrived at this understanding, we then need to appreciate the fact that the concept actually starts to lose its meaning and significance in the advanced stage of capitalism that we are now in. (R. Rikowksi, 2004b: 1)

Furthermore, with regard to the intellectual labourer:

> Ideas can materialise at any time of the day or night ... [is the knowledge worker] sitting there thinking up something wonderful to benefit the company, or are they just dreaming about their forthcoming night out, or a football match? (R. Rikowski, 2004b: 2)

Many argue that the knowledge worker is empowered, but I very much challenge this notion in my article. This is because the knowledge worker, or more accurately, the intellectual labourer, still has to sell their labour-power as a commodity in the marketplace, in the same way as any other labourer does. For this, the intellectual labourer is paid a wage, but they also create 'added' value over and above the value that already exists. But, as Marx says, this is:

> ...very advantageous to the capitalist inasmuch as it preserves the existing value of his capital. So long as trade is good, the capitalist

is too much absorbed in money-grabbing to take notice of this gratuitous gift of labour. (Marx, 1867: 200)

Thus, as I say:

> In regard to the concept of the 'working day'... this concept becomes a nonsense when applied to intellectual labour. This is because, with the need to engender an environment that encourages intellectual thinking and with the need for more flexible ways of working etc., it becomes impossible to determine the length of the working day for intellectual labour. (R. Rikowski, 2004b: 8)

And so, 'all that is solid melts into air' (Marx and Engels, 1883: 83).

The problem here is that as it becomes impossible to determine the length of the working day for intellectual labour, it is also difficult to easily 'manage' the creation and extraction of value from intellectual labour. By this, I mean that the intellectual labourer cannot be managed in the same way that the manual labourer can be. While it is possible to have a production target for the manual labour, such as the production of ten small parts for a car, in one hour, it is not possible to have a similar type of production target for intellectual labour. The capitalist/manager cannot insist that the intellectual labourer produces five ideas an hour, for example. Bater and Cabos also make this point in their chapter in this book, saying:

> ...'manage' no longer means what it did under the old mechanical model of business. Managers in the knowledge economy lead rather than command. They look to the longer term rather than the shorter, and address a holistic vision of outcomes, rather than isolated 'objectives'.

Thus, it becomes necessary to try to think about other ways of 'managing' intellectual labour. The answer lies in the implementation of effective KM practices. We come full circle!

Intellectual labour and manual labour

In conclusion, when labourers labour they undertake two types of labour: manual and intellectual labour. They must, of necessity, always undergo both types of labour. If one is doing a highly manual job, some thinking is still required, even if this is at a minimalist level. On the other hand, if one is performing a very intellectual job, some manual work will also be required. However, in the industrial revolution, the emphasis was on manual labour – it was the physical work that the labourer underwent, such as going down the coal mines and digging up the coal, which exhausted the labourer. And the value that was extracted from labour in the industrial revolution was largely from this manual labour.

In the knowledge revolution in the modern developed world, however, the picture has changed. It is largely the intellectual work that creates the additional value to sustain capitalism, and it is the intellectual work that exhausts the labourer.

It is for all these reasons that KM is so important today, particularly given the fact that this intellectual labour and the ideas that intellectual labourers can have, can be so difficult to capture, and that it becomes, indeed, impossible to determine the length of the working day for intellectual labour in the same sort of way. Because of this impossibility, being able to manage knowledge effectively becomes imperative.

Objectification of labour

In capitalism, labour is objectified and as Postone says:

> Value ... is the objectification of abstract labor ... Value is ... a category of mediating: it is at once a historically determinate, self-distributing form of wealth and an objectified, self-mediating form of social relations ... value is a category of the social totality: the value of a commodity is an individual moment of the objectified general social mediation. Because it exists in objectified form, this social mediation has an objective character, is not overtly social, is abstracted from all particularly, and is independent of directly personal relations. (Postone, 1996: 154)

Thus, 'as the objectified form of abstract labor, value is an essential category of capitalist relations of production' (Postone, 1996: 154).

Postone explains how both labour and value become objectified, saying that:

> Value ... is unfolded by Marx as the core of a form of social mediation that constitutes social objectivity and subjectivity, and is intrinsically dynamic; it is a form of social mediation that necessarily exists in objectified, materialized form, but is neither identical with, nor an inherent property of, its materialized form,

whether in the shape of money or goods. The way in which Marx unfolds the category of capital retrospectively illuminates his initial determination of value as an objectified social relation, constituted by labor, that is carried by, but exists 'behind' the commodities as objects. This clarifies the thrust of his analysis of the commodity's twofold character and its externalization as money and commodities. (Postone, 1996: 269)

Bensaid's words are also very illuminating. He shows how humans are not only objectified but alienated, saying:

> In labour, human beings are not only objectified, but also alienated. Their bodies are literally stolen from them, and their existence is reduced to its economic function. The separation of labour from its natural conditions results in the destruction of the natural condition of humankind, living off the earth and its own labour ... In a word, it [labour] must become abstract, objectified, alienated, become abstract general labour that makes individuals mere 'instruments of labour'. (Bensaid, 2002: 321)

Thus, an appreciation of the objectification, exploitation and alienation of labour and how value is derived from the objectification of abstract labour is crucial for the development of a theoretical critique of capitalism.

Human beings labour, but in capitalism this labour becomes objectified and then dominates the labourer themselves. People cannot really feel a part of the world that they have created; they cannot relate to it and can no longer appreciate the fact that the alien world in which they live is of their own making, constructed by their own labour. Thus, the labourer becomes dominated by her/his own labour, and becomes alienated. This is true, even if people do not have an appreciation of this and say that they are not alienated, and that they can relate to the world they have created. This merely demonstrates the extent of the alienation, because objectively they are alienated – their labour-power is sold for a price and generates surplus value for capitalism. Furthermore, and even more disturbingly, in the knowledge revolution today, unconscious tacit knowledge is even being derived from intellectual labour for the creation of value – ideas and knowledge that people did not even know that they had. Furthermore, intellectual labour is being transformed into human capital and intellectual capital and ultimately into structural capital.

Traditional Marxism versus Open Marxism

The section will briefly consider the benefits of Open Marxism over the more traditional Marxist approach. Open Marxism is a school of thought to which I adhere. Postone's book *Time, Labour and Social Domination* (1996) provides a reinterpretation of traditional Marxism. Postone argues that we need to move beyond a traditional Marxist approach and, instead, he provides a critique and a dynamic reinterpretation of Marxism. Postone's contribution to Marxism is very profound indeed, and furthermore, his theories and ideas help to prevent us from deifying Marx, which I am sure that Marx himself would not have wanted. Instead, Marx would have wanted people to use his theories and build on them, as Postone has done, in order to help to bring about socialism/communism. Postone builds on Marx's work, and takes us on to a new dimension with it, illustrating in particular, the dynamic and transformative nature of capitalism. He argues that traditional Marxists have used Marxist terminology in rather a sterile, category-engendered, box-like fashion, and that in this way they have misinterpreted Marx. This has sometimes made Marx appear to be too deterministic (unfairly so, as he did not write in a 'box-like' fashion himself), but it has enabled others to criticise him. Instead, we need to appreciate the power of Marx's concepts and terminology, and the fact that when they are used dynamically and in an interactive way they uncover the mystery and the essential characteristics of capitalism itself. Furthermore, Marx's theory, including his theory of value, is specific to capitalism. Without this dynamic approach we will never be able to uncover the real essence of capitalism and seek to move beyond it. I do not think that the importance of Postone's work has, as yet, been fully appreciated. Other Open Marxists include John Holloway and Werner Bonefeld.

Social scientific theory and Marxist theory

Postone emphasises how his reinterpretation not only calls into question traditional Marxism but also raises questions for social theory in general. He says:

> In conclusion, it should be noted that the interpretation I have presented here not only calls into question traditional Marxist

approaches but also raises issues of significance for social theory in general. I have presented Marx's theory as a self-reflexive, historically determinate theory, as an approach that is conscious of the historical specificity of its categories as well as of its own theoretical form. In addition to being historically determinate, the Marxian critique is a theory of social constitution... (Postone, 1996: 398)

Indeed, he calls for a re-examination of social theory itself:

The question of the adequacy of Marx's theory, then, is not only a question of the viability of his categorical analysis of capitalism. It also raises more general questions regarding the nature of social theory. Marx's critical theory, which grasps capitalist society by means of a theory of the constitution of labor of a directionally dynamic, totalizing mediation that is historically specific, is a brilliant analysis of this society; and, it is, at the same time, a powerful argument regarding the nature of an adequate social theory. (Postone, 1996: 399)

Postone considers Marx's theory further in general:

...the Marxian theory is also a social theory of consciousness and subjectivity, one that analyzes social objectivity and subjectivity as intrinsically related; it grasps both in terms of determinate forms of mediation, objectified forms of practice. (Postone, 1996: 398)

Furthermore, Marx's theory questions 'meaning' and 'implies that meaning is not necessarily constituted in the same way in all societies, and thereby calls into question transhistorical and transcultural theories of the constitution of meaning, and, hence, of "culture"' (Postone, 1996: 398).

In addition, it is a theory that is very much grounded within capitalism itself, and it is historically specific.

...Marx's category of capital can ground socially the directional dynamic of capitalist society, the character of economic 'growth' and the nature and trajectory of the production process in capitalism. His analysis implicitly demands of other theoretical positions that they provide a social account of these features of capitalist society. (Postone, 1996: 399)

Thus, all these issues are very important for the development of social theory in general, as well as providing a reinterpretation of Marxism, which enables us to uncover more fully the dynamics of capitalism itself, and its interrelationships. It is also important for the development of value theory specifically, as it demonstrates how value becomes 'reconstituted structurally as the core of capitalism' (Postone, 1996).

In essence, it demonstrates the power of Marx's theory over other social scientific theories, and illustrates how Marx's theory forces other social scientific theorists to question and critique their own positions. As Postone says, Marx's analysis implicitly demands that other theoretical positions need to be as 'rigorous' as his. He argues that 'more generally, Marx's approach implicitly is critical of all transhistorical theories, as well as of theories that address either social structure or social practices without grasping their interrelations' (Postone, 1996: 399).

Overthrowing capitalism and abolishing value as its means of sustenance

Thus, labour is exploited, alienated and objectified in capitalism. By this means, value is created for the perpetuation of capitalism. In order to release humans from this nightmare, value must cease to be embedded in the commodity, and to be the means for creating social wealth, and capitalism itself must be overthrown.

As Postone makes clear, in order to overthrow capitalism, value created by labour must cease to be the means for creating social wealth, because by this means social wealth is created in capitalism and is perpetuated. Indeed, 'for Marx, overcoming capitalism involves the abolition of value as the social form of wealth, which, in turn, entails overcoming the determinate mode of producing developed under capitalism' (Postone, 1996: 27).

Postone refers to the 'mystification' of value in capitalism, and how this can only be demystified through socialism, saying:

> Value, in Marx's analysis, both expresses and veils a social essence – in other words, as a form of appearance, it is 'mystifying'. Within the framework of interpretations based upon the notion of 'labor', the function of critique is to demystify (or defetishize) theoretically, that is, to reveal that, despite appearances, labor is actually the transhistorical source of social wealth and the regulatory principle of society. Socialism, then, is the practical 'demystification' of

capitalism ... Demystification ... is understood as a process whereby the essence openly and directly appears. (Postone, 1996: 61)

Postone then refers to various ways in which this nightmare can be overcome, arguing that 'in socialism ... labor would emerge openly as the regulatory principle of social life, which would provide the basis for the realization of a rational and just society, based on general principles' (Postone, 1996: 64).

Postone refers to the abolition of value and how this can liberate humans. He says, for example:

With regard to the structure of social labor ... the Marxian contradiction should be understood as a growing contradiction between the sort of labor people perform under capitalism and the sort of labor they could perform if value were abolished and the productive potential developed under capitalism were reflexively used to liberate people from the sway of the alienated structures constituted by their own labor. (Postone, 1996: 35)

So, the aim is to abolish alienated labour:

...for Marx, overcoming the value form of social relations would mean overcoming alienated social necessity ... In Marx's view, then, the abolition of alienated labor would entail overcoming historical necessity, the historically specific social necessity constituted in the capitalist sphere of production; it would allow for historical freedom. (Postone, 1996: 382)

Furthermore, people need to consider how they want to shape their world:

...the issue is not so much whether people should try to shape their world – they already are doing so. Rather, the issue is the way in which they shape their world and, hence, the nature of this world and its trajectory. (Postone, 1996: 384)

Postone also says that currently, knowledge as capital dominates people, but in a post-capitalist society people would 'begin to control what they create rather than being controlled by it'. So:

Central to Marx's conception of the overcoming of capitalism is his notion of people's reappropriation of the socially general knowledge and capacities that had been constituted historically as capital. We have seen that, according to Marx, such knowledge and capacities, as capital, dominate people; such reappropriation, then, entails overcoming the mode of domination characteristic of capitalist society, which ultimately is grounded in labor's historically specific role as a socially mediating activity. Thus, at the core of his vision of a post-capitalist society is the historically generated possibility that people might begin to control what they create rather than being controlled by it. (Postone, 1996: 373)

So, people need to find a way to use their knowledge as a way to liberate them rather than dominate them. In conclusion, Postone says that 'rethinking the nature of capitalism means reconceptualizing its overcoming' (Postone, 1996: 392).

Once society understands itself more, we will be moving towards communism. And so we need to look towards a better world, and as I say in my globalisation book, 'Let humans rejoice ... in the world that they have developed with their labour – do not let them be dominated by it. Let us look towards a better future and a brighter world' (R. Rikowksi, 2005a: 336).

(The preceding sections have largely been taken from R. Rikowski, 2003c.)

Conclusion

Throughout this chapter, I have examined Marx's theory of value and the commodity in some detail, and have also sought to re-interpret it in the light of Postone's work, which emphasises the fact that Marxism is dynamic and transformative, and is not static. This has been necessary in order to understand the significance that KM plays today in capitalism, particularly in the developed world.

In conclusion then, following on from Marx, our analysis of capitalism must begin with the commodity. Humans labour (undertaking both manual and intellectual labour) and value is created from their labour. This value becomes embedded in the commodity and this commodity is then sold in the marketplace. Profits are derived from the value that is created from labour (and value can only ever be created from labour). However, in the knowledge revolution, in the developed world, there is a greater exertion of intellectual labour and less exertion of manual labour. Thus, creating more value from intellectual labour becomes increasingly important in the knowledge revolution that we find ourselves in today – this being the latest phase of capitalism. Effective and enforceable knowledge management practices become essential for the successful extraction of value from intellectual labour – i.e. from the ideas and knowledge that they have. By all these means, global capitalism is maintained and perpetuated.

We should try to use KM, and in particular, our knowledge and intellect in general, in a different way, I would suggest – in a way that will help to liberate labour rather than exploit it further. But we can only start to do this once we have a firm grasp and understanding of the social universe in which we find ourselves, and from this, we can then start to look towards a future beyond capitalism. We can then use our knowledge, intellect and understanding towards this end, rather than for the continued creation of value for the furtherance of capitalism. In this way, our labour can begin to liberate us, rather than to dominate us. Let us look towards a better future and a brighter world.

Conclusion
Ruth Rikowski

This book has covered a number of important themes running through knowledge management (KM), and I hope it has given the reader food for thought and a desire to explore some of these topics in more depth. It has also aimed to look at the topic from a somewhat different angle, in comparison with many more traditional KM books. In particular, I hope that I have been able to convince the reader of the need for a deeper theoretical analysis of KM.

All of the contributors make a very valuable contribution to the KM literature, but obviously I do not agree with everything that everyone says. This, indeed, is the beauty of an edited collection; that it provides the opportunity for different views and perspectives to be aired within one book.

Yet, while fully wishing to respect the work and ideas of others, I am also very keen to push my own ideas and theories forward. For this reason, I have written a critique, and have outlined some of the ways in which my views differ from some of the other contributors. I also suggest how the work of the contributors could, perhaps, be developed (and this includes ideas for developing my own work, as I continually seek to be critical of my own work and to seek ways in which I can improve it). This critique is available on the Rikowski website, 'The Flow of Ideas' at *www.flowideas.co.uk*, in the 'Articles' section, and is entitled 'KM critique'. It seemed more appropriate to put this critique on our website, rather than to include it in this final chapter. If others want to contribute to the debate, then they can place comments in the website 'Forum' and/or write an article themselves for insertion on our website. I can be contacted through the e-mail on our website in this regard, or at *rikowskigr@aol.com*. Thus, this concluding chapter of the book is quite short, and focuses on a few key points in the book.

Professor Bruce Lloyd's opening chapter provides an interesting and thought-provoking start to the book, and it encourages us to think about KM in a deeper and more philosophical way. In addition, Lloyd emphasises the importance of further considering the role of wisdom for practical effective decision making. Thus, I am grateful to Lloyd for his contribution, for raising the topic of wisdom and emphasising how the concept of wisdom is often excluded from much of the KM literature. Lloyd refers to 'values', in contrast to the objective meaning of 'value', which has been the focus of my work. I would suggest that further consideration needs to be given to the difference between 'values' (a subjective/personal definition) and 'value' (an objective definition). Lloyd has laid some of the groundwork and this can now be built on, and the meaning and significance of wisdom within KM can be considered at a deeper and a more theoretical and philosophical level.

Meanwhile, Bob Bater and Isabelle Cabos have provided a valuable contribution both to the KM literature in general, and to wider considerations in regard to the economy, with their examination of value and intangibles. They emphasise the fact that we are in the knowledge economy today, that the ideas and knowledge in people's heads are of ever-increasing importance, and that more consideration needs to be given to intangible value. In addition, they stress that knowledge workers cannot be managed in the same way that manual workers can be managed, and furthermore that companies today, in general, are taking corporate responsibility more seriously. I very much agree with Bater and Cabos in regard to the changes that are taking place, although personally I do not think that all this is leading to a lasting, more enlightened form of capitalism, that many more people can benefit from. Rather, I think that labour continues to be exploited. Nevertheless, Bater and Cabos have made a very valuable contribution to the literature on intangibles, value and KM and have drawn people's attention to many important points. Their work is of real significance, and it provides us with the opportunity to now build on this.

Mandy Webster and Paul Catherall focus on some practical issues in regard to KM, and provide much valuable information in this regard. Webster considers how librarians and information professionals working within the context of the library and information centre can, and should, work more effectively with KM. She gives many examples about how this is currently being done, and how this can be built on in the future. Webster also emphasises, though, that the library still needs to be able to offer a quiet place to work. I very much agree with Webster, that the library and information profession should be moving more into KM.

However, the traditional library and all that it has to offer also needs to be cherished. Meanwhile, Catherall provides a very valuable contribution to the KM literature, giving the reader a wealth of useful and detailed information regarding IT and web-related issues for KM, with its focus on web accessibility and usability. It is also a practical guide, as well as providing some useful legal information for disabled people, in particular, concerning web accessibility. Catherall's work in this area could, perhaps, also be developed further, by relating IT to wider social, economic and political issues.

In my chapters on culture and KM, I cover a number of different areas, helping to place KM within an international/global context. This includes an examination of cultural theories, focusing in particular on the work of Hofstede and relating this to KM; KM in the developing and the developed world; knowledge transfer across cultures; communities of practice and globalisation and KM.

Dr Leburn Rose aims to bring science and social science together in his chapter, and relates thermodynamics, energy and principles to knowledge and KM. His alternative schema for knowledge creation in an organisation, where he suggests that there are four processes through which knowledge is transferred, namely, conduction, convection, radiation and combustion, is very innovative. Furthermore, his suggestion that there are four knowledge zones, namely, tacit-organic, tacit-rigid, explicit-organic and explicit-rigid, is new, providing a more adequate analysis of the different types of knowledge, rather than just focusing on the traditional tacit and explicit knowledge divide. Rose focuses very much on the organisation, though, and I think it would be very useful if he were now to consider thermodynamics, knowledge and energy in relation to the commodity, because, as I make clear in this book, in my view, following on from Marx, any analysis of capitalism must begin with the commodity. In sum, Rose has focused on a very important topic, relating KM to energy and thermodynamics, and his work is of real significance, if not ground-breaking, and hopefully further work can be undertaken on this area in the future.

In my theoretical chapter, I briefly consider the relationship between value and energy, and emphasise the importance of bringing science and social science together more in this regard. I then go on to develop an Open Marxist theoretical perspective on KM and highlight the importance of the knowledge worker/intellectual labourer in the knowledge revolution and the need for effective KM practices within this context. Furthermore, I argue that the labourer still has to sell their labour-power as a commodity in the marketplace, and that value is extracted from labour, so the knowledge worker is not empowered, but is still exploited, alienated and objectified in this knowledge revolution, this being the latest phase of capitalism. I need to continue to develop my work in these areas, and to give further consideration to topics such as the difference between value and profit.

In conclusion, I hope this can all now be built on; that the practical sections offer some useful information and guidelines and that the importance of an examination of knowledge, knowledge management and the knowledge economy/knowledge revolution at a deeper level can be more fully appreciated and explored.

Bibliography

Abell, A. (1998) 'Skills for the 21st century', *Journal of Librarianship and Information Science*, 30(4): 211–14.

Abell, A. and Oxbrow, N. (2001) *Competing with Knowledge: The Information Professional in The Knowledge Management Age*, London: Library Association Publishing.

Allee, V. (2002) 'A value network approach for modeling and measuring intangibles'. Paper prepared for presentation at Transparent Enterprise, Madrid, November; available at: *http://www .vernaallee.com/value_networks/A_ValueNetworkApproach_white_ paper.pdf* (accessed 15 July 2006).

Amidon, D. M. and Macnamara, D. (2001) '7 C's of knowledge leadership: innovating our future', *Entovation International: Delivering Knowledge Innovation*; available at: (accessed 18 July 2006).

Anon (2006) 'Reframing sustainable sources of energy for the future: the vital role of psychosocial variants'. Draft paper prepared on the occasion of the meeting of the Energy Technology Foresight Network (EFONET), 11th March; available at: *http://www.laetusinpraesens .org/musings/enerfut.php* (accessed 17 July 2006).

Bailey, F. G. (1971) 'The peasant view of the bad life', in Teodor Shamin (ed.) *Peasants and Peasant Societies*, Harmondsworth: Penguin.

Baker, H. J. and Baker, G. A. (2001) 'Leadership, culture and knowledge management', *We Lead Online Magazine*; available at: *http://www .leadingtoday.org/Onmag/sepoct01/h-gbsepoct01.html* (accessed 20 July 2006).

Barth, S. (2000) 'Managing knowledge across borders', *Knowledge Management* (May); available at: *http://www.destinationkm .com/print/default.asp?ArticleID=832* (accessed 20 July 2006).

Bennis, W. G. (1989) *On Becoming a Leader*, Boston: Addison-Wesley.

Bensaid, D. (2002) *Marx for Our Times: Adventures and Misadventures of a Critique*, London: Verso.

BIC (2005a) 'Business in the community's corporate responsibility index: companies that count'; available at: *http://www.bitc.org.uk/programmes/key_initiatives/corporate_responsibility_index/* (accessed 15 July 2006).

BIC (2005b) 'Business in the community: a director's guide to corporate responsibility reporting', July 2005; available at: *http://www.bitc.org.uk/document.rm?id=1880* (accessed 15 July 2006).

Bird, A. and Metcalf, L. (year unknown) 'Integrating twelve dimensions of negotiating behaviour and Hofstede's work-related values: a six-country comparison'; available at: *http://blake.montclair.edu/~cibconf/conference/DATA/Theme4/Usa1.pdf* (accessed 19 July 2006).

Birkinshaw, J. and Crainer, S. (2002) *Leadership the Sven-Goran Eriksson Way: How to Turn Your Team into Winners*, Oxford: Capstone.

Blair, T. (1999) Speech to the CBI conference in Brighton, 2 November; available at: *www.number-10.gov.uk/public/news/features.feature_display.asp?id-680* (accessed November 2000).

BOND (2003) 'Learning from work: an opportunity missed or taken?', BOND survey, London: British Overseas NGOs for Development; available at: *www.bond.org.uk/lte/think.htm* (accessed 19 July 2006).

Bonac, V. A. (2001) 'The forbidden knowledge of the unconscious', *International Journal of Communicative Psychoanalysis and Psychotherapy* 15(1). (This is a slightly modified version of the paper first presented at the Annual Conference of the International Society of Communicative Psychoanalysis and Psychotherapy, in New York City, held 26–28 October 2001); available at: *http://www.ejcpsa.com/articles_and_essays/Forbid_Knowedge_Art.htm* (accessed 18 July 2006).

Boyett, J. H. and Boyett, J. T. (2001) *Guru Guide to the Knowledge Economy*, Chichester: John Wiley.

British Dyslexia Association (2005) 'What is dyslexia?'; available at: *http://www.bda-dyslexia.org.uk/extra329.html* (accessed December 2005).

Broadbent, M. (1998) 'The phenomenon of knowledge management: what does it mean to the information profession?', *Information Outlook* (May): 23–6.

Buckley, P. and Carter, M. (1999) 'Managing cross-border complementary knowledge', *International Studies of Management and Organization*, 29(1): 80–104.

Buus, I. (year unknown) 'Leadership development: a Scandinavian model', *Business Leadership Review*; available at: *http://www.mbaworld.com/blrprintarticle.php?article=12* (accessed 18 July 2006).

Byers, S. (1999) Speech to CBI London Region Annual Lunch, 26 February; available at: *www.dti.gov.uk/Minspeech/byers05099.htm* (accessed March 2000).

Byers, S. (2000) Speech to the Mansion House, 1 February.

Cap Gemini Ernst and Young (1999) 'Center for Business Innovation's Measures That Matter: a survey of financial executives at Global 500 corporations'.

Capra, F. (1982) *The Turning Point: Science, Society and the Rising Culture*, New York: Bantam Books.

Carlsson, J. (1998) 'Organisation and leadership in Africa', in L. Wohlgemuth, J. Carlsson and H. Kifle (eds) *Institution Building and Leadership in Africa*, Uppsala: Nordic Africa Institute.

Cashman, K. (1997) 'Authentic leadership', *Innovative Leader* 6(11): 305; available at: *http://www.winstonbrill.com/bril001/html/article_ index/articles/301-350/article305_body.html* (accessed 18 July 2006).

Catherall, P. (2004) *Delivering E-Learning for Information Services in Higher Education*, Chandos Publishing: Oxford.

Challenge Forum (year unknown) 'Leadership'; available at: *http://www.chforum.org/methods/xc415.html* (accessed 2005).

Chillingworth, M. (2005) 'Marxism mires debate: globalization is unjust, unfair and threatens the existence of libraries, according to this controversial title: Book review of Ruth Rikowski's *Globalisation, Information and Libraries: The Implications of the World Trade Organisation's GATS and TRIPS Agreements*', *Information World Review*, No. 219 (December): 61.

CMS Wiki (2004) 'Knowledge management'; available at: *http://www .cmswiki.com/tiki-index.php?page=Knowledge Management* (accessed 18 July 2006).

Collison, J. (1998) 'Female bosses rate higher as effective leaders: what must employers and males do', *HRMadeEasy*; available at: *http://www.employerhelp.org/jimcollison/stories/female_bosses.htm* (accessed 18 July 2006).

Daum, J. (2004) 'Interview with Jeremy Hope: The origins of Beyond Budgeting and of the Beyond Budgeting round table (BBRT)'. *New Economy Analyst Report*, 10 January; available at: *http://www .juergendaum.com/news/01_10_2004.htm* (accessed 21 June 2006).

Davenport, T. and Prusak, L. (1998) *Working Knowledge: How Organizations Manage what They Know*, Boston, MA: Harvard Business School Press.

Davies, R. (1998) 'Order and diversity: representing and assisting organisational learning in non-government aid organisations'. PhD thesis, Swansea: Centre for Development Studies, University of Wales; available at: *www.mande.co.uk/docs/thesis.htm* (accessed 19 July 2006).

Derber, C. (2003) *People Before Profit: The New Globalisation in an Age of Terror, Big Money, and Economic Crisis*, London: Souvenir Press.

Dilts, R. and Dilts, J. (year unknown) 'Leadership and success factor modelling: discovering the factors of success in the new economy'; available at: *http://www.journeytogenius.com/DSG/Leadership/Article/SFM_Article.html* (accessed 18 July 2006).

DIRKS (2003) 'The DIRKS manual: a strategic approach to managing business information'. National Archives of Australia; available at: *http://www.naa.gov.au/recordkeeping/dirks/dirksman/dirks.html* (accessed 21 June 2006).

Disability Rights Commission (2004a) 'Code of practice – rights of access goods, facilities, services and premises'; available at: *http:// www.drc-gb.org/open4all/law/code.asp* (accessed December 2005).

Disability Rights Commission (2004b) 'The Web: access and inclusion for disabled people – a formal investigation conducted by the Disability Rights Commission'; available at: *http://www.drc-gb .org/publicationsandreports/report.asp* (accessed December 2005).

Drucker, P. F. (2001) *Management Challenges for the 21st Century*, New York: HarperBusiness.

Dyspraxia Foundation (2005) 'What is dyspraxia?'; available at: *http://www.dyspraxiafoundation.org.uk/services/dys_dyspraxia.php* (accessed December 2005).

Eade, J. (ed.) (1997) *Living in the Global City: Globalization as Local Process*, London: Routledge.

Economic and Social Research Council (2005) 'Disability in the UK'; available at: *http://www.esrcsocietytoday.ac.uk/ESRCInfoCentre/facts/index42.aspx?ComponentId=12640&SourcePageId=6970* (accessed December 2005).

Edozien N. N., Almeida Freire, I., Geier, J., Miedzinski, M. and Susiarjo, G. (year unknown) 'tt20-project: Knowledge transfer across cultures'; available at: *http://onevillagefoundation.org/ovf/downloads/pdfs/tt30-WSIS_KTproject.pdf* (accessed 19 July, 2006).

Edwards, M. (1994) 'NGOs in the age of information', *IDS Bulletin* 25(2): 117–24.

Einstein, A. (1949) 'Why Socialism?', *Monthly Review* 1(1); available at: *http://www.monthlyreview.org/598.einst.htm* (accessed 17 July 2006).

Elkington, J. (1998) 'Cannibals with forks: the triple bottom line of twenty-first century business', Gabriola Island, BC: New Society Publishers.

Employers' Forum on Disability (2005) 'Disability in the UK'; available at: *http://www.employers-forum.co.uk/www/guests/info/statistics.html* (accessed December 2005).

Everest, K. (2001) 'Knowledge management: a view from the field', *2001–2002 KBE Speaker Series*, 5 October, Queen's University, Kingston, ON.

Executive Advisory Group to CILIP (2002) *CILIP in the Knowledge Economy: A Leadership Strategy*, London: The Chartered Institute of Library and Information Professionals.

Figge, F., Hahn, T., Schaltegger, S. and Wagner, M. (2002) 'The Sustainability Balanced Scorecard'; available at: *http://www.strategyguide.org/Pdfs/Banks/TheSustainablyBalancedScorecard TheoryandApplicationofaToolforValueBasedsustainabilityManagement.pdf* (accessed 21 June 2006).

FOLDOC, Free On-Line Dictionary of Computing (2005a) 'ARPA'; available at: *http://foldoc.org/?query=ARPA+&action=Search* (accessed December 2005).

FOLDOC, Free On-Line Dictionary of Computing (2005b) 'Visual programming language'; available at: *http://foldoc.org/foldoc .cgi?query=visual+programming+language* (accessed December 2005).

Ford, D. P. and Chan, Y. E. (2002) 'Knowledge sharing in a cross-cultural setting: a case study', Working Paper, WP 02-09, Queen's KBE, Centre for Knowledge-Based Enterprises, Queen's School of Business; available at: *http://business.queensu.ca/knowledge/ workingpapers/working/working_02-09.pdf* (accessed 19 July 2006).

Formica, P. (2005) 'Analyzing knowledge policymaking in managed and free-market economies'. Association of Knowledgework; available at: *http://www.kwork.org/Stars/formica.html* (accessed 15 July 2006).

Fukuyama, F. (1995) *Trust – The Social Virtues and The Creation of Prosperity*, London: Hamish Hamilton.

Galbraith, J. K. (1958) *The Affluent Society*, London: Hamish Hamilton.

Gao, F. and Li, M. (2003) 'Why Nonaka highlights tacit knowledge: a critical review', *Journal of Knowledge Management* 7(4): 6–14.

Geertz, C. (1973) *Interpretation of Cultures*, New York: Basic Books; p. 5.

Goleman, D., Boyatzis, R. E. and McKee, A. (2002) *The New Leaders: Transforming the Art of Leadership into the Sciences of Results*, London: Time Warner.

Grant, R. (1996) 'Prospering in dynamically competitive environments: organizational capability as knowledge integration', *Organization Science* 7(4): 375–87.

Grey, D. (2004) 'Community of one?' Knowledge-at-work web-log (15 February); available at: *http://denham.typepad.com/km/2004/02/index.html* (accessed 5 August 2006).

GRI (year unknown) Global Reporting Initiative; available at: *http://www.globalreporting.org/* (accessed 15 July 2006).

Gudykunst, W. B. and Ting-Toomey, S. (1988) *Culture and Interpersonal Communication*, Newbury Park, CA: Sage.

Guinomet (1999) 'Linkages between economic, environmental and social indicators', working paper to the United Nations CSD V expert group.

Gushurst, K.-P. (2004) 'The new leadership – sober, spirited and spiritual: leadership styles today combine the classic values of discipline and execution with the contemporary values of openness and natural expression'; available at: *http://www.strategy-business.com/enewsarticle/enews010804?pg=all* (accessed 18 July 2006).

Hagberg, R. (2003) 'Corporate culture: the distorted view from the top', *LeaderValues*; available at: *http://www.leader-values.com/Content/detail.asp?ContentDetailID=61* (accessed 18 July 2006).

Hailey, J. and James, R. (2002) 'Learning leaders: the key to learning organisations', *Development in Practice* 12 (3/4): 398–406.

Halestrap, J. (2005) 'Is information the DNA of the modern business world?', *Managing Information* 12(3): 48–52.

Hamilton, S, (2002) 'Internet accessible information and censorship, intellectual freedom and libraries – a global overview', *IFLA Journal* 28 (4): 190–7.

Handy, C. (1996) *Beyond Certainty*, London: Arrow Books.

Hannerz, U. (1990) 'Cosmopolitans and locals in world culture', in M. Featherstone (ed.) *Global Culture*, London: Sage; pp. 237–51.

Haralambos, M. and Holborn, M. (2004) *Sociology: Themes and Perspectives* (6th edn), London: HarperCollins.

Harness, J. and Levene, S. (2005) Profiting through knowledge, *Society for Computers and Law Magazine* 16 (1).

Hatch, M. J. (1997) *Organization Theory: Modern Symbolic and Post Modern Perspectives*, Oxford: Oxford University Press.

Heeks, R. (2002) 'Failure, success and improvisation of information systems projects in developing countries', *Development Informatics Working Paper* 11, January. Manchester: Institute for Development Policy and Management, University of Manchester; available at: *http://unpan1.un.org/intradoc/groups/public/documents/NISPAcee/UNPAN015601.pdf* (accessed 21 July 2006).

Helgesen, S. (1995) *The Female Advantage: Women's Ways of Leadership*, New York: Doubleday, Random House.

Henczel, S. (2001) *The Information Audit A Practical Guide*, Munchen: KG Saur.

Heylighen, F. (2005) *Web Dictionary of Cybernetics and Systems*, available at: *http://pespmc1.vub.ac.be/ASC/indexASC.htm* (accessed 8 August 2006).

Hickford, A. (year unknown) 'Leadership in the new economy: are you listening?' Available at: *http://www.providersedge.com/docs/leadership_articles/Leadership_in_the_new_economy.pdf* (accessed 18 July 2006).

Hofstede, G. (1980) *Culture's Consequences: International Differences in Work-Related Values*, Beverley Hills, London: Sage Publications.

Hofstede, G. (2001) *Culture's Consequences: Comparing Values, Behaviours, Institutions and Organizations across Nations*, Thousand Oaks: Sage Publications.

Hofstede, G. (2003) *Cultures and Organizations: Software of the Mind – Intercultural Cooperation and its Importance for Survival*, London: Profile Books.

Hofstede, G. and Bond, M. (1988) 'Confucius and economic growth: new trends in culture's consequences', *Organizational Dynamics* 16(4): 4–21.

Hofstede, G. and Usunier, J.-C. (1996) 'Hofstede's dimensions of culture and their influences on international business negotiations', in P. Ghauri and J. C. Usunier (eds) *International Business Negotiations*, Oxford: Pergamon.

Holden, N. J. (2002) *Cross-Cultural Management: A Knowledge Management Perspective*, Harlow: Pearson Education.

Home Office (1995) *Disability Discrimination Act*, London: HMSO.

Home Office (2001) *Special Educational Needs and Disability Act*, London: HMSO.

House of Lords, Select Committee on Economic Affairs (2002) Globalisation: Session, 1st Report, London: HMSO.

Horton, B. and Maynard, L. (2005) 'Knowledge returns', *Society for Computers and Law Magazine* 16 (2).

Hovland, I. (2003) 'Knowledge management and organizational learning: an international development perspective' Working Paper 224, Overseas Development Institute: London; available at: *http://www.odi.org.uk/publications/working_papers/wp224.pdf* (accessed 19 July 2006).

Huntington, S. P. (1993) 'The clash of civilizations', *Foreign Affairs* 73(3): 22–49.

Hustings, K. and Michailova, S. (2004) 'Facilitating knowledge sharing in Russian and Chinese subsidiaries: the role of personal networks and group membership', *Knowledge Management* 8(2): 84–94.

Hutton, W. (2000) 'The murder of manufacturing: and who is guilty of this crime? The City of course, but most culpably, the Government', *Observer*, 7 March.

Interface (year unknown) 'Interface sustainability'; available at: *http://www.interfacesustainability.com/whatis.html* (accessed 15 July 2006).

Internet World Stats (2005) 'Usage and Population Statistics'; available at: *http://www.internetworldstats.com/list2.htm* (accessed December 2005).

Irlen Institute (2005) 'What is Irlen syndrome?'; available at: *http://www.irlen.com/index_sss.html* (accessed December 2005).

Ives, T. (2003) 'Implementing 'communities of practice' and 'after action reviews'; available at: *http://66.102.9.104/search?q=cache:9WYFMyZ85gIJ:www.acs.org.au/Certification/Documents/KM/2003KM1-ImplementingCoPs.pdf+ives+and+implementing+communities+of+practice&hl=en&ie=UTF-8* (accessed 21 July 2006).

Kakabadse, N. K., Kakabadse, A. K. and Kouzmin, A. (2003) 'Reviewing the knowledge management literature: towards a taxonomy', *Journal of Knowledge Management* 7(4): 75–91.

Kaplan, R. S. and Norton, D. P. (1992) 'The Balanced Scorecard – measures that drive performance', *Harvard Business Review* 70(1): pp. 71–9.

Kaplan, R. S. and Norton, D. P. (1996) *The Balanced Scorecard*, Boston: Harvard Business School Press.

Kaplan, R. S. and Norton, D. P. (2004) *Strategy Maps – Converting Intangible Assets into Tangible Outcomes*, Boston: Harvard Business School Press.

Kim, S. (1999) 'The roles of knowledge professionals for knowledge management', Conference Proceedings for 65th IFLA Council and General Conference, Bangkok, 20–28th August.

King, K. (2001) 'Knowledge agencies: making the globalisation of development knowledge work for the world's poor?', Learning to Make Policy, Working Paper 9. Edinburgh: Centre of African Studies, University of Edinburgh; available at: *www.ed.ac.uk/centas/fgpapers.html.* (Accesed 2005).

LaBarre, P. (2000) 'Do you have the will to lead?', *Fast Company*, Issue 32 (February); available at: *http://www.fastcompany.com/online/32/koestenbaum.html* (accessed 19 July 2006).

Lambe, P. (2002) 'The blind tour guide: leadership in the new economy', *Digital Divide*; available at: *www.greenchameleon.com*.

Landsberg, M. (2003) *The Tools of Leadership*, London: Profile Books.

Leadbeater, C. (1999) *Living on Thin Air*, London: Viking, Penguin.

Leeds, C. A. (year unknown) 'Managing conflicts across cultures: challenges to practitioners', *International Journal of Peace Studies*

2(2); available at: *http://www.gmu.edu/academic/ijps/vol2_2/leeds.htm* (accessed 19 July 2006).

Lev, B. (1999) 'Seeing is believing – a better approach to estimating knowledge capital'; available at: *http://www.cfoasia.com/archives/9905-42.htm* (accessed 15 July 2006).

Lev B. (2002) 'Intangibles: management, measurement and reporting'. Brookings Institution, Washington; available at: *http://www.icgrowth. com/resources/documents/Brookings-Lev-Intangibles-01.02.20.pdf* (accessed 15 July 2006).

Lloyd, B. (1999) 'Does knowledge have any value without wisdom?', *Professional Manager* (July): 6.

Lloyd, B. (2003) 'Leadership and wisdom', in Adel Safty (ed.) *Value Leadership*, Istanbul: Bahceshir University Press, pp. 348–61.

Lloyd, B. (2006) 'Knowledge management: what has wisdom got to do with it?', paper presented at the Gurteen Knowledge Café, London South Bank University, 24 January; available at: *http://www.gurteen .com/gurteen/gurteen.nsf/id/L001903/* (accessed: 20 June 2006).

Lowendahl, B. (1997) *Strategic Management of Professional Service Firms*. Copenhagen: Copenhagen Business School Press.

Manville, B. (2002) 'Organizing enterprise-wide e-learning and human capital management'; available at: *http://www.clomedia.com/ content/anmviewer.asp?a=170&print=yes* (accessed 19 July 2006).

Manz, C. C. and Sims, H. P. (2001) *The New SuperLeadership: Leading Others to Lead Themselves*, San Francisco: Berrett-Koehler Publishers.

March, J. G. (1991) 'Exploration and exploitation in organizational learning', *Organization Science* 2(1): 71–87.

Martin, J. (1992) *Culture in Organisations*, New York: Oxford University Press.

Marx, K. (1858) [1973] *Grundisse*. Middlesex: Penguin.

Marx, K. (1867) [1954 – text reproduced from English edition of 1887] *Capital: A Critique of Political Economy*, Vol. 1, London: Lawrence and Wishart.

Marx, K. (1975) *Early Writings*, London: Pelican.

Marx, K. and Engels, F. (1846) [1964] *The German Ideology*, Moscow: Progress Publishers.

Marx, K. and Engels, F. (1848) [1967] *The Communist Manifesto*, Hardmonsworth: Penguin Books.

Matarazzo, J. M. and Connolly, S. D. (eds) (1999) *Knowledge and Special Libraries*, Oxford: Butterworth Heinemann.

McDermott, R. (2000) 'Knowing in community: 10 critical success factors in building communities of practice', *IHRIM Journal*

(March): 19–26; available at: *http://64.233.183.104/search?q=cache: qw3v BppN9vMJ:www.communispace.com/documents/KnowingIn Community.pdf+McDermott+and+Knowing+in+Community&hl=en &gl=uk&ct=clnk&cd=1&ie=UTF-8* (accessed 19 July 2006).

McFarlane, A. (1998) 'Information, knowledge and learning', *Higher Education Quarterly* 52(1): 77–92.

Merritt-Gentry Group (year unknown) 'BrainMining'; available at: *http://www.merritt-gentry.com/brainmining.htm* (accessed 19 July 2006).

Meyer, C. (2000) 'What's the matter? No longer does bigger, heavier, and more solid mean more value', *Business 2.0* (March): 193–8.

Michailova, S. and Husted, K. (2002) 'Managing the dynamic interfaces between culture and knowledge: a research agenda', Working Paper, WP 11/2002, May. Department of Management, Politics and Philosophy, Copenhagen Business School; available at: *http:// econpapers.repec.org/paper/hhbcbslpf/2002_5F011.htm* (accessed 19 July 2006).

Milton, N. (2000) 'The knowledge you don't know you know', *Knowledge Management* (May): 16–18.

Morgan, G. (1986) *Images of Organization*, California: Sage Publications.

Mosse, D. (2002) 'The Western India Rainfed Farming Project: Seminar and Discussion', PARC Document 8, presented at a DFID learning organisation seminar, 5 July. Birmingham: Performance Assessment Resource Centre, International Organisation Development Ltd; available at: *http://64.233.183.104/search?q=cache:u1wOItgtPcsJ: www.livelihoods.org/post/Docs/WIRFP.doc+Western+India+Rainfed+ Farming+Project+and+Mosse&hl=en&gl=uk&ct=clnk&cd=1&ie=U TF-8)* (accessed 19 July 2006).

Mougayar, W. (2000) 'Aggregation nation: a nontrivial pursuit: turning information into electronic markets', *Business 2.0* (March): 253–8.

Moussa, A. and Schware, R. (1992) 'Informatics in Africa: lessons from World Bank experience', *World Development* 20(12): 1737–52.

Mumford, E. (1996) *Systems Design: Ethical Tools for Ethical Change*, London: Macmillan.

National Electronic Library for Health (2001) 'Communities of practice: what are communities of practice?' available at: *http://www.nelh.nhs. uk/knowledge_management/km2/cop_toolkit.asp*.

Neary, M. and Rikowski, G. (2002) 'Time and speed in the social universe of capital', in G. Crow and S. Heath (eds) *Social Conceptions of Time: Structure and Process in Work and Everyday Life*, London: Palgrave; pp. 53–65.

Newell, S., Robertson, M., Scarborough, H. and Swan, J. (2002) *Managing Knowledge Work*, Hampshire: Palgrave.

Nonaka, I. (1991) 'The knowledge-creating company', *Harvard Business Review* 69(6): 96–104.

Nonaka, I. and Takeuchi, H. (1995) *The Knowledge-Creating Company: How Japanese Companies Create the Dynamics of Innovation*, New York: Oxford University Press.

Oppenheim, C. (2005) 'Review of Ruth Rikowski's book – Globalisation, Information and Libraries', *Journal of Documentation* 61(5): 681–4.

OPSI, The Office of Public Sector Information (1995) *Disability Discrimination Act*; available at: *http://www.hmso.gov.uk/acts/acts1995/1995050.htm* (accessed December 2005).

OPSI, The Office of Public Sector Information (2001) *Special Educational Needs and Disabilities Act (SENDA)*; available at: *http://www.hmso.gov.uk/acts/acts2001/20010010.htm* (accessed December 2005).

OPSI, The Office of Public Sector Information (2002) *The Disability Discrimination Code of Practice (Goods, Facilities, Services and Premises)*; available at: *http://www.hmso.gov.uk/acts/acts1995/1995050.htm* (accessed December 2005).

Oram, H. (2001) 'Leadership in the new economy: are you listening?' available at: *http://www.eyeforpharma.com/index.asp?news=20071* (accessed 19 July 2006).

Orna, E. (2005) *Making Knowledge Visible*, Aldershot: Gower Publishing.

Pandya, M. (2004) 'Leadership in e-commerce: what does it take to lead an e-commerce venture?'; available at: *http://leadership.wharton.upenn.edu/e-ommerce/articles/Wharton_E-commerce_Forum.shtml* (accessed 19 July 2006).

Parise, S. and Sasson, L. (2002) 'Leveraging knowledge management across strategic alliances', *Ivey Business Journal,* (March/April); available at: *http://www.iveybusinessjournal.com/view_article.asp?intArticle_ID=378)* (accessed 20 July 2006).

Patterson, V. (year unknown) 'Breaking the glass ceiling: what's holding women back?', *CareerJournal.com*; available at: *http://careerjournaleurope.com/myc/climbing/19980113-patterson.html* (accessed 19 July 2006).

Pocket Oxford Dictionary in Oxford Reference Shelf (1994) [Computer Program], Oxford: Oxford University Press.

Polanyi, M. (1966) *The Tacit Dimension*, New York: Anchor Day Books.

Postone, M. (1996) *Time, Labour and Social Domination: A Reinterpretation of Marx's Critical Theory*, Cambridge: Cambridge University Press.

Potter, D. (1999) 'Wealth creation in the knowledge economy of the next millennium'. Third Millenium Lecture, Downing Street, 27 May; available at: *http://www.number10.gov.uk/output/Page3051.asp* (accessed 19 July 2006).

Powell, M. (2003) *Information Management for Development Organisations* (2nd edn), *Oxfam Development Guidelines Series*, Oxford: Oxfam.

Prakash, P. (2003) 'A Bhopal, le poison court toujours'. Libération.fr. Available for purchase at: *http://www.liberation.fr/page.php?Article=162048* (accessed 18 February 2006).

Rikowski, G. (2001) 'Transfiguration: globalisation, the World Trade Organisation and the national faces of the GATS', *Information for Social Change*, No.14 (Winter); available at: *http://www.libr.org/ISC/articles/14-Glenn_Rikowski.html* (accessed 21 July 2006).

Rikowski, G. (2002) 'Fuel for the living fire: labour-power!' in A. C. Dinerstain and M. Neary (eds) *The Labour Debate: an investigation into the theory and reality of capitalist work*, Aldersgate: Ashgate, pp. 179–202.

Rikowski, G. (2003) 'Alien life: Marx and the future of the human', *Historical Materialism* 11(2): 121–64.

Rikowski, G. (2005) 'In the dentist's chair: a response to Richard Hatcher's critique of habituation of the nation – part two'; available at: *http://www.flowideas.co.uk/index.php?page=articles&sub=In%20the%20Dentist[a]s%20Chair:%20Part%20Two&searched=reductionism* (accessed 21 July 2006).

Rikowski, R. (2000a) 'The knowledge economy is here – but where are the information professionals? (Part 1)' *Business Information Review* 17(3): 157–67.

Rikowski, R. (2000b) 'The knowledge economy is here – but where are the information professionals? (Part 2)', *Business Information Review* 17(4): 227–33.

Rikowski, R. (2003a) 'The role of the information professional in knowledge management: the beginning of the end or the end of the beginning for the library and information professional', *Managing Information* 10(4): 44–7.

Rikowski, R. (2003b) 'Value – the life blood of capitalism: knowledge is the current key', *Policy Futures in Education* 1(1): 163–82; available at: *http://www.wwwords.co.uk/pdf/viewpdf.asp?j=pfie&vol=1&issue=*

1&year=2003&article=9_Rikowski_PFIE_1_1&id=195.93.21.68 (accessed 21 July 2006).

Rikowski, R. (2003c) 'Value theory and value creation through knowledge in the knowledge revolution'. Research MA dissertation, University of Greenwich.

Rikowski, R. (2004a) 'Creating value from knowledge in the knowledge revolution', *Information for Social Change*, Winter, Issue 20; available at: *http://libr.org/isc/articles/20-R.Rikowski.html* (accessed July 2006).

Rikowski, R. (2004b) 'On the impossibility of determining the length of the working-day for intellectual labour', *Information for Social Change*, Issue 19 (Summer); available at: *http://libr.org/isc/articles/19-R.Rikowski-2.html* (accessed 21 July 2006).

Rikowski, R. (2005a) *Globalisation, Information and Libraries: The Implications of the World Trade Organisation's GATS and TRIPS Agreements*, Chandos Publishing: Oxford.

Rikowski, R. (2005b) 'New ideas in globalisation, information and libraries: the implications of the World Trade Organisation's GATS and TRIPS Agreements, Part 1'; available at: *http://www.flowideas. co.uk/?page=articles&sub=New%20Ideas%20in%20Ruth%20Rik wski[a]s%20Book%20-%20Part%201* (accessed 19 July 2006).

Rondinelli, D. (1993) *Development Projects as Policy Experiments: An Adaptive Approach to Development Administration*, London: Routledge.

Samek, T. (2005) 'Book Review: Ruth Rikowski's *Globalisation, Information and Libraries: the implications of the World Trade Organisation's GATS and TRIPS Agreements*', *Feliciter* 51(5): 246.

Schein, E. H. (1992) *Organisational Culture and Leadership* (2nd ed), San Francisco: Jossey-Bass.

Schumpeter, J. A. (1951) *The Theory of Economic Development*, Cambridge, MA: Harvard University Press.

Schumpeter, J. A. (1952) *Capitalism, Socialism and Democracy*, London: George Allen and Unwin.

Schiller, H. I. (1979) 'Transnational media and national development'. In K. Nordenstreng and H. I. Schiller (eds), *National Sovereignty and International Communication*, Norwood, NJ: Ablex, pp. 21–32.

Schiller, H. I. (1985) 'Electronic information flows: new basis for global domination?' in P. Drummond and R. Paterson (eds) *Television in Transition*, London: BFI Publishing, pp. 11–20.

Scott, P. (ed.) (2004) *Practice Management Handbook*, London: The Law Society.

Semler, R. (1993) *Maverick!* London: Century Random House.

Senge, P. (1990) *The Fifth Discipline: The Art and Practice of The Learning Organisation*, New York: Doubleday/Currency.

Sharpe, R. (2000) 'As leaders, women rule: New studies find that female managers outshine their male counterparts in almost every measure', *BusinessWeekOnline*; available at: *http://www.businessweek.com/2000/00_47/b3708145.htm?scriptFramed* (accessed 19 July 2006).

Short, C. (2001) 'Making globalisation work for poor people', *Education International* 7(2): 17.

Simonin, B. (1999) 'Transfer of marketing know-how in international strategic alliances: an empirical investigation of the role and antecedents of knowledge ambiguity', *Journal of International Business Studies* 30(3): 463–90.

SiteScape (2002) 'Collaboration models pure and hybrid', White Paper; available at: *http://www.realmarket.com/requiredsitescape1.pdf* (accessed 8 August 2006)

Skyrme, D. J. (1998) 'Developing a knowledge strategy', *Strategy* (January); available at: *http://www.skyrme.com/pubs/knwstrat.htm* (accessed 19 July 2006).

Smith, A. (1776) *The Wealth of Nations* (Books I–III), London: Penguin.

Smith, A. (1991) *National Identity*, London: Penguin.

Starovic, D. and Marr, B. (2003) *Understanding Corporate Value: Managing and Reporting Intellectual Capital*, London: Chartered Institute of Management Accountants.

Sunday Times (2005) 'Companies that count: measuring, managing and reporting responsible business practice. *Sunday Times* supplement, 3 April.

Surr, M., Barnett, M., Duncan, A., Speight, M., Bradley, D., Rew, A., Toye, J. (2002) *Research for Poverty Reduction: DFID Research Policy Paper*, London: Department for International Development; available at: *http://www.dfid.gov.uk/pubs/files/povredpolpaper.pdf* (accessed 20 July 2006).

Sveiby, K.-E. (2005) 'Methods for measuring intangible assets'; available at: *http://www.sveiby.com/articles/IntangibleMethods.htm* (accessed 3 March 2006).

TechDis (2005) 'Pre-requisite presentation – what is accessibility?'; available at: *http://www.techdis.ac.uk/resources/sites/staffpacks/Staff%20Packs/Intro%20to%20web%20accessibility/What%20is%20Accessibility.xml* (accessed December 2005).

TFPL (2003) 'The knowledge proposition', A report by participants of the Sixth CKO Summit for the private sector, 5–7 October,

Luttrellstown Castle, Dublin; available at: *http://www.tfpl.com/ resources/cko_summit_2003.cfm* (accessed 19 July 2006).

Tomlinson, J. (1999) *Globalization and Culture*, Cambridge: Polity Press.

Torrey, B. and Datta, V. (1998) 'Knowledge across the globe, cultural implications for sharing knowledge', *Knowledge Management* 1(5); available at: *http://www.ikmagazine.com/xq/asp/sid.DF9B49BA-FBC8-446B-B86B-C316A05FDE16/articleid.F26808B2-824A-4409-8AA3-621A473C88CA/qx/display.htm* (accessed 20 July 2006; whole article available by subscription).

Triandis, H. C. (1989) 'Cross-cultural studies of individualism and collectivism', in J. Berman (ed.) *Nebraska Symposium*, Lincoln, NE: University of Nebraska Press; pp. 41–130.

Trompenars, F. and Hampden-Turner, C. (1998) *Riding the Waves of Culture: Understanding Diversity in Global Business* (2nd edn), New York: McGraw-Hill.

Truch, E. (2004) *Leveraging Corporate Knowledge*, Aldershot: Gower Publishing.

Uphoff, N. (1992) *Learning from Gal Oya: Possibilities for Participatory Development and Post-Newtonian Social Science.* Ithaca, NY: Cornell University Press.

Van der Boon, M. (year unknown) 'Global workforce: women, technology and leadership in the new millennium'; available at: *http://www.globaltmc.com/Articles%20html/glob.workforce.html* (accessed 19 July 2006) [This article first appeared in *Woman Abroad* magazine].

Van Heel, O. D., Elkington, J., Fennell, S. and van Dijk, F. (2001) 'Buried treasure'; available at: *http://www.sustainability.co.uk/insight/ businesscase-article.asp?id=141* (accessed 15 July 2006).

Volkow, N. (1998) 'Strategic use of information technology requires knowing how to use information', in C. Avgerou (ed.) *Implementation and Evaluation of Information Systems in Developing Countries.* Proceedings of the Fifth International Working Conference of the International Federation for Information Processing, Working Group 9.4, 18–20 February, Bangkok.

Ward, R and Taylor, S. (2005) 'The human value of knowledge', *Society for Computers and Law Magazine* 15 (6).

Webb, S. (1998) *Knowledge Management: Linchpin of Change*, London: Aslib.

Welch, R. (2000) 'Knowledge management in a deconstructing economy: treating KM as another fad ignores its key role in the new economy', *Knowledge Management* (May): 10.

Wenger, E. (1999) *Communities of Practice: Learning, Meaning and Identity*, Cambridge: Cambridge University Press.

Wenger, E. (2002) Cultivating *Communities of Practice: A Guide to Managing Knowledge*, Boston, MA: Harvard Business School Press.

Wenger, E. C. and Snyder, W. M. (2000) 'Communities of practice: the organizational frontier', *Harvard Business Review* (Jan–Feb): 139–45.

Wenger, E. and Lave, J. (1991) *Situated Learning: Legitimate Peripheral Participation*, Cambridge: Cambridge University Press.

Wick, C. (2000) 'Knowledge management and leadership opportunities for technical communications', *Technical Communication Online: Applied Theory* 47 (4): 515–29.

Wikipedia (2005) 'Mondragón Cooperative Corporation'; available at: *http://en.wikipedia.org/wiki/Mondragón_Cooperative_Corporation* (accessed 15 July 2006).

Willis, P. (1977) *Learning to Labour*, Farnborough: Saxon House.

World Wide Web Consortium (1997) 'W3C leads program to make the Web accessible for people with disabilities'; available at: *http://www.w3.org/Press/WAI-Launch.html* (accessed December 2005).

World Wide Web Consortium (1999a) 'Web Content Accessibility Guidelines 1.0'; available at: *http://www.w3.org/TR/WAI-WEBCONTENT/* (accessed December 2005).

World Wide Web Consortium (1999b) 'Checklist of checkpoints for Web Content Accessibility Guidelines 1.0'; available at: *http://www.w3.org/TR/WCAG10/full-checklist.html* (accessed December 2005).

World Wide Web Consortium (2000) 'Web content techniques'; available at: *http://www.w3.org/TR/WCAG10-HTML-TECHS/* (accessed December 2005).

World Wide Web Consortium (2005a) 'HyperText Markup Language (HTML) home page'; available at: *http://www.w3.org/MarkUp/* (accessed December 2005).

World Wide Web Consortium (2005b) 'Document object model (DOM)'; available at: *http://www.w3.org/DOM/* (accessed December 2005).

World Wide Web Consortium (2005c) 'Cascading style sheets home page'; available at: *http://www.w3.org/Style/CSS/* (accessed December 2005).

World Wide Web Consortium (2005d) 'Browser statistics: what is the trend in browser usage, operating systems and screen resolution?'; available at: *http://www.w3schools.com/browsers/browsers_stats.asp* (accessed December 2005).

Yoo, Y., Ginzberg, M. and Ahn, J. H. (1999) 'A cross-cultural investigation of the use of knowledge management systems', *Academy of*

Management Review; pp. 501–5; available at: *http://66.249.93.104/ search?q=cache:ur14jZ4r7m0J:is.lse.ac.uk/support/ICIS/2000/pdffiles/ 1999/papers/Rip9917.pdf+Yoo,+Ginzberg+and+Ahn+and+cross-cultural+investigation+of+use+of+knowledge+management+systems &hl=en&gl=uk&ct=clnk&cd=13&ie=UTF-8* (accessed 20 July 2006).

Young, K. (2005) 'Share and share alike', *Legal IT* 6(5): 32–6.

Zack, M. H. (1999a) *Knowledge and Strategy*, Massachusetts: Butterworth and Heinemann.

Zack, M. H. (1999b) Managing Codified Knowledge, *Sloan Management Review* 40(4): 45–58.

Index